OECD Economic Surveys:
European Union
2009

OECD

ORGANISATION FOR ECONOMIC CO-OPERATION AND DEVELOPMENT

The OECD is a unique forum where the governments of 30 democracies work together to address the economic, social and environmental challenges of globalisation. The OECD is also at the forefront of efforts to understand and to help governments respond to new developments and concerns, such as corporate governance, the information economy and the challenges of an ageing population. The Organisation provides a setting where governments can compare policy experiences, seek answers to common problems, identify good practice and work to co-ordinate domestic and international policies.

The OECD member countries are: Australia, Austria, Belgium, Canada, the Czech Republic, Denmark, Finland, France, Germany, Greece, Hungary, Iceland, Ireland, Italy, Japan, Korea, Luxembourg, Mexico, the Netherlands, New Zealand, Norway, Poland, Portugal, the Slovak Republic, Spain, Sweden, Switzerland, Turkey, the United Kingdom and the United States. The Commission of the European Communities takes part in the work of the OECD.

OECD Publishing disseminates widely the results of the Organisation's statistics gathering and research on economic, social and environmental issues, as well as the conventions, guidelines and standards agreed by its members.

ISBN 978-92-64-05445-5 (print)
ISBN 978-92-64-05446-2 (PDF)

ISSN 0376-6438 (print)
ISSN 1609-7513 (online)

Also available in French.

Photo credits: Cover © Pat O'Hara/The Image Bank/Getty Images.

Corrigenda to OECD publications may be found on line at: *www.oecd.org/publishing/corrigenda*.
© OECD 2009

Table of contents

This Survey is published on the responsibility of the Economic and Development Review Committee of the OECD, which is charged with the examination of the economic situation of member countries.

The economic situation and policies of the European Union were reviewed by the Committee on 28 May 2009. The draft report was then revised in the light of the discussions and given final approval as the agreed report of the whole Committee on 8 July 2009.

The Secretariat's draft report was prepared for the Committee by Nigel Pain and Jeremy Lawson under the supervision of Peter Hoeller. Research assistance was provided by Isabelle Duong.

The previous Survey of the European Union was issued in September 2007.

This book has...

StatLinks
A service that delivers Excel® files from the printed page!

Look for the *StatLinks* at the bottom right-hand corner of the tables or graphs in this book. To download the matching Excel® spreadsheet, just type the link into your Internet browser, starting with the *http://dx.doi.org* prefix.
If you're reading the PDF e-book edition, and your PC is connected to the Internet, simply click on the link. You'll find *StatLinks* appearing in more OECD books.

BASIC STATISTICS OF THE EUROPEAN UNION, 2008

	EU15	EU12	EU27
LAND AND PEOPLE			
Area (thousand km^2)	3 238	1 088	4 326
Population (million)	394.1	103.3	497.4
Number of inhabitants per km^2	119.9	94.0	113.4
Population growth (1998-2008, annual average % rate)	0.5	-0.2	0.3
Labour force (million)	258.8	71.6	330.4
Unemployment rate (%)	7.1	6.5	7.0
ACTIVITY			
GDP (billion EUR, current prices)	11 526	981	12 507
Per capita GDP (current PPS)	27 700	15 200	25 100
In per cent of GDP:			
Gross fixed capital formation	20.8	25.0	21.1
Exports of goods and services	40.0	55.0	41.1
Imports of goods and services	39.4	59.2	40.9
PUBLIC FINANCE			
(per cent of GDP)			
General government:			
Revenue	45.0	39.0	44.5
Expenditure	47.2	42.1	46.8
Balance	-2.2	-3.2	-2.3
Gross public debt (end-year)	63.9	33.5	61.5

EXTERNAL TRADE IN GOODS
(main partners, % of total flows)

	Exports	Imports
United States	19.1	12.0
Other Europe (incl. Russia)	28.7	27.8
China	6.0	16.0
Japan	3.2	4.8
Other Asia	20.8	19.5
Other	22.2	19.9

Executive summary

The European Union is facing severe challenges from the financial crisis and the worst global recession in the past fifty years. The Community has responded to the crisis proactively, consistent with the broad framework for policy actions provided by the European Economic Recovery Plan. Actions have been taken to stabilise financial markets and support the economy. An ambitious agenda for financial services reform is underway to improve macro- and micro-prudential regulation and supervision, and the ECB has cut its policy rate significantly.

It is essential that policy actions to support economic activity during the crisis do not imperil the prospects for recovery or endanger the single market and, where necessary, some measures must be withdrawn once the economy recovers. Fiscal measures should ideally offer dual benefits; mitigating the impact of the recession on output and jobs as well as providing longer term benefits. Structural reforms must be accelerated in the years ahead to help prevent future financial crises, enhance resilience to adverse economic shocks and improve both longer term growth prospects and the long-term sustainability of the public finances.

Strengthening innovation. Despite numerous policy initiatives, research and innovation in Europe still lag behind that in the United States and Japan. An integrated labour market for researchers, a Community patent and a Unified Patent Litigation System would help to stimulate innovation. Tackling obstacles to the funding of innovation and encouraging research co-operation would improve the practical use of research results and accelerate their diffusion. New measures of innovation outputs should be developed to sharpen policy design and evaluation in this area, including education.

Deepening the single market. The single market programme has already brought long-term benefits, but more can be done to enhance competitive pressures. The Services Directive needs to be implemented in a timely and effective manner and actions should be taken to ensure proper implementation of single market rules. Competition in financial services, energy markets and network industries can be raised further, and continued efforts are needed to simplify regulations and improve assessments of policy proposals.

Implementing energy policy and the transition to a low-carbon economy. Europe is taking important steps towards becoming a low-carbon economy. Policies to reduce greenhouse gas emissions, promote low-emission technologies and reduce energy consumption should focus on correcting genuine market failures and be flexible to cope with future economic and technological changes. Faster liberalisation of EU electricity and gas markets is necessary to increase competition, improve energy security, and send clearer price signals through the EU Emission Trading Scheme. Regarding external energy policy, it is important that the Union speaks with a single voice.

Further improving external access to European markets. The EU must continue to resist the rise in protectionist sentiment and continue to push for global trade liberalisation. Reductions in tariffs would send a powerful free trade message to the rest of the world and improve consumer welfare. The rules of origin in the EU's preferential trade agreements could be further simplified and *thresholds for domestic content lowered, particularly for developing countries, and it should be ensured that they are fully consistent with both the EU's trade and development goals. Recent reforms have reduced distortions in the Common Agricultural Policy. Support could be further decoupled from production and payments better targeted to achieve income support objectives and encourage the provision of public goods such as improving the rural environment.*

Assessment and recommendations

Europe has experienced its worst post-war recession but must pursue its reform agenda to return to sustainable growth

The European Union is facing severe challenges from the financial crisis and the deep recession. The European economy has been heavily affected by ongoing financial turmoil and the associated deep and synchronised recession in the global economy, reflecting the strong commercial and financial linkages between European economies and between Europe and the rest of the world. Output is projected to decline by around 4% this year, making this Europe's worst post-war recession. The actions taken by central banks, member state governments, the Commission and other EU institutions have stabilised financial markets and supported the economy. It is important that these policy actions do not imperil the prospects for subsequent recovery or endanger the single market. The recession itself will result in a considerable loss of capacity in the European economy, adding to the pressures on long-term growth prospects that will come from population ageing, and has disrupted the progress that was being made towards achieving the objectives of the renewed Lisbon Strategy for Growth and Jobs. Reforms undertaken through the Lisbon strategy since 2005 have helped the EU to improve the resilience of its economy. These results can be attributed to the overhaul of the Strategy in 2005 marked by the introduction of clear "governance" mechanisms. There have also been improvements in the fiscal position in many countries that allowed for a co-ordinated fiscal impulse to support demand and boost confidence as part of the EU's recovery plan. The speed and depth of reforms, however, still vary among member states. This can be remedied by further improving governance which would bring more ownership and a substantial policy response of the member states to these policy recommendations. Tackling these "delivery disparities" should be a key objective for the upcoming revision of the Lisbon Strategy for the period after 2010. Structural reforms remain essential for the European economy, and the Lisbon Strategy will need to ensure that reforms are accelerated and deepened, thereby limiting the medium-term effects of the crisis on potential output. This Survey reviews recent developments and the measures introduced in response to the economic and financial crisis. It then identifies some of the key structural policy challenges that the European economy will face in the coming years. These include strengthening innovation performance, deepening the single market, making the transition to a low-carbon economy and further opening European markets to the rest of the world.

Prompt and effective implementation of the
European Economic Recovery Plan is essential

The crisis presents substantial challenges to European policymakers, with prompt action needed to revive financial markets and cushion the impact of the recession on demand and employment. EU-level actions have also been needed to provide additional financial support to some of the member states that have faced considerable economic and financial headwinds since the onset of the financial crisis. The short-term challenges to European policymakers are magnified by the need to press ahead with the implementation of structural reforms that will help to prevent future financial crises, enhance resilience to adverse economic shocks and improve both longer term growth prospects and the long-term sustainability of the public finances, in the context of ageing populations.

The Commission has a central role in monitoring and co-ordinating the actions taken by member states in response to the economic crisis and ensuring they are implemented effectively. The European Economic Recovery Plan, which combined short-term measures with an acceleration of structural reforms as set out in the Lisbon strategy country specific recommendations was a welcome answer to the crisis. Total support to demand from member states and EU-level authorities will amount to around 5% of EU GDP in 2009 and 2010. Discretionary fiscal measures in these two years amount to a total of 1.8% of GDP, augmenting the significant stimulus coming from the relatively large automatic stabilisers in the EU. Past structural reforms and, in particular, fiscal consolidation in good times, have allowed most member states to launch fiscal stimuli within the framework of the European Economic Recovery Plan. Measures taken to underpin the financial sector and direct assistance from the Commission and other European bodies are also supporting activity. Further measures may be announced by member states that have sufficient budgetary scope. However, taking into account the contingent liabilities linked to the financial sector rescue operation and the implicit liabilities related to ageing, the fiscal space has been narrowing across the EU. In some member states, fiscal space has been virtually exhausted owing to already high budget deficit and public debt levels, which are reflected in rising interest rate spreads on government bonds. It is vital that the Commission and the Council, through the Stability and Growth Pact, ensure that clear and credible plans for fiscal consolidation are implemented by the member states.

The crisis is an opportunity to promote
structural reforms

Past experience shows that growth-enhancing structural reforms are often initiated at times of economic crisis. But careful thought is necessary in designing such reforms to ensure that they offer long-term benefits rather than just a short-term palliative. The European Economic Recovery Plan rightly combines short-term measures with structural reforms in order to meet the Union's medium-term objectives. In particular, it is essential that policies to support local jobs and businesses do not endanger the European single market or hamper external access to the European Economic Area. The Commission has already intervened promptly against measures that favour selected subgroups of companies and violate single market principles and must continue to do so. The Commission also needs to stand ready to ensure time-limited state aid and other fiscal supports are withdrawn promptly at the appropriate juncture as the economy recovers.

Nonetheless, the fiscal easing underway in many European economies has provided an opportunity to facilitate some worthwhile structural reforms. Well-founded investments in infrastructure, including broadband and new low-emission technologies will offer long-term supply-side and environmental benefits as well as a short-run boost to activity. The activation of labour market programmes, development and better matching skills with the market needs, reductions in social security contributions and support for low-income households will dampen the impact of the recession on labour markets and the necessary adjustments that will arise from other structural reforms. Maintaining, and even increasing, investment in education and training is a lever for helping to get through, and overcome, the challenges of the recession, thus helping to ensure that the workforce holds on to and upgrades its skills, and that people are equipped for opportunities that will arise once the crisis is over. The Commission needs to continue to monitor the effectiveness of these measures, provide guidance on policy design and facilitate the exchange of information about policy experiences.

Progress is being made towards implementing an EU-wide system of financial supervision

While most financial market segments have become well integrated, financial supervision has remained predominantly national in scope. This may hinder the single market for financial services and increase the chances that financial risks related to the EU-wide activities of systemically important cross-border institutions will not be detected and acted upon. It also complicates financial crisis management and resolution, as the financial crisis has revealed. In early 2009, the de Larosière Group made proposals on how the European financial supervisory system could be improved, including: i) measures to establish a European System Risk Council (ESRC) to oversee the stability of the financial system as a whole, and ii) for the supervision of individual financial institutions, a European System of Financial Supervisors (ESFS), consisting of three European Supervisory Authorities (ESA), replacing the existing three Level 3 committees and working in tandem with the national financial supervisors. The ESRC would pool and analyse all information relevant for financial stability, and a macro-prudential risk warning system would be put in place. The ESFS would represent an evolutionary reform. The ESAs would have, in cases clearly specified in Community legislation, the means to ensure coherent application of Community legislation, including the power to resolve disputes between national supervisors. They would also be given the responsibility for the authorisation and supervision of certain entities with pan-European reach, such as credit rating agencies. This should better balance the interests of home and host supervisors and better take into account the EU-wide impact of cross-border activities The ESRC should make it more likely that systemic risks are quickly recognised and acted upon. In May 2009, the Commission published a Communication fleshing out the recommendations put forward by the de Larosière Group. The intention of the Commission is to present all necessary legislative proposals in the course of autumn 2009. It is essential that the proposed powers and independence of the new authorities are retained in the legislative proposals.

The Commission has announced further measures to counteract the financial crisis and has set out an ambitious agenda for financial services reform. Based on earlier roadmaps, many measures have been adopted, including a Regulation on Credit Rating Agencies and a review of the Capital Requirements Directive (CRD). Furthermore, the Commission has indicated how it intends to apply state aid rules to state support schemes and individual assistance for financial institutions; has provided guidance on the treatment of asset relief and impaired assets; and has presented proposals for establishing regulatory and supervisory standards for alternative investment fund managers. Further revisions to the CRD will be proposed in October 2009. As regulatory changes are made it will be important to remember that unnecessary or badly-designed regulation could impair the functioning of financial markets and increase instability. In the shorter term, concerns that the scale of impaired assets has not been fully recognised and that banks may be insufficiently capitalised to deal with a further deterioration in economic conditions need to be addressed.

The measurement of innovation
and the evaluation of innovation policies
need to be strengthened

In 2000, the Lisbon agenda included a commitment to make Europe the most dynamic and competitive knowledge-based economy in the world. Enhancing investment in knowledge and innovation is now one of the four priority areas of the renewed Lisbon Strategy. The Commission set out a broad-based innovation strategy in 2006 and member states have committed to achieving an integrated European Research Area by 2020. Increasing attention is now being given to the concept of "creativity", although this concept has not yet been clearly defined or measured.

Despite the wide range of policy initiatives, progress to date has been slow, with research and innovation still lagging behind the United States and Japan. The target of raising research and development (R&D) expenditure to 3% of GDP by 2010 will not be met in the EU as a whole and appears unlikely to be achieved anytime soon. While the target is an aggregate level benchmark that has encouraged policy action during the past decade, it is less clear that it should be retained as such, because it depends largely on private sector actions, and tends to emphasize innovation inputs rather than outputs and the use of innovations. EU member states have already set themselves their own specific targets within the framework of the National Reform programmes. The understanding of the innovation process is also changing, with non-technological innovations and open innovations (such as open-source software) becoming more important and research efforts more likely to involve co-operation across national borders. These all change the link between national R&D efforts and innovation outcomes. The Commission is taking steps to improve the statistical information available about innovative and creative activities in order to make greater use of output-based measures, allowing innovation policies to be developed from a more appropriate knowledge base. Support for R&D by the EU member states should be at least maintained during the current recession.

Improvement in measurement would also be an important step towards better evaluation of the effectiveness of the innovation policies pursued by the Commission. The Commission has been commendably prompt in introducing policy support for innovation. The policy initiatives are tied together by the vision of the future European Research Area (ERA) and a broad-based innovation strategy. But there is a need for priority setting amongst the initiatives and better quantification of the importance of each in accounting for differences in innovation across countries. The policies adopted reflect the perceived need for favourable framework conditions such as well-functioning product and financial markets and an adequate supply of human resources for science and technology. Without these, the effectiveness of specific innovation-related initiatives and attempts to foster demand for innovations may be constrained. Better measurement of innovation outcomes would aid the evaluation of Commission-funded research programmes. The Commission should also take further steps to improve the development and use of common evaluation methodologies and techniques for all innovation programmes.

Developing an integrated labour market for researchers and an integrated intellectual property system should be priorities

Improvements in the framework conditions for innovation and progress towards an integrated research area will underpin the free movement of knowledge across national borders (the so-called "fifth freedom"). Achieving a fully integrated labour market for researchers, a Community patent and a Unified Patent Litigation System will be important. The Commission is already taking actions to improve education and training policies to raise the long-term supply of human resources for science and technology. But such resources remain smaller in the EU than elsewhere and a significant share of university graduates, doctorate recipients and postdoctoral students graduating in Europe migrate to work elsewhere. The international orientation of European researchers should, in principle, enhance knowledge flows to the EU economy. However, steps need to be taken to enhance the circulation of EU and non-EU researchers. The Commission has launched the European Partnership for Researchers and should ensure that the priority actions are implemented on schedule by end-2010. Some of these are a matter for member states, but the Commission can ensure that publicly-funded research positions and research grants are open to qualified nationals of all member states and that researchers have the freedom to take research grants across national borders when changing jobs. Obstacles to short-term mobility in national pension and social security schemes should be removed. A Blue Card scheme is also to be introduced to encourage inflows of highly-skilled migrants by simplifying application procedures, provided that they have sufficient experience and a job offer with a salary above a certain threshold. The scheme is a welcome step forward, but the immediate benefits of it may not be large, especially since the Card will not grant rights to permanent residency and member states retain the right to set quotas that limit the numbers of cards issued. It will be important to monitor the impact of the scheme and explore possible extensions to the rights granted to Card holders to further promote mobility.

The European patent system, and hence the cross-border markets for technology and knowledge, is currently fragmented. Patent protection can be obtained in multiple European countries by receiving a "European patent" from the European Patent Office. But such patents require validation by national patent offices, which often requires translation into another language. Furthermore, the "European patent" is subject to litigation in the national courts. The costs of validating and maintaining a patent in many European countries are thus much higher than in either the United States or Japan, with the burden being especially high for small and medium-sized enterprises. Therefore, to reduce such costs, a simplified system, with a single "Community patent" that would be valid automatically in all member states and a centralised Patent Litigation Court for both European and Community patents should be implemented.

*Funding for innovation should be enhanced
and research co-operation should be encouraged*

The market for high-risk capital, such as private equity and venture capital, plays an important role in the financing of innovation, especially for young, innovative companies, but is underdeveloped in Europe. The Commission and other Community-level bodies have thus taken steps in the European Economic Recovery Plan to ensure that financing of such companies is supported during the ongoing recession. Further ahead, the Commission will need to follow through on plans to tackle obstacles to cross-border venture capital provision. It should enhance the effectiveness of innovation policy design and delivery by tackling overlaps between the numerous Community-level programmes that offer funding for innovation, by looking for unexploited synergies and by reducing the presently high cost of research grant applications.

Innovation activities increasingly involve co-operation between different groups. Yet European innovation surveys indicate that public research organisations are a key information source for only a relatively small number of companies. This could mean that there are only a few commercial applications of the basic research undertaken in Europe, but is more likely to indicate that there are obstacles preventing firms from either being aware of the work undertaken in publicly-funded research organisations or from accessing it. The Commission produced guidelines for universities and research institutions to improve their links with European companies in 2007 and is to upgrade the status of the EU Forum for University-Business Dialogue. In 2008 it adopted a Recommendation on the management of intellectual property in knowledge transfer activities and a Code of practice for universities and other public research organisations. The rules for participation in Community-level R&D funding programmes should be extended to ensure that all applicants have to submit plans for dissemination of research findings as part of their research projects. Consideration should also be given to ways in which the European Union might further strengthen research and innovation links with other regions.

*The single market is moving ahead,
but more remains to be done*

The single market programme has already delivered many benefits to the European economy and improved longer term growth prospects, by raising competitive pressures. But much more remains to be done, especially in service sectors and some network industries. OECD product market regulation indicators show that such regulations remain relatively stringent and that competitive pressures are lower than they could be. Intra-EU trade in goods and services is growing only modestly and price convergence between member states appears to have stalled, with the exception of the new member states. Some important past reforms are awaiting full implementation by member states. There has been an improvement in the rate of transposition of legislation, but as of the end of 2008 there were 92 single market directives (6% of the total) that had not been transposed fully by all member states by the due date. Some were several years overdue. There are also many cases of directives either being transposed incorrectly or incorrectly applied. In all, over 1 200 infringement cases remained open as of the end of 2008. Assessment of the quantitative importance of such infringements is difficult, but actions should be taken to limit their number. The Commission should press ahead with measures to identify best practices amongst member states, particularly with regard to the application of single market rules and administrative co-operation on single market issues, and continue to pursue infringement proceedings where necessary.

The Services Directive needs to be implemented in a timely and effective manner

The Services Directive should bring a marked improvement in competition, provided it is implemented in a timely and effective fashion, as intended, by the end of 2009. Implementation is a demanding task for member states as numerous legislative changes are required and new procedures have to be introduced to reduce administrative and regulatory costs. Information on the state of progress is sparse, but there are indications that some member states may find it difficult to meet the deadline. The Commission is already providing advice to member states and has drawn up plans to continue collaboration through a "mutual evaluation exercise" that will take place with member states in 2010. The Commission will need to act decisively in introducing follow-on actions if member states do not meet the transposition deadline. Assessments of the state of transposition could be helped by the development of a centralised website with timely information on measures adopted by member states.

The single market needs to be extended further

Increasingly, the focus of single market activity appears likely to turn towards monitoring and implementation, but further steps will need to be taken to ensure that obstacles to cross-border retail financial services are tackled and that further liberalisation takes place in EU energy markets. The adoption of the third Postal Directive marks the commitment of EU member states to fully open their postal markets by the end of 2010 (with the possibility for some member states to postpone full market opening by two more years as a maximum, accounting for the remaining 5% of the EU postal market). Previously untouched sectors, such as port services, also have to be tackled. Increasingly, the Commission will need to strengthen the evidence base for single market initiatives and identify the importance of specific barriers for market size and productivity growth. Without these, the impact of past legislation and the need for follow-up measures will be impossible to assess effectively. The Market Monitoring exercises recently begun by the Commission are an important step towards achieving this.

Continued efforts should be made to simplify regulations and improve assessments of new policy proposals

The business environment can be further improved by continuing efforts to simplify the administrative burdens resulting from Community law. Considerable progress has already been made by the implementation of the Better Regulation agenda since 2005, which includes proposals to simplify more than 130 regulations. A programme is now in place to reduce administrative burdens by an estimated 25% by 2012. It is important that this is pursued vigorously, with high quality *ex post* evaluation of the resulting measures being undertaken. More could also be done to improve the quality of *ex ante* impact assessments of new legislative proposals. Impact assessments of Commission proposals are always made, but are rarely revisited after amendments are made by the European Parliament and the European Council. This complicates effective evaluation of the final policies introduced.

The transition to a low-carbon economy needs to occur in a cost-effective way

Europe is taking important steps towards a successful transition to a low-carbon economy and making an effective contribution to the world's efforts to mitigate climate change. The goal of reducing Europe's carbon footprint is underpinned by concrete targets for reducing greenhouse gas emissions by 20% by 2020, raising the share of renewable energy consumption to 20% by 2020 and reducing energy consumption by 20% by 2020. In addition to addressing the wedge between the social and private cost of greenhouse gas emissions, policy has to overcome other market failures, including, for instance, capital market imperfections, monitoring and enforcement costs or incentives for free-riding. It is essential that the instruments that are chosen are efficient, correct genuine market failures and are flexible to cope with future economic and technological changes. Policies that unnecessarily raise the cost of carbon abatement need to be avoided. For the most part the EU is doing this, but, there are ways to improve the current policy mix. It is widely acknowledged that emission trading schemes (ETS) are more efficient and equitable if they cover as many sectors of the economy as can be done cost effectively, and that allocating free emission allowances to installations should occur when the cost of such allowances cannot be passed on and when auctioning could therefore lead to an increase in greenhouse gas emissions in third countries where installations would not be subject to a comparable carbon constraint. In principle, incentives for abatement should be aligned across all sectors of the economy. The EU should seriously consider including all transport sectors in the ETS when practical and appropriate. The EU plans to improve the way that emission allowances are allocated partly by auctioning. However, only sectors rigorously identified as being at a significant risk of carbon leakage should continue to receive free allowances until 2020. Thresholds for determining which trade-exposed sectors should receive free allowances were determined without an impact assessment. However, the risk of carbon leakage is being assessed on the basis of quantitative and qualitative criteria laid down in the Directive and there will be a review following a comprehensive global agreement on future climate action.

Although additional support for the research, development and deployment of low-emission technologies may be necessary to counteract market failures, many member states already offer generous subsidies to the renewable energy sector. Such policies are likely to increase the overall cost of greenhouse gas abatement, particularly in the short run. There are a number of ways to ensure that the 20% renewable energy target is met in the most cost effective way, including the options implemented with the new directive on renewable energy sources. In the longer term, restrictions on importing renewable energy should be abolished and a single, harmonised European low-emission energy support mechanism should be considered when practical. It should be ensured that the development of renewable energy in the transport sector is achieved as sustainably and cost-effectively as possible, through a combination of European production and greater use of imported biofuels. Given the high cost of biofuel technologies, it will be important to ensure that the 10% renewable transport fuel target efficiently achieves its objectives of reducing greenhouse gas emissions, ensuring sustainability and increasing security of supply. At the very least, tariffs on imported biofuels should be reduced significantly. Funding for low-emission technology R&D should be stepped up as current levels of Community support are likely to fall short of what is necessary, particularly in an economic environment where firms are cutting back on non-essential investment. Moreover, it is essential that the social benefits of policies to reduce energy consumption exceed the costs. Mandatory labelling standards are an effective way of overcoming information failures, but mandatory performance standards need to be carefully designed so that they focus on performance rather than specific technologies and are re-assessed to ensure ongoing incentives for innovation.

Energy market reform and investment in cross-border capacity is necessary to deliver a single and secure energy market

Further liberalisation of EU electricity and gas markets is necessary to deliver efficient retail electricity and gas prices, increase incentives to innovate and invest in new generation and transmission capacity and improve energy security. A fully competitive single market for gas and electricity has been a long-time goal but liberalisation has progressed unsatisfactorily. The EU's third liberalisation package forces more effective unbundling through the creation of independent Transmission System Operators (TSOs). They can remain part of vertically-integrated companies, but there will be detailed rules governing the autonomy, independence and investment of TSOs. Full ownership unbundling is also an option, even though voluntary. Another option is the creation of an independent system operator where the ownership of the TSO assets remains with the vertically-integrated company, but the system operation is effectively separated from the assets. It is important that the review of the independent TSO option that the Commission intends to undertake does take place as planned, and that if the expected improvement in competition does not occur, full ownership unbundling is required.

A well-functioning internal energy market also requires effective institutions for overseeing cross-border co-operation between national supervisors and managing cross-border investments. The EU proposal for an Agency for the Co-operation of Regulators (ACER) is welcome. ACER will have decision-making powers in specific cross-border matters in order to achieve a single, competitive market. In any case, it is essential that the strengthened national regulators co-operate within a harmonised European regulatory framework. ACER will also need to be adequately staffed, while the Commission should have binding oversight over the certification procedures for TSOs. Increasing investment in cross-border transmission networks is also critical; without sufficient interconnection capacity foreign suppliers cannot exert competitive pressure on national incumbents. The earlier approach of leaving member states to voluntarily develop joint schemes for congestion management has delivered insufficient progress. Under the third liberalisation package, operators of the main gas and electricity transportation networks will be obliged to co-operate and co-ordinate the operation of their networks through the European Networks of Transmission System Operators. The Commission will need to monitor cross-border investment and be prepared to take measures should investment be inadequate.

Security of supply is a key component of the Lisbon Strategy and a key objective of the EU integrated energy and climate change policy. The EU's "20-20-20 by 2020" objectives and energy market liberalisation policies will improve security of supply by diversifying energy supply and increasing internal trade. The EU's Energy Security and Solidarity Action Plan provides complementary measures focusing on: infrastructure needs and the diversification of energy supplies; external energy relations; oil and gas stocks and crisis response mechanisms; energy efficiency; and making the best use of the EU's own energy sources. Increasing investment in gas pipelines and other energy infrastructure to diversify supply is critical, as illustrated by the recent stand-off between Russia and the Ukraine. Additional investment will help reduce countries' exposure to energy supply shocks from individual supplier countries. A number of projects have been identified under the Trans-European Networks-Energy programme. However, as of 2008 only a small proportion of projects with a European interest have been finalised, in part because incentives for investors to guarantee security of supply are not always sufficient. Consequently, for implementation of such projects, obligatory minimum security of supply standards for gas and a fast implementation of the third internal market package, which will ensure greater independence of transmission and trading interests, are important. The Ukraine/Russia stand-off also highlighted the need for improved procedures for dealing with gas emergencies, and in particular, for co-ordinating emergency policies amongst member states. Regarding external energy policy it is essential that EU member states speak with a single voice. Although diversifying EU energy supply is an important policy goal, it is important that policies to achieve this do not unnecessarily raise the cost of energy inputs.

Further improving foreign access to European markets will improve efficiency and help buffer against the economic crisis

These are testing times for European and global trade policy. Progress on the Doha round of world trade negotiations stalled, global trade has collapsed and the economic crisis is creating political pressure to raise protection for domestic firms. As the world's largest trading power, the EU has a significant interest in resisting protectionist pressures and securing further trade liberalisation. While the successful completion of Doha is not assured, there is much that the EU and other OECD countries can do to promote freer trade. Although average non-agricultural most-favoured-nation (MFN) tariffs are low, at around 4%, average MFN agricultural tariffs are considerably higher, at just under 15%. The EU remains committed to its offer to undertake a significant reduction of the border protection of its agricultural sector as part of a comprehensive multilateral trade agreement. As is the case with other OECD countries, further trade liberalisation by the EU would send a powerful free trade message to the rest of the world. In addition to its efforts in the multilateral sphere, the EU also pursues its trade policy objectives through reciprocal bilateral and regional preferential trade agreements (PTAs). Although the limited available evidence suggests that the EU's web of PTAs has been welfare enhancing overall, more can be done to raise trade creation. Further simplification of rules of origin requirements and, where appropriate to enhance development, lowering of the thresholds for the necessary value added in partner countries should be actively considered. The argument has been made that Europe's trade defence instruments, such as anti-dumping policies, should be updated to reflect the increasingly global supply chain of European firms. However, there is no consensus among the member states about whether or how such a reform should be carried out.

There is further scope to improve agricultural policy

The Common Agricultural Policy (CAP) represents around 40% of the total EU budget (the total support estimate – encompassing price support and budgetary transfers – is estimated at 0.9% of GDP), and just over a quarter of gross farm receipts. A series of important reforms, including the 2008 Health Check, have significantly reduced distortions where the linkages between payments and production have been cut. The use of market price support measures has also been scaled back for many agricultural commodities. Moreover, the CAP has also become marginally more equitable as payments for landowners receiving more than EUR 5 000 under the Single Payment Scheme have been further reduced and the savings generated transferred to the Rural Development Plan. Nevertheless, there is further scope to improve the CAP. Full decoupling should be extended to the livestock meat production sector, if adverse social and environmental impacts can be addressed through more targeted support measures. Payments across agricultural producers should be flattened further, in line with the Health Check recommendations. Despite the increase in modulation following the Health Check, the CAP could better target those farmers in need of income support. In part, the unequal distribution of CAP payments is due to the way that farmland and past production patterns were distributed in Europe. But, this is exacerbated by the loose definition of income support and stabilisation objectives, the poor measurement of farm households' profitability and wealth, and the failure to separately quantify the magnitude of payments that are necessary to correct market failures relating to public goods and externalities. The Commission should consider moving to a more effective mechanism for providing income support, whether that be through subsidised private insurance targeted at farmers exposed to significant income variability, or a system of income-contingent loans. Most importantly, payments for the provision of public goods should be separated from payments to support incomes to the extent that it is possible to measure public goods produced, taking into account transaction costs.

Chapter 1

Policies to overcome the crisis

The EU economy experienced a deep economic slump. Monetary policy has eased and fiscal stimulus provided to revive the economy. Past experience shows that economic crises can provide momentum for introducing longer term structural reforms by demonstrating the limitations of existing policies and by weakening the resistance to change. The crisis has already triggered reforms to tackle weaknesses in the financial system which, if implemented effectively, should support financial stability and longer term growth prospects. Pursuing structural reforms in the context of the Lisbon strategy will also be important as the recession could result in a considerable loss of capacity in the European economy, adding to the pressures on long-term growth prospects that will soon come from population ageing.

The shadow of the global financial and economic crisis and recession now hangs over the EU

The near-term economic outlook for the EU has changed rapidly since the previous *Survey* was completed in 2007. At that time, the EU was enjoying what appeared to be strong and sustainable growth, supported by a robust world economy. The optimism of 2007 has now dissipated as the global economic crisis, combined with home-grown macroeconomic imbalances in some member states, have sent the European economies into a deep recession (Figure 1.1). Activity is expected to pick up only slowly in 2010, as the tensions in financial markets are gradually unwound and the full effects of policy stimulus are felt. The projected contraction of EU output by close to 4½ per cent in 2009 (OECD, 2009a) would make this the worst post-war recession in Europe. Inevitably, this has already begun to be reflected in widespread job losses and a sizeable jump in unemployment.

Figure 1.1. **Contributions to EU27 GDP growth**

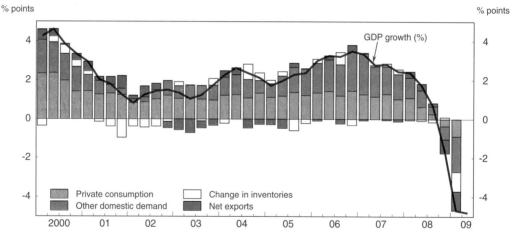

Source: Eurostat.

StatLink http://dx.doi.org/10.1787/712121550120

Although the crisis initially had its greatest effect on those European economies with over-heated housing markets and banking sectors with direct exposure to the US sub-prime mortgage market, the recession was widespread (Figure 1.2). Once again, the inter-connectedness of European economies, both with each other and with the broader global economy, has been clearly demonstrated. Another feature of the downturn is that many of Europe's earlier best performers such as Ireland, Spain and some countries in Eastern Europe, have been hit especially hard, suggesting that their strong growth was not sustainable. The severe difficulties of some member states have raised questions about whether and how EU level support should be provided. This is

Figure 1.2. **Projected cumulative GDP growth in 2009-10**
Per cent

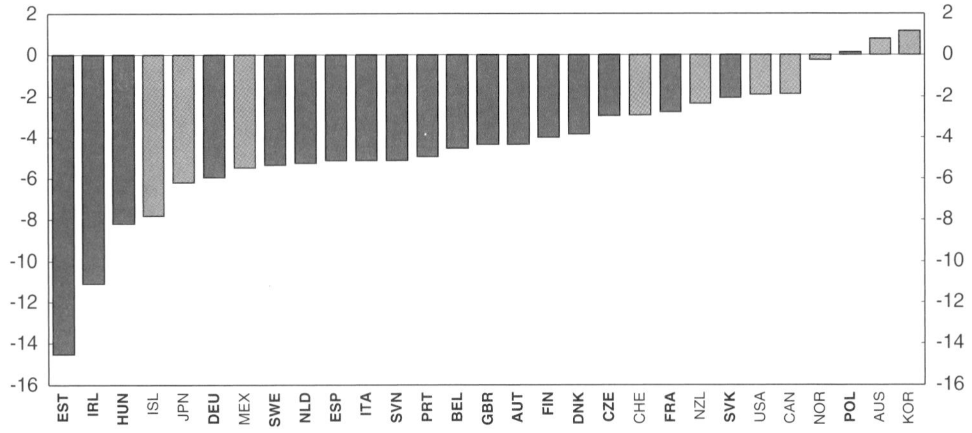

Source: OECD, OECD Economic Outlook 85 database.

StatLink http://dx.doi.org/10.1787/712135540818

challenging the Union and its institutions to find new ways of co-ordinating policy and assisting each other through the hard times.

The first priorities of EU-level bodies and the member states are to return the balance sheets of their financial institutions to health, so that financial conditions ease and lending can rise to support economic activity, and at the same time to provide support to aggregate demand through concerted monetary and fiscal policy actions. The EU has started down this road with measures to provide liquidity and additional capital to distressed financial institutions, together with the European Economic Recovery Plan, which provides for fiscal expansion across member states that is closely connected to the four priority areas of the Lisbon Strategy (people, business, infrastructure and energy, and research and innovation). Most member states have allowed the automatic stabilisers to work, partly cushioning the effects of the fall in private-sector aggregate demand, and have introduced new discretionary fiscal measures to support demand. Total support to demand from member states and EU-level authorities is projected to amount to a little over 5% of EU GDP in 2009 and 2010. Discretionary fiscal measures in these two years are expected to amount to a total of 1.8% of EU GDP (Figure 1.3). These measures have not prevented sharp output declines, but should help to underpin activity in the latter half of 2009 and in 2010. Some member states continue to have budgetary scope to provide additional fiscal stimulus in the short term. However, in other member states, the fiscal space has been virtually exhausted, with high public deficit and debt levels and rising sovereign bond spreads. All member states also need to formulate clear and credible plans to ensure medium-term fiscal sustainability, with budgetary stimulus being withdrawn rapidly once the recovery takes hold.

There has been an unprecedented easing of monetary policy by European central banks, and the operation of liquidity management has also helped to bring down overnight rates in recent months. However, financial market tensions have dampened the transmission of lower policy rates to money market and retail interest rates. More needs to be done to improve the functioning of credit markets. Disinflationary pressures imply that there should be a commitment to maintain rates at this level for

Figure 1.3. **Decomposition of cumulative changes in government balance**
2009-10[1]

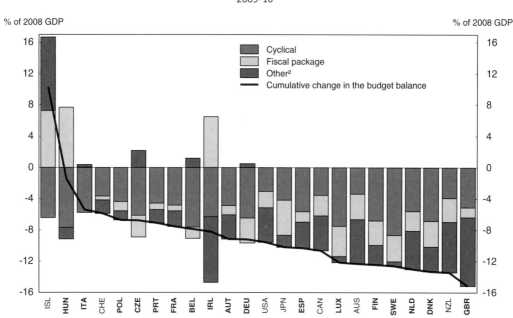

1. Sum of 2009 and 2010 deviations from 2008 levels of government balances.
2. Cumulative changes in deficit minus the sum of the fiscal package and the cyclical components. This captures effects such as discretionary fiscal policy measures other than those in response to the crisis and the disappearance of exceptional revenue buoyancy.

Source: OECD, OECD Economic Outlook 85 database.

StatLink http://dx.doi.org/10.1787/712167336286

as long as is warranted, and European central banks should continue to implement credit and liquidity easing policies.

In many EU countries, uncertainties remain regarding the extent of the impaired assets problems on banks' balance sheets and concerns persist that banks may be insufficiently capitalised to deal with a further deterioration in economic conditions. This will need to be addressed. In April 2009 the IMF estimated that European banks (excluding those from the United Kingdom) were facing potential write-downs on their assets of up to USD 1.1 trillion, and that if the leverage of euro area banks was to return to the levels of the mid-1990s (6% tangible common equity over tangible assets) additional capital of USD 725 billion would be required. In June 2009 the ECB estimated that euro area banks were facing losses of around USD 650 billion, and had written off only just over half of these losses so far. The difference between both estimates stems from different methodologies and coverage of assets held by EU banks, with the IMF applying US coefficients to EU data and the ECB using the available euro area data. The ECB's smaller estimate is based on euro area specific assumptions about future loan default rates. This ongoing uncertainty calls for further action: systematic, rigorous and transparent stress tests are necessary to clarify the capital needs of individual European banks. Although the Committee of European Banking Supervisors (CEBS) is overseeing an EU-wide forward-looking stress testing exercise of the EU banking system, it will not identify individual recapitalisation needs and the parameters and assumptions underpinning the tests have not been made public – and will not be made public in line with the current mandate given by the Economic and Financial

Committee (EFC). Nevertheless, individual member state supervisors are also undertaking their regular stress tests (in accordance with Basel II) and in only a small number of cases institution specific details have been made public (for example in the financial stability reports of some national central banks). When necessary, recapitalisation should occur swiftly, while supervisors should also monitor the soundness of the banks' management, business plan, funding, risk management practices and compensation policies (IMF, 2009). For institutions that supervisors identify as non-viable, governments should consider either winding them up in an orderly manner or merging them with viable institutions (IMF, 2009). Failure to deal with banks' balance sheet problems adequately could inhibit the functioning of the financial system as well overall economic growth, for some time.

Structural reforms must continue to be pursued

Structural reforms remain essential in the European Union. Before the onset of the recession, the EU was already facing the difficult challenge of accelerating its structural reform agenda, set out in the renewed Lisbon Strategy for Growth and Jobs of 2005, in order to lift its long-term economic performance. The deep recession and its concurrence with a prolonged global financial crisis make this task even more important, as the recession will result in a considerable loss of capacity in the European economy, adding to the pressures on long-term growth prospects that will soon come from population ageing (EC, 2009a).

Recessions are usually associated with temporary reductions in potential output growth, as labour supply and capital accumulation are temporarily pushed down. However, deep recessions may have long-lasting effects as well, especially when associated with financial crises (Box 1.1). In addition, in the wake of past European recessions structural unemployment has risen, as negative shocks have interacted with inflexible labour markets and insufficient employment incentives. Accelerating structural reforms in the years ahead would not only improve longer term growth prospects, but also help to reduce the likelihood of similar financial crises and enhance resilience to adverse economic shocks (Duval and Vogel, 2008).

Box 1.1. **Possible effects of the recession on potential output and unemployment**

A critical question is the extent to which the economic crisis will temporarily or permanently reduce the level and growth rate of potential output. Long-lasting effects would not only reduce growth in European living standards, but also put additional long-term pressure on already stretched public finances as revenue growth is reduced and welfare spending increases. Different paths for potential output will also have important implications for output gaps and hence monetary and fiscal policy.

A number of channels can lower the trajectory of potential output. Recessions can reduce potential labour supply by discouraging labour force participation and generating hysteresis effects whereby the long-term unemployed lose skills and become detached from the labour market. Policy responses to recessions can also raise structural unemployment if changes to labour market institutions aimed at protecting workers reduce firms' demand for labour or welfare policies discourage labour supply. Logeay and Tober (2005) show that structural unemployment in Europe increased significantly following each recession since the early 1970s, and declined only gradually in subsequent recoveries (Figure 1.4). Blanchard and Wolfers (2001) argue that this stylised fact is explained

---

Box 1.1. **Possible effects of the recession on potential output and unemployment** (cont.)

by the interaction of negative shocks with inflexible labour market institutions. Nickell et al. (2005) argue that many European governments have tended to increase the generosity of unemployment benefits, install tighter employment protection legislation and increase tax wedges following recessions that contributed most to the trend increase in the NAIRU. That said, many countries have implemented reforms to make their labour markets more flexible during the current downturn and there is no evidence so far that these reforms are being reversed (Figure 1.5).

Figure 1.4. **Unemployment rates in the EU**[1]

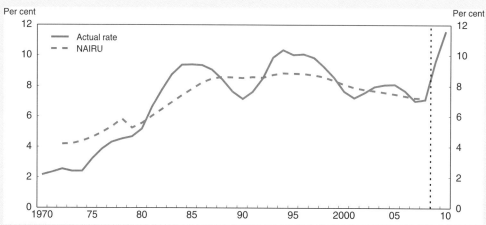

1. Aggregate including only EU countries also members of the OECD. OECD projections for 2009 and 2010.
Source: OECD, OECD Economic Outlook 85 database.

StatLink ⟶ http://dx.doi.org/10.1787/712168344832

Recessions and financial crises can also lower potential output by lowering the capital stock and its efficiency. During recessions investment plunges and, as firms go out of business, scrapping may rise. Also, the high fiscal deficits and rising public debt may crowd out investment. Financial crises add a special dimension to this effect, by impairing financial intermediation (Furceri and Mourougane, 2009) and forcing otherwise viable firms out of business. The financial services sector's share of economic activity also increased noticeably in a number of European countries in the lead up to the current crisis and measured productivity in this sector was relatively high. As the share of the financial services sector in economic activity falls and the earlier estimates of productivity growth in the sector are revised, estimates of potential output could be revised down.

The impact of recessions and financial crises on the level and growth rate of potential total factor productivity (TFP) is more ambiguous. In endogenous growth models, recessions can lower the trajectory of TFP by reducing the research and development (R&D) intensity of the economy as firms cut back on such investment spending. This effect could be amplified during a financial crisis due to the increase in borrowing constraints. Cash strapped governments may also lower spending in growth-enhancing areas such as education, public R&D and infrastructure. On the other hand, recessions may force the least productive firms out of business, increasing average productivity across the economy.

The small empirical literature examining the long-run implications of financial crises and recessions suggests that there may be permanent effects. Looking at post-war

Box 1.1. **Possible effects of the recession on potential output and unemployment** (cont.)

Figure 1.5. **Overall employment protection legislation (EPL)**[1]

Index scale of 0-6 from weakest to strongest protection

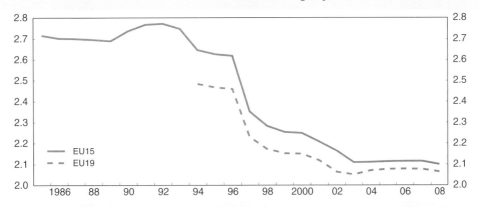

1. The EU aggregate (excluding Ireland and Luxembourg due to lack of data over a long time period) has been obtained by weighting each member's EPL with the employment data.

Source: OECD (2009), Employment Protection Legislation database and OECD Employment Outlook, forthcoming.

StatLink http://dx.doi.org/10.1787/712172347135

US data, Campbell and Mankiw (1987) show that output shocks have been highly persistent, with a 1% shock to GDP changing the optimal ten-year ahead forecast for GDP by more than 1%. Piger et al. (2005) apply a Markov switching model and find that recessions have had only small permanent effects in the United States, but larger permanent effects in European countries. Cerra and Saxena (2007) examine whether economic contractions are followed by rapid recoveries. They find that the losses are not regained, though in many cases potential output returns to its earlier growth rate. Recent OECD research is also consistent with persistent effects from financial crises. Furceri and Mourougane (2009) show that past financial crises have on average been accompanied by permanent reductions in potential output of around 1.5 to 2%, with severe crises associated with effects twice as large. Haugh et al. (2009) find that the 1990s banking crisis in Japan was associated with lower potential growth, likely due to the failure to deal quickly with banking problems. In contrast, they find that because the Nordic banking crises of the early 1990s were resolved more quickly, the Nordic countries experienced only a temporary decline in potential growth.

All of this evidence needs to be digested cautiously. Not only does the global nature of the current crisis make it hard to compare with previous episodes, but financial crises have often been associated with earlier unsustainable booms. This means that comparing the path of trend output following crises with the path leading up to crises may not be appropriate because the latter may be over-estimated. Moreover, even if it is likely that the recession will have permanent effects on potential output, determining the magnitude of the effect is fraught with difficulty, especially in real time.

Nevertheless, the significant welfare and policy implications of different paths for potential output make it essential for policymakers to estimate the impact of the current economic and financial crisis on potential output. The OECD uses a production function to estimate potential output, which requires the use of projections for potential employment, capital and total factor productivity. In the June Economic Outlook (OECD, 2009a), the OECD revised down its projections for potential output from 2009 to 2017 for all OECD countries, including the euro area. The largest contributions to the downward

Box 1.1. **Possible effects of the recession on potential output and unemployment** (cont.)

revision come from a lower capital stock and lower potential employment. The capital stock is held down by large falls in investment in 2009 and 2010, as well as higher capital costs related to expectations of a permanent increase in risk aversion. Potential employment is reduced due to an expected increase in the NAIRU due to hysteresis effects acting through higher long-term unemployment rates. Overall, the cumulative reduction in projected potential output in 2009 and 2013 is 3.7%. This is similar in magnitude to recent estimates from the European Commission, which also uses a production function approach, though the Commission also revised down its estimates of potential output for 2007 and 2008 (Figure 1.6). However, as stated earlier, there is considerable uncertainty surrounding these projections.

Figure 1.6. **Euro area potential GDP**
Index 2007 = 100

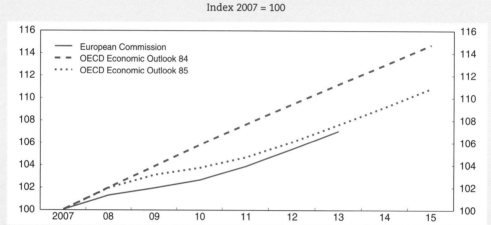

Source: European Commission (2009), "Impact of the Current Economic and Financial Crisis on Potential Output", *European Economy,Occasional Papers 49*, June, and *Annual Macroeconomic database*; OECD, *OECD Economic Outlook 84 and 85 databases.*

StatLink ⟶ http://dx.doi.org/10.1787/712183236067

The potential for the current recession to have permanent effects underscores the importance of accelerating the EU's structural reform agenda.

GDP per capita in the EU is a third lower than that in the United States, with only limited progress having been made towards convergence over the past decade, especially by the long-standing member states (OECD, 2009b). In accounting terms, around two-fifths of the shortfall can be attributed to differences in labour utilisation, with the rest being attributable to a lower level of labour productivity. However, there are member states where income convergence has proceeded rapidly in recent years, providing an indication of what might be possible if structural reforms were pursued more actively throughout the Union (Arnold *et al.*, 2009). One of the main challenges for the upcoming revision of the Lisbon strategy will be to reduce disparities in the speed and depth with which member states have implemented the structural reforms recommended by the (European) Council to member states.

Detailed growth accounting exercises can shed some light on the factors underlying differences in labour productivity and labour utilisation (Mourre, 2009; Duval and de la Maisonneuve, 2009). For the EU as a whole, the primary source of the labour productivity gap is due to differences in total factor productivity, rather than shortfalls in either physical or human capital, although both of these also matter (Figure 1.7), with low capital intensity

Figure 1.7. **The sources of differences in GDP per capita**

Difference to the US in percentage points

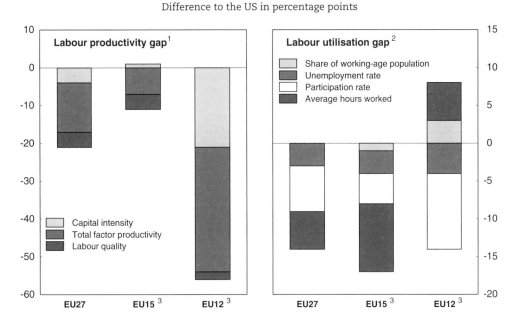

1. GDP per hour worked.
2. Total hours worked per capita.
3. EU15 refers to member states who joined the Union before 2004. EU12 refers to the new member states who have joined the Union since 2004.

Source: Mourre, G. (2009), "What Explains the Differences in Income and Labour Utilisation and Drives Labour and Economic Growth in Europe? – A GDP Accounting Perspective", European Economy, Economic Papers 354, January.

StatLink ⧉ http://dx.doi.org/10.1787/712230411320

being an especially important factor in the new member states (EU12). The importance of total factor productivity provides a clear indication that economic efficiency in the EU needs to improve. At the sectoral level, the underperformance of the EU is especially marked in many market service sectors and in sectors in which production and use of information and communication technologies are important (van Ark et al., 2008). These are sectors in which there has been limited progress made towards a fully integrated European market.

The labour utilisation gap between the EU and the United States is mostly attributable to a lower level of labour force participation in Europe and a lower number of average hours worked per employee. Whilst many policy options are available to improve participation and affect decisions over working hours, especially in the areas of taxation and social security, the majority are the responsibility of member states, rather than of the Community. Therefore, co-ordination of reforms can yield additional dividends, giving the Commission an important role to play even when it cannot implement reforms directly. The Lisbon strategy is intended to help align national efforts to implement structural reforms. Since the 2005 renewal, the strategy has successfully helped to set out a common direction for reforms, and highlighted the importance of policy integration.

The Lisbon Agenda

The key structural policy agenda for the EU is set out in the Lisbon Strategy for Growth and Jobs. It was initially established in 2000, but simplified and relaunched in 2005 with a view to enhance ownership at national level and to focus more clearly on the ultimate objectives of strengthening long-term growth prospects and raising employment. The Lisbon Strategy is organised around a partnership between the Commission and member states.

The overhaul of the Strategy in 2005 was marked by the introduction of clear "governance" mechanisms, with the EU setting the direction of reforms which are then implemented by member states through their national reform programmes. Progress in the implementation of these national reform programmes is monitored yearly by the Commission. Since 2007, the Commission has issued "country-specific recommendations", which are subject to multilateral surveillance prior to their endorsement by the European Council. However, the speed and depth of reforms still vary among member states. This suggests that further improvements in governance are needed, giving member states more ownership over the policy recommendations. Tackling such "delivery disparities" should be a key objective for the upcoming revision of the Lisbon strategy for the period after 2010.

The current Lisbon strategy has four domestic priority areas, with actions being proposed by the Commission, adopted by the European Council and then implemented at national level. The priority areas are: investing in people and modernising labour markets; improving the business environment, especially for SMEs; investing in knowledge and innovation; and energy and climate change. Actions are needed in all of these areas to strengthen the European economy. The strategy also has an external dimension, focusing on maintaining open markets for trade and investment.

A broad range of policies were launched in the first phase of the Community Lisbon Programme (CLP) from 2005 to 2008. While progress was made in some important areas (notably the establishment of a long-term agenda for reducing business regulations) the overall impact of the measures implemented is difficult to assess, since one key action, the Services Directive introduced in 2006, is only due to be implemented fully by the end of 2009. If this is achieved, it will provide a marked boost to competitive pressures within the EU economy. The second phase of the CLP, covering actions for 2008-10, saw a more focused agenda being adopted around the four domestic policy priorities of the Lisbon strategy, with additional initiatives to support the EU external agenda (EC, 2008). Important initiatives that have emerged over the past 18 months include the establishment of long-term agendas for the development of an integrated European Research Area and the development of a comprehensive energy and climate policy strategy, further measures to improve the business environment, such as the enhanced Better Regulation agenda and new initiatives on tackling remaining regulations in some network industries.

Key areas for further reforms

This *Survey* focuses on some of the key structural policy challenges that the European economy faces in the coming years to improve the prospects for stronger productivity growth. These include strengthening innovation performance, deepening the single market, making the transition to a low-carbon economy and opening European markets to the rest of the world. As emphasised by the Lisbon strategy, progress in achieving reforms in each of these areas will not only have a direct effect on longer term growth prospects but will also have additional indirect effects by providing more favourable economy-wide conditions for progress in other areas. For instance, further steps towards the single market from tackling anti-competitive product market regulations in previously untouched service sectors and network industries will intensify competitive pressures on companies and improve business efficiency and productivity growth. But, it will also do much to enhance incentives to innovate. A much broader set of actions will also be needed to ensure that innovations can be developed, diffused and used effectively throughout an integrated European research area. Progress in this area will be vital to support longer run productivity growth and also boost workforce skills and human capital. It is also vital that the capital stock in Europe is decarbonised in the coming decades to help combat climate change. However, carbon pricing and other mitigation policies must be implemented efficiently to limit potential adverse effects on growth prospects. Finally, the EU must continue to push for further global trade liberalisation, and could further this agenda by doing more unilaterally, especially in agriculture. Enhanced international openness would provide a direct boost to economic growth (OECD, 2003) and facilitate the diffusion of knowledge into and out of the EU.

A common theme developed throughout the *Survey* is the need for better measurement in many of the areas in which reforms are planned, and better evaluation of the policies that have been introduced. These needs are recognised by the Commission and the member states, and progress is being made to improve impact assessments and *ex post* evaluations. But more could be done. The recession provides a challenging backdrop against which reforms have to be introduced, and it is all the more important to ensure that priorities are chosen on the basis of clear evidence of market failures and specific policy objectives whose impacts are rigorously analysed and enforced. Regulatory and other policy measures should be targeted and proportional to the market failures themselves. The recession will also affect the optimal sequencing of reforms, as discussed below. The spring European Council has recently emphasised that full use should be made of the renewed Lisbon Strategy for Growth and Jobs in the current situation, and that the short-term initiatives introduced by member states should remain consistent with their longer term reform objectives.

The Commission has emphasised the importance of education and training policies in helping to alleviate the impact of the recession on employment. If member states are able to maintain, or even increase, their investment in education and training, it will help to ensure that the workforce holds on to and upgrades its skills, thus equipping people for opportunities that will arise once the crisis is over. It will also help to tackle rising youth unemployment. Efforts by member states to offer a learning place to all youngsters and to offer re-training programmes that focus on skills, employability and adaptability, will be crucial. More generally, for the most hard-to-place unemployed, targeted hiring and the provision of subsidies to help pay for in-job work experience would also help. Over the longer term, current Commission policies emphasise the need to shift education systems from focusing on knowledge to a focus on skills.

Reform of the European financial regulatory and supervisory framework is especially critical

The benefits of both short-term policy stimulus and longer term structural reforms will be enhanced by a well functioning financial system. The financial system has a critical role in fostering economic growth by directing savings to the most productive investment projects, and helping households and firms smooth their access to financing for consumption and investment following temporary income shocks. However, as the current financial crisis has demonstrated all too clearly, financial markets are subject to a range of market failures that can inhibit this role and lead to bouts of financial instability with significant economic and social costs. Well-designed prudential regulation and supervision should protect depositors and the stability of the financial system, while not impeding improvements in efficiency or hindering competition. Prudential supervision has both a micro dimension, ensuring that depositors' interests are protected and that individual institutions do not pose a risk to the financial system, and a macro dimension, limiting distress in the financial system as a whole in order to protect the overall economy from significant losses in real output. Assessing micro and macro risks correctly is very difficult. As discussed in the recent euro area *Survey* (OECD,

2009c), the European Union faces additional challenges from having an integrated capital market that operates with a supervisory framework that is primarily national, albeit within a common framework. This raises issues about the resilience of the single market for financial services and the risks that arise for the European financial system, because the centralisation of key risk management functions within cross-border financial groups and the ongoing integration of EU financial markets make it increasingly difficult to organise financial supervision and crisis management on a predominantly national basis. Reform of the European financial regulatory and supervisory framework is thus essential for the longer term health of the European economy.

As discussed in the last *Economic Survey of the Euro Area* (OECD, 2009c), the current fragmented approach to supervision in the EU may increase the potential for financial instability by making it more difficult to assess fully the activities of systemically important cross-border institutions. There are substantial differences in the powers granted to national supervisors in the different member states, both in respect of what they can do by way of supervision and in respect of enforcement actions (including sanctions). In most member states, crisis management and resolution are not supervisory tasks, and EU legislation does not harmonise restructuring procedures. The fragmented approach also complicates crisis management and resolution. The lack of convergence in national frameworks also means that cross-border financial institutions can face a considerable regulatory burden, adding to their costs. Although colleges of supervisors for cross-border financial institutions are being set up,[1] it may still be difficult for national supervisors to gain access to adequate information and, currently, there are no established mechanisms for resolving disputes between home and host supervisors, or sharing the financial burden of cross-border failures. The Commission will issue a consultation document on a bank stabilisation and resolution framework in the EU. Proposals have been put forward by the Commission to strengthen the overall supervisory architecture in Europe, as discussed below.

The macro-prudential framework should also be developed further. The ECB currently publishes a *Financial Stability Review* which draws attention to the main risks and vulnerabilities, and assesses whether the euro area financial system is capable of withstanding shocks and disruptions that are severe enough to significantly impair its intermediation function. Macro-prudential analysis is mainly undertaken by the Banking Supervision Committee of the European System of Central Banks (ESCB).[2] It also reviews structural developments in the EU banking sector that are relevant to central banks and supervisory authorities, publishing a separate annual report. This means that the existing approach to macro-prudential policy is largely confined to providing information on risks, although significant informational gaps remain. In addition, the overall arrangements place too much emphasis on the supervision of individual firms, and there is little in the way of concrete instruments to ensure that warnings about the build-up of systemically important risks are acted upon by national supervisors.

After reviewing the existing European regulatory and supervisory framework, the 2009 *OECD Economic Survey of the Euro Area* (OECD, 2009c) recommended a number of reforms to strengthen the European financial supervisory framework including: moving toward a more centralised structure for the supervision of large complex financial institutions; and investigating possibilities to reduce the pro-cyclicality of financial markets, such as counter-cyclical adjustments to capital ratios. The European Commission has been very active over the past year in taking steps to improve the financial regulatory and supervisory architecture, both in response to the financial crisis and in line with longer term reform priorities. ECOFIN adopted a roadmap in December 2007 to enhance the functioning of the Lamfalussy framework, especially the functioning of the Committees of Supervisors. ECOFIN has also drawn up a list of policy responses to the recent financial market crisis. Another roadmap was adopted in October 2007 to strengthen the financial stability framework, and in particular crisis management arrangements. A third roadmap was set out in October 2007, in response to the financial turmoil. This roadmap focused on improving: i) transparency, ii) valuation standards of complex financial instruments, iii) prudential rules, in view of encouraging better risk management, and iv) market functioning, notably the role of credit rating agencies.

Most importantly, the de Larosière Group was set up to examine how the European financial supervisory system can be improved to provide better macro and micro-prudential oversight. The final report was completed in February 2009. The following key recommendations were made for improving micro-prudential oversight:

- A decentralised European System of Financial Supervisors (ESFS) should be set up by 2012 and colleges of supervisors should be set up for all cross-border institutions.

- Three new European authorities should be set up, replacing the Level 3 Lamfalussy Committees – the Committee of European Banking Supervisors (CEBS), the Committee of European Insurance and Occupational Pensions Supervisors (CEIOPS) and the Committee of European Securities Regulators (CESR). The new Authorities would be the European Banking Authority (EBA), the European Insurance and Occupational Pensions Authority (EIOPA) and the European Securities Authority (ESA).

- The ESFS should be independent of political authorities but accountable to them. The Authorities should be managed by a board comprised of the chairs of the national supervisory authorities. The chairpersons and directors general of the Authorities should be full-time independent professionals. The ESFS should rely on a common set of harmonised rules and have access to high-quality information.

- The Authorities should have the following key competencies: legally binding mediation between national supervisors; adoption of binding supervisory standards; adoption of binding technical decisions applicable to individual financial institutions; oversight and co-ordination of colleges of supervisors; licensing and supervision of specific EU-wide entities including credit rating agencies; and binding co-operation with the European Systemic Risk Council to ensure adequate macro-prudential supervision.

The following key recommendations were made by the de Larosière Group for improving macro-prudential oversight:

- A new body called the European Systemic Risk Council (ESRC) should be set up. The ESRC should be chaired by the ECB President and the ECB should provide logistical support. The ESRC should be composed of members of the General Council of the ECB, the chairpersons of the key micro-prudential authorities (EBA, EIA and ESA) and a representative from the European Commission.

- The ESRC should pool and analyse all information relevant for financial stability pertaining to macroeconomic conditions and to macro-prudential developments in all financial sectors. A proper flow of information between the ESRC and the micro-prudential supervisors must be ensured.

- An effective risk warning system should be put in place under the auspices of the ESRC and of the Economic and Financial Committee (EFC). The ESRC should be responsible for issuing macro-prudential risk warnings. There should be mandatory follow-up and, where appropriate, action taken by the relevant competent authorities in the EU. If the risks are serious the ESRC should inform the chairman of the EFC. The EFC, working with the Commission, will implement a strategy ensuring that the risks are addressed. If the ESRC judges that the response of a national supervisor to a risk warning is inadequate, it will inform the chairman of the EFC with a view to action being taken against that supervisor.

In May 2009, the Commission published a Communication on European Financial Supervision, for decision at the June European Council. This Communication sets out the basic architecture for a new European financial supervisory framework, fleshing out the recommendations put forward in the de Larosière report. At the June Council, European leaders reached an agreement retaining most of the Commission's proposals, while resolving earlier divergences. The agreed text retains the European System of Financial Supervisors' binding decision making powers to resolve disputes between home and host supervisors. However, there was no agreement on burden sharing with the text stating clearly that decisions made by the European Supervisory Authorities should not have fiscal consequences for member states. The agreed text also retains the role foreseen by the Commission for the European Systemic Risk Board. However, rather than being chaired by the ECB president, the European Council concluded that the chair should be elected by the members of the ECB's General Council. When implemented, the reforms will significantly strengthen the European regulatory and supervisory framework. A key advantage of the ESFS is that it would be an evolutionary reform of the existing European micro-prudential framework and not require any Treaty changes. Home country national supervisors with existing relationships and understanding of cross-border institutions would retain primary supervisory responsibility. Yet by proposing binding oversight on specific EU-wide institutions (i.e. credit rating agencies and post-trading financial market infrastructures) and dispute resolution powers for the European authorities, the ESFS should ensure that the interests of host countries and the European-wide dimension of cross-border institutions' operations are better taken into account. It will be essential that the binding powers and independence of the Authorities are retained in the final legislation. The new European Supervisory Authorities will have to be monitored to ensure that they appropriately balance the interests of home and host countries and adequately resolve disputes between them. European authorities will also have to ensure that the implied proliferation of colleges of supervisors does not become unwieldy. If these issues are not satisfactorily resolved, steps toward a single supervisor for all systemically important financial institutions may need to be considered in the longer term. It is essential that member states eventually agree to more concrete mechanisms to clarify financial crisis management/resolution systems, including guarantee schemes and burden sharing.

On the macro-prudential side, the ESRC, renamed European Systemic Risk Board (ESRB) by the Council, and the close involvement it will have with the micro-prudential regulatory authorities should significantly improve the flow of information between the two levels of prudential supervision and increase the likelihood that signs of systemic risk are quickly recognised and acted upon. However, the rules governing how micro-prudential supervisors are to respond to specific ESRB recommendations will have to be designed very carefully to ensure that concrete actions are taken following such recommendations.

The Commission has also outlined other measures to counteract the financial crisis and has been implementing an ambitious agenda for broader financial services reform since the intensification of the financial crisis in October 2008. In November, the Commission outlined proposals to more effectively regulate credit rating agencies by ensuring that they comply with rigorous rules, are not affected by conflicts of interest, remain vigilant on the quality of the rating methodology and the ratings, and act in a transparent manner. The proposal, which has subsequently been adopted by the European Parliament and Council also includes a surveillance regime whereby a college of European securities regulators will supervise credit rating agencies.

The Commission has adopted three major guidance documents on measures taken in response to the financial crisis: the Banking Communication of 13 October 2008, the Recapitalisation Communication of 5 December 2008 and the Communication on the treatment of impaired assets of 25 February 2009. These Communications explain how state aid rules will be applied in the exceptional circumstances of the current crisis. The Communication on restructuring is forthcoming. These Communications were intended to provide guidance on how to take effective measures to stabilise financial markets and ensure sustained lending to the real economy without creating undue distortions of competition by simply exporting problems from one member state to the others. The methodology set out in these guidance documents has permitted the swift design and approval of a high number of national schemes and individual measures to tackle the crisis whilst trying to avoid harmful economic imbalances between banks and between member states. The Commission will need to remain vigilant to ensure that member state support schemes continue to be consistent with the spirit of a single European market for financial services.

In response to the de Larosière report, in March 2009 the Commission presented a Communication announcing an ambitious programme of further regulatory reforms to be implemented by the end of 2009. In April 2009, the Commission announced a legislative proposal establishing regulatory and supervisory standards for alternative investment fund managers. It also outlined recommendations on the remuneration of directors and broader financial services remuneration, and issued a communication on retail investment products to strengthen the effectiveness of marketing safeguards. A revision of the Capital Requirements Directive (CRD) is expected to increase the quality and quantity of prudential capital for trading book activities and tackle complex securitisation (alongside the Basel initiative). Initiatives on tools for early intervention (bank stabilisation and resolution framework) and a report on derivatives and other complex structured products will also be issued.

In the second half of 2009, the Commission plans: further revisions of the CRD to supplement existing risk-based requirements and to issue a report on the CRD's procyclicality; a review of the Market Abuse Directive; a report on sanctioning regimes for financial market wrongdoing; measures on responsible lending and borrowing; a review of deposit guarantee schemes in banking, insurance and securities markets; and measures to strengthen the voice of European investors in financial services policymaking.

A detailed review of Europe's response to the financial crisis and this broad legislative, regulatory and supervisory agenda will be undertaken in the next euro area *Survey*, scheduled for 2010. It is very welcome that the European authorities are addressing the failures in the existing regulatory and supervisory system so comprehensively. Still, it should be remembered that regulating the financial industry is complicated by the absence of clear standards against which regulation can be judged. There is often a trade-off between promoting soundness on the one hand, and innovation and wealth creation on the other. Unnecessary regulation may damage the functioning of financial markets, stifle innovation and hamper economic growth. Badly-designed regulation can also enhance instability through regulatory arbitrage or by encouraging excessive risk taking. Moreover, because of information asymmetries, it will always be challenging for regulators and supervisors to stay informed about the institutions they supervise and to keep pace with innovations and their potential impact on the stability of financial institutions. For these reasons, regulation (and changes to regulations) should proceed cautiously with a clear sense of its own limits, the market failures it is trying to offset, and how it will address such failures. It is welcome that legislative initiatives will be accompanied by impact assessments and consultations, in line with the better regulation principles. These procedures aim to improve the quality of the Commission's policy proposals in terms of their efficiency, effectiveness and coherence. To be fully effective, such impact assessments should be revisited if legislative amendments are made by the European Parliament and the European Council.

Tackling the crisis and supporting structural reforms

Past experience shows that economic crises can provide a propitious moment to introduce longer term structural reforms by demonstrating the limitations of existing policies and by weakening the resistance to change (OECD, 2007a and 2009b). The crisis has already triggered reforms to tackle weaknesses in the financial system which, if achieved and implemented effectively, should support longer term growth prospects. As set out in the European Economic Recovery Plan, it is also possible that short-term fiscal measures to support demand through the recession can offer longer term supply-side benefits. Where possible, such reforms are to be preferred to ones that offer only short-term demand stimulus, although the latter remain important if they offer a particularly timely and large stimulus because of the need to support private sector demand. Fiscal easing may also help to offset any short-term economic slack associated with structural reforms.

Short-term policies with long-run benefits

The fiscal easing underway in many European economies has provided an opportunity to facilitate some worthwhile structural reforms in member states. In particular, well-founded additional investments in infrastructure, including broadband roll-out, and new low-emission technologies will offer long-term supply-side and environmental benefits as well as an immediate boost to activity. In several member states, it has proved feasible to bring forward the timing of previously planned infrastructure projects that have been identified after a careful cost-benefit analysis. The Commission has also announced that some of the financial assistance available to lower-income regions under the current structural fund programmes (from 2007 to 2013) is to be brought forward to provide financial support for infrastructure projects. As of March 2009, new measures to support investment activity represented approximately one-third of the total number of structural measures introduced by all EU member states since the onset of the economic crisis (EC, 2009b).

Careful thought is necessary in designing structural measures at a time of crisis to ensure that market failures are indeed being addressed and that the policies do not endanger the European single market or hamper external access to the European Economic Area. All EU member states have introduced actions to support industrial sectors and businesses. In total, these also account for a third of the number of structural actions taken since the onset of the crisis (EC, 2009b). Some measures are clearly designed to tackle particular market failures, such as the difficulties being experienced by small and medium-sized enterprises (SMEs) in accessing financial support. Others are, in effect, direct subsidies to support particular sectors of the economy. Such measures need to be evaluated on a case-by-case basis. In some instances, they provide support to a systemically important sector, such as support and implicit guarantees for financial institutions. But other measures could potentially distort competition and resource allocation by delaying the exit of non-competitive producers. It is welcome that the Commission has demonstrated a clear willingness to intervene promptly against proposed fiscal and financial support by member states that would violate single market principles by favouring particular companies over others. It is essential that the Commission and member states prepare exit strategies setting out a clear agenda for ending emergency support measures to companies as the economy begins to recover.

The remaining third of the structural measures support the functioning of the labour market and household purchasing power. Such measures have become increasingly important, with unemployment rising rapidly in the EU since mid-2008. The European Employment Summit, held in May 2009, set out a series of actions to be implemented at national and European levels to mitigate the labour market effects of the recession and improve the prospects for job creation in the medium term. At the national level, emphasis was placed on maintaining employment by adjusting working hours, improving the efficiency of labour market programmes and national employment services, developing and better matching skills with the market needs, reductions in social security contributions and support for low-income households. At the European level, the Commission is to build on the "New Skills for New Jobs" initiative, introduced in 2008, to help identify new job opportunities and skill needs in the EU labour market. Additional funds are also being made available to support business start-ups, and the European Social Fund and the European Globalisation Adjustments Fund have been revised to maximise the financial support available to member states to alleviate the employment and social consequences of the crisis. If implemented effectively and promptly, these measures should all help to dampen the impact of the recession on labour markets and the necessary adjustments that will arise from other structural reforms. The Commission needs to continue to monitor the effectiveness of these measures and provide guidance on policy design and facilitate the exchange of information about policy experiences.

Overcoming barriers to reforms

Structural reforms can be difficult to adopt and implement because they typically involve clear and substantial up-front redistribution away from incumbents in protected sectors in return for future efficiency gains that will fully materialise only over a considerable period (OECD, 2007a). The adjustments arising from such reforms may be especially high during a recession. Thus, the sequencing and synergies between structural policies are especially important, with past experience of reform efforts currently offering important guidance for European policymakers. In particular, successful product market reforms have often been found to facilitate subsequent labour market reforms, with additional competitive pressures, augmented by supportive macroeconomic policies, helping to stimulate new job creation (OECD, 2007a). This emphasises the importance of pushing ahead with measures to deepen the single market in Europe and maintain the external openness of the European economy. Additional expenditure on active labour market programmes and carefully-designed policies that provide short-term compensation to displaced workers for their foregone earnings can also help to facilitate adjustment and acceptance of reforms (OECD, 2007b).

The experience of OECD countries points to a number of additional steps that governments can take to overcome barriers to reform (Arnold *et al.*, 2009). First, binding external commitments can help, a fact that underlines the continuing importance of the Commission taking active steps to ensure prompt and effective transposition of single market legislation. Secondly, reform is easier where the costs of the *status quo* are well understood by stakeholders and the public. This points to the need for comprehensive and transparent explanations of the short- and long-run costs and benefits of reforms by the European Commission, as well as member states, underpinned by solid research. Finally, individual regulatory reforms tend to be harder to resist when rolled out in the context of a wide-ranging regulatory reform. Such a strategy needs to be based on clear principles, such as competitive neutrality, structural reform of public monopolies, removal of legislative restrictions on competition except where they can clearly be shown to promote the public interest and the establishment of non-discriminatory access regimes for public infrastructure. A broad consensus on such principles can make regulatory privileges harder to defend while creating a presumption in favour of reducing entry barriers and pro-competitive reforms. Thus the Better Regulation agenda and the single market programme remain the key for successful reform efforts in Europe.

Fiscal policy after the crisis

Public finances are coming under severe pressure during the downturn as falls in economic activity and asset markets have driven down revenues, whilst placing upward pressure on cyclical spending. Discretionary measures introduced to support demand and the assistance provided to the financial and other sectors have also weakened fiscal positions. The EU average general government budget deficit is projected to rise to over 7% of GDP in 2010 from less than 1% of GDP in 2007 at the onset of the financial market disruption. Government debt is rising rapidly, reflecting not only the budgetary deterioration but also debt incurred to finance capital injections into financial institutions. Additional implicit assistance has been provided through government guarantees to the financial sector. Further ahead, budgetary pressures from ageing in Europe are set to rise substantially. The latest estimates by the European Commission suggest that ageing will raise public expenditure by 4½ per cent of GDP over the next 50 years (EC, 2009a). These estimates could be even larger once allowance is made for a longer lasting effect of the economic crisis on potential output. In many member states, deteriorating public finances have already been reflected in higher interest rates.

To ensure long-run fiscal sustainability, it is vital that member states now begin to set out clear and credible plans for fiscal consolidation and implement these promptly once the recession ends. Early announcement of plans will help to anchor the medium-term expectations of savers and investors, and thus help to hold down the costs associated with the need to finance much higher debt levels. In this context, the Stability and Growth Pact (SGP) and the associated requirements placed on member states to produce medium-term convergence programmes will continue to have an important role to play. Most member states will have budget deficits well in excess of the 3% deficit threshold and face a steadily rising stock of government debt by 2010. Prompt action can be taken to withdraw some forms of fiscal stimulus introduced during the recession, but other forms of expenditure, such as additional infrastructure investments, and guarantees for the financial sector, could be in place for several years. A cyclical upturn will also help to bring some budgetary improvements, but these are unlikely to prove sufficient to ensure long-run sustainability. In addition, structural fiscal measures will be required in many member states and effective implementation of the SGP will thus remain essential in the years ahead. But it will be challenging, not least because of the need to take due account of the recession and its effects on potential output when making judgements about the need for changes in the fiscal plans of member states. In particular, downward revisions to potential output will enhance the need for fiscal tightening, at least in the medium term. It will also be important to ensure that consolidation measures are carefully chosen to minimise any negative impact on longer term growth prospects. Potential options include steps to reduce public expenditure that is not growth-enhancing, or tax increases that are broadly-based and do not adversely affect the economic incentives of consumers and companies.

More generally, as discussed in the last *Economic Survey of the euro area* (OECD, 2009c), there remain several areas in which the SGP could be improved. The approaching impact of ageing on public finances in a context of reduced fiscal space reinforce the need for country-specific medium-term budgetary objectives to take due account of contingent and implicit liabilities. Additional weight will also need to be given to asset prices and other financial factors in fiscal assessments. Greater attention will also need to be placed on the quality of the public finances. The efficiency of government intervention can contribute to raising living standards, with key factors including the ways in which money is spent and the design of the tax system.

Notes

1. Regarding the major financial groups in the EU, colleges already exist.

2. Other bodies are now also involved in the assessment of financial stability. The EU Committees of Supervisors (CESR, CEBS and CEIOPS), also play a role by providing a bi-annual assessment of micro-prudential trends, potential risks and vulnerabilities to the Commission. These assessments are required to include a classification of the main risks and vulnerabilities and indicate to what extent such risks and vulnerabilities pose a threat to financial stability and, where necessary, propose preventative or remedial actions. The Economic and Financial Committee (EFC) also contributes through its Financial Stability Table.

Bibliography

Arnold, J., P. Hoeller, M. Morgan and A. Wörgötter (2009), "Structural Reforms and the Benefits of the Enlarged EU Internal Market: Much Achieved and Much to Do", *OECD Economics Department Working Paper*, No. 694, OECD, Paris.

Blanchard, O. and J. Wolfers (2001), "The Role of Shocks and Institutions in the Rise of European Unemployment: The Aggregate Evidence", *The Economic Journal*, Vol. 110, Issue 462.

Campbell, J.Y. and N.G. Mankiw (1987), "Are Output Fluctuations Transitory?", *The Quarterly Journal of Economics*, November.

Cerra, V. and S.C. Saxena (2007), "Growth Dynamics: The Myth of Economic Recovery", *BIS Working Papers*, No. 226.

Duval, R. and L. Vogel (2008), "Economic Resilience to Shocks: The Role of Structural Policies", *OECD Journal: Economic Studies*, Vol. 2008, pp. 201-238, OECD, Paris.

Duval, R. and C. de la Maisonneuve (2009), "Long-run GDP Growth Framework and Scenarios for the World Economy", *OECD Economics Department Working Paper*, No. 663, OECD, Paris.

EC (2008), "Implementation Report for the Community Lisbon Programme 2008-2010", *European Commission Communication*, COM(2008) 881 final.

EC (2009a), "The 2009 Ageing Report: Economic and Budgetary Projections for the EU-27 Member States (2008-2060)", *European Economy*, April.

EC (2009b), "Driving European Recovery", *European Commission Communication*, COM(2009) 114 final.

Furceri, D. and A. Mourougane (2009), "Financial Crises: Past Lessons and Policy Implications", *OECD Economics Department Working Paper,* No. 668, OECD, Paris.

Haugh, D., P. Ollivaud and D. Turner (2009), "The Macroeconomic Consequences of Banking Crises in OECD Countries", *OECD Economics Department Working Paper,* No. 683, OECD, Paris.

IMF (2009), *Global Financial Stability Report – Responding to the Financial Crisis and Measuring Systemic Risks,* IMF, Washington DC.

Logeay, C. and S. Tober (2005), "Hysteresis and NAIRU in the Euro Area", *IMK Working Paper* 4/2005.

Mourre, G. (2009), "What Explains the Differences in Income and Labour Utilisation and Drives Labour and Economic Growth in Europe? A GDP Accounting Perspective", *European Economy Economic Paper*, No. 354.

Nickell, S., L. Nunziata and W. Ochel (2005), "Unemployment in the OECD Since the 1960s: What Do we Know?", *Economic Journal,* Vol. 115, No. 500.

OECD (2003), *The Sources of Economic Growth in OECD Countries*, OECD, Paris.

OECD (2007a), *Going For Growth*, OECD, Paris.

OECD (2007b), "OECD Workers in the Global Economy: Increasingly Vulnerable?", *OECD Employment Outlook*, OECD, Paris.

OECD (2009a), *OECD Economic Outlook*, June, OECD, Paris.

OECD (2009b), *Going For Growth*, OECD, Paris.

OECD (2009c), *OECD Economic Surveys: Euro Area*, OECD, Paris.

Piger, J., J. Morely and C. Kim (2005), "Nonlinearity and the Permanent Effects of Recessions", *Journal of Applied Econometrics*, Vol. 20, Issue 2.

van Ark, B., M. O'Mahony and M. Timmer (2008), "What Drives the Productivity Gap Between Europe and the United States: Trends and Causes", *Journal of Economic Perspectives*, Winter.

Chapter 2

Strengthening research and innovation

The central importance of investing in knowledge and innovation for long-term growth is recognised in the Lisbon strategy. R&D expenditure in the EU is well below that in the United States and Japan and, despite the target for EU-wide R&D expenditure of 3% of GDP by 2010, limited progress has occurred in recent years. The Commission introduced a broad-based innovation strategy in 2006 and initial steps have been taken towards the formation of a European Research Area. More recently, the focus of policy has also turned towards encouraging and promoting the broader concept of "creativity". A key challenge for the Commission is to improve the measurement of creative and innovative activities and the evidence base regarding the key policy influences on these activities. Further steps should be taken to strengthen the European Research Area and encourage cross-border research co-operation and the mobility of researchers. Progress in completing the internal market should also stimulate innovation.

In 2000, the Lisbon agenda included a commitment to make Europe the most dynamic and competitive knowledge-based economy in the world, reflecting a recognition of the need to raise investment in knowledge-based activities to boost longer term growth prospects. The Barcelona Council meeting in 2002 subsequently agreed that research and development (R&D) expenditure at the EU-wide level should be raised to 3% of GDP by 2010, with two-thirds being funded by the business sector. This objective was motivated by a perceived need to raise R&D expenditure in the EU to the levels in the United States and Japan.

Following the meeting of the European Council in spring 2006, investment in knowledge and innovation has become one of the four priority areas of the renewed Lisbon strategy. The overall target for EU-wide R&D expenditure of 3% of GDP by 2010 was reaffirmed, and member states set their own specific targets within the framework of the National Reform Programmes. Detailed comparisons of their respective innovation performance are now being made in the annual Innovation Scoreboard. An annual assessment of the progress towards a more efficient European research environment is also made (EC, 2008a). An EU-level broad-based innovation strategy was introduced in 2006, bringing together a range of different policy areas and broadening the focus of policy to consider innovation outputs and the use made of innovations as well as research and development.

Within the current Community Lisbon Programme, two key objectives are to improve the framework conditions for innovation and to take action to further the creation of an integrated European Research Area, thus making possible the free movement of knowledge within the EU (the so-called "fifth freedom"). The broad-based innovation strategy is part of the policy mix for achieving these objectives. More recently, the focus of policy has also turned towards encouraging and promoting the broader concept of "creativity", with 2009 being designated the European year of creativity and innovation. The design and implementation of innovation-related policies raise issues that cut across a large number of directorates at the European Commission, and many policies have potential synergies, making policy coherence a difficult, but vitally important task.

Despite all the initiatives that have been introduced in recent years, tangible progress has been limited to date, with research efforts and innovation activities in the EU continuing to lag behind those in the United States and Japan. To some extent this may not be surprising, since many innovation policies will only yield benefits in the longer term. But it might also reflect gaps in policy coverage or areas where improvements can usefully be considered.

This chapter reviews the innovation policies pursued by the European Commission and focuses in detail on five key issues – the labour market for researchers, intellectual property, financial support, linkages between universities and businesses, and new measures to support the demand for innovations. All are areas where a better policy mix could be expected to improve the prospects for innovation. Of course, improved innovation outcomes will not be achieved through specific innovation policies alone. Completion of the single market programme and the elimination of anti-competitive product market regulation are especially important, given the favourable effects of competitive pressures and financial integration on innovation performance in OECD economies, particularly when catching-up with other economies (Aghion *et al.*, 2005; Jaumotte and Pain, 2005a). Maintaining and promoting free trade, while ensuring continued investment in skills at all levels and ages, including schools and vocational training, are also essential if new knowledge is to be created, diffused and utilised effectively.

The sharp recession is likely to curtail private sector innovation activities in the near term. Economic uncertainty has risen, as has the cost of external finance. In this environment, it is likely that firms will curtail investments with a long and uncertain payback. However, the public sector can make up for at least some of this likely shortfall by incorporating forward-looking structural measures that will continue to support innovation in the mix of policies being adopted to tackle the economic downturn. The European Economic Recovery Plan includes: measures to finance additional investment in broadband networks, which are an important infrastructure for many forms of innovation activity and the diffusion of knowledge; funding for research into new technologies to promote greater energy efficiency; enhanced support for small and medium-sized enterprises (SMEs); and investment financed through the structural funds. Continued efforts to reduce regulatory burdens and open markets will also support future innovation activities. It will be important to account for these measures, and the impact of the recession, when assessing future progress towards the various goals of innovation policy.

A snapshot of innovation performance

The share of research and development (R&D) spending in GDP is one of the most widely used indicators to compare the research activities of different countries, although it is only an indicator of inputs into the innovation process. In recent years, the share has largely stagnated in most OECD economies, including the EU (Figure 2.1, left panel). R&D amounted to just over 1.8% of GDP in the EU economies in 2006, unchanged from the level in 2000 and well below the level in other large economies, such as the United States and Japan. There has not been any progress towards the stated objective of an EU-wide 3% R&D ratio by 2010, and there appears little chance that this will be met in the near future.

Figure 2.1. **Gross domestic and business enterprise expenditure on R&D**

As a percentage of GDP

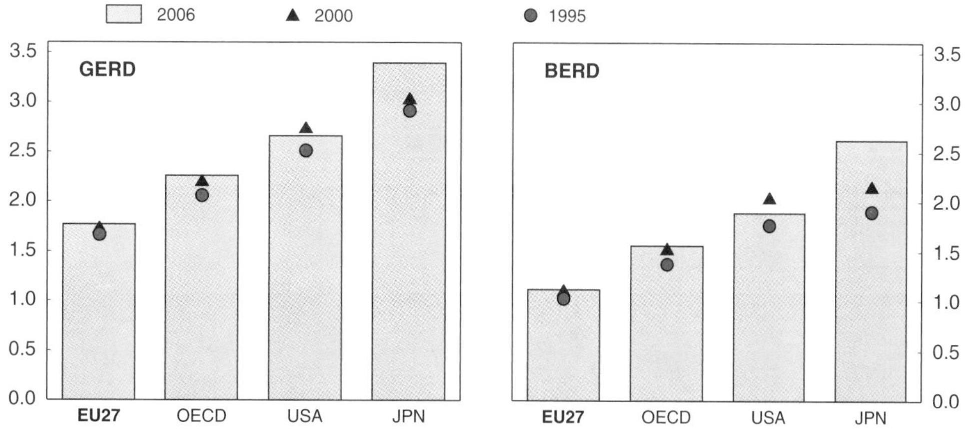

Source: OECD (2008), *Main Science and Technology Indicators*, Vol. 2008/2.

StatLink http://dx.doi.org/10.1787/712251534572

However, the gap between R&D intensity in the EU and the United States has narrowed since 2000 (although the gap with Japan has not) because R&D intensity in the United States has declined. Some progress has been made within the EU, with R&D intensity rising in 17 EU Member States over the period 2000-06. However, most of these countries are ones with comparatively low levels of R&D intensity. This has been offset by stagnation or small falls in other member states with comparatively high R&D intensities. To this extent, the range of innovation policies introduced in recent years by the Commission and the member states may have provided some marginal near-term gains.

At the national level, R&D spending varies widely in Europe, although only two member economies, Sweden and Finland, have a higher aggregate R&D ratio than both Japan and the United States. The variation in state-level R&D expenditures in the United States is also broad, but the median R&D intensity is much higher than in the EU. In 2006, seven US states had an R&D intensity greater than that of the most research-intensive EU economy (van Pottelsberghe, 2008). On average over 1995-2003, the gap between the EU and the United States was present in most main industrial sectors, with R&D intensity in the EU being higher only in the electricity, gas and water sector (EC, 2008b). Although part of the differences between R&D intensity in the EU and other large OECD economies is accounted for by a different mix of business sectors (because of differences in the R&D intensities of different sectors (Guellec and Sachwald, 2008), this is not the sole factor behind the lower level of R&D in Europe. There are also structural differences in the propensity to invest in research and development in some sectors, particularly high-tech ones. The single largest share of national R&D is performed in the business sector, which is also the major source of the cross-country dispersion in aggregate R&D expenditure. Not surprisingly, expenditure in the EU is again much weaker than that in other OECD economies, and especially than in Japan (Figure 2.1, right panel).

At the EU level there has been little progress towards the implicit objective of having 1% of GDP public funding for R&D (implied by the objective of having two-thirds of the 3% R&D objective financed by the business sector), even though this can be more directly controlled by member states (Figure 2.2, left panel). Indeed, the amount of EU-wide public funding for R&D has continued to decline relative to GDP since 2000. Again, there have been marked

Figure 2.2. **Government-financed GERD and higher education expenditure on R&D**
As a percentage of GDP

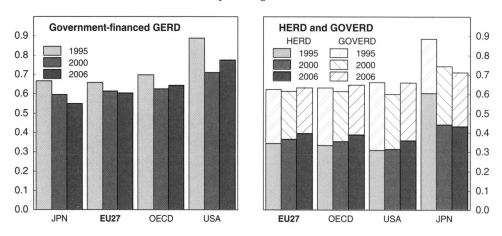

Source: OECD (2008), *Main Science and Technology Indicators*, Vol. 2008/2.

StatLink http://dx.doi.org/10.1787/712281454502

differences across countries, with government funding for R&D as a percentage of GDP rising in 14 member states, but stagnating or falling in other member states. In addition, there is a clear shift by many EU member states away from direct funding of private sector research *via* grants and subsidies to indirect funding through tax credits for R&D outlays. The latter, which offers a more effective means of support for R&D (Jaumotte and Pain, 2005a) has a clear budgetary cost, but is not reflected in the R&D funding data.

Higher education institutions and government research institutes also undertake R&D, funded either by government or the private sector. Here, the comparative performance of the EU is somewhat better (Figure 2.2, right panel), especially in the higher education sector, where R&D intensity (HERD) has risen over time and is similar to that in other OECD economies. This development is encouraging, given evidence of the longer term positive benefits of public sector research for private sector innovation (Jaumotte and Pain, 2005a; van Pottelsberghe, 2008). In contrast, the amount of R&D undertaken within the public sector (GOVERD) has edged down relative to GDP in the EU, and remains lower than in the other large economies.

The overall picture provided by the R&D data seems to be representative of the broader innovative capacity of Europe. An alternative indicator of innovation activities is the OECD data on triadic patents.[1] Patents per capita have increased in all countries over the past two decades, although there has been comparatively little change in the most recent years for which data are available (Figure 2.3, left panel). Again, patenting levels in the EU lag behind those in the other major economies.[2] There are also fewer patents with foreign (non-EU) co-inventors in the EU27 than in the United States (OECD, 2008a), suggesting that the European Research Area may be less open than that of the United States. The patent data are based on the country of residence of the applicant. Thus, even if non-European countries have a comparative advantage in undertaking research, with European companies choosing to locate R&D activities outside the EU, the resulting location of the patent applicant would still be shown as the EU. Similarly, patent applications in Europe by non-EU enterprises who undertake research in the EU would be registered as non-EU applications.

Figure 2.3. **Triadic patents and scientific articles**

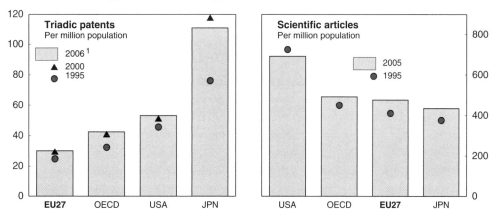

1. Or latest available year.

Source: OECD (2008), *Main Science and Technology Indicators*, Vol. 2008/2; OECD (2008), *OECD Science, Technology and Industry Outlook 2008*; OECD (2008), *National Accounts*.

StatLink ⟶ *http://dx.doi.org/10.1787/712282518571*

The number of scientific publications, another indicator of research outputs, has also risen rapidly over the past 10 to 15 years (Figure 2.3, right panel). However, publications per capita in the EU lag well behind those in the United States. Highly-cited researchers are also much more likely to work in the United States rather than in the EU (Bauwens *et al.*, 2007 and EC, 2008a). Thus, across a variety of different international indicators of innovation activity, it appears clear that innovation in the European Union is some way below that in other major economies.

R&D investment-related indicators are largely an input measure into the overall innovation process, although they also provide a signal of the overall attractiveness of the EU as a research location. Patents and publications are intermediate outputs. The formal definition of innovation, set out in the OECD Oslo Manual, is output-based, reflecting the successful commercial introduction of new products and processes. Direct output indicators of firm-level innovation performance in Europe are available from the successive waves of the Community Innovation Survey (CIS), which provides indicators of direct relevance to European policymakers. Expenditure on innovation includes not just R&D, but also investment in new machinery and equipment and expenditure on training necessary for the innovative activity. Companies can also undertake design and organisational innovations (although these are not always included in survey-based measures of innovation). The fourth CIS (CIS4) found that around 40% of all enterprises in the EU undertook some kind of innovative activity (Eurostat, 2008). Innovative companies were larger on average than non-innovative companies, accounting for around two-thirds of total employment. Three-quarters of the innovative companies invested in advanced machinery and equipment, and around half in R&D and training. R&D expenditure accounted for only a little over a half of total expenditure on innovation (by innovating companies).[3] When questioned about the factors hampering innovative activities, the costs of innovation, uncertainty about demand, a lack of qualified personnel and a lack of partners to co-operate with, were the four most important factors. Although it is difficult to compare all of the CIS data directly with data from surveys in other countries (OECD, 2008a), the available micro-data evidence suggests that the proportion of firms undertaking innovation activities in Europe are not different from other OECD economies.

The concept of "creativity" has begun to receive greater policy attention in Europe, with the Commission designating 2009 as the Year of Creativity and Innovation. There is an urgent need to define and measure creativity at individual, regional and national level. Work on this has already begun. However, there are significant challenges involved defining and measuring creativity (Box 2.1), and until these are overcome, any policy initiative should proceed only cautiously. In the first instance, efforts should concentrate on establishing whether it is feasible to measure creativity and, if so, identify the necessary steps required to be able to conduct large scale surveys to obtain data on the development and levels of creative skills. Indicators that measure the extent of organisational, design and marketing innovations in the EU will be needed for policy and strategy making. CIS4 data suggest that around two-fifths of European enterprises introduced organisational and/or marketing innovations (Eurostat, 2008), a similar proportion to the numbers introducing other forms of innovation.

More generally, there is a clear need for the Commission to work towards obtaining more timely and comprehensive measures of all forms of innovation activities, especially in service sectors. As things stand, evidence of the effects of the recession on innovative activities will not emerge for some time, making it difficult to identify areas that may need

Box 2.1. **Creativity**

The objective of "European Year" initiatives is to stimulate political debate and raise public awareness of the issues involved. 2009 has been termed the Year of Creativity and Innovation. Creativity is viewed as a driver of innovation, as well as a concept that encompasses the range of workforce skills and attributes that are needed in an increasingly knowledge-based economy. The launch report on creativity and innovation had the key message that investment in education and in the skills and creative capacity of Europe should be the top priority of EU institutions and governments.

The focus on creativity can be seen as an acknowledgement of the central importance of skills, knowledge and life-long learning for innovation outcomes. It is also a reflection of the changing nature of innovation, with non-technological innovations and user-driven open innovations becoming increasingly prevalent sources of innovation, as well as the rapid growth of intellectual property covered by design, trademark and copyright protections. Much of this form of innovation takes place in service sectors, including business and cultural services.

A clear definition of creativity or any widely-accepted agreement on how it could be measured is needed. Without this, well-founded policymaking in this area is impossible. To the extent that it focuses attention on the skills needed for innovation and the importance of education policies, creativity is a useful concept. But the need for creativity should certainly not be taken as a rationale for policy support for non-profit "creative industries".

One approach to measuring creativity is based on estimates of the overall economic importance of the creative industries. While there are differences in the approaches adopted in different economies, creative industries are generally estimated to account for between 4-8% of GDP in most European economies (Hölzl, 2006). Another possible approach would be to make use of concepts already identified in existing statistics, such as balance of payments statistics for trade in services, to monitor the activities of sectors in which creativity is especially important. For example, it is possible to identify trade in categories such as royalties and license fees, research and development services, architectural and engineering services and audiovisual services. In 2006, exports of this group of activities represented just over 0.5% of GDP for the EU (extra-EU trade) and just under 0.7% of GDP in the United States (OECD, 2008b).

These approaches focus on only a handful of sectors of the economy. The emphasis on skills for innovation would suggest that a much broader economy-wide concept be employed if creativity is to be a focus for policymakers, with use being made of survey-based indicators of skills. This is something that the Commission is presently working on, with an initiative that aims to provide a list of a limited number of indicators covering the various dimensions of creativity (derived from existing statistical sources). The OECD is also currently exploring this, as part of the ongoing work on the OECD innovation strategy. Until such indicators are developed more fully, making use of the data on non-technological innovations in the Community Innovation Survey, and possibly expanding the range of information collected about such innovations, might prove a practical way forward (DTI, 2005).

support. More comprehensive measures of innovation outputs would also facilitate evaluation of innovation policy initiatives and provide a clearer indication of the range of factors that constrain the innovative capabilities of European companies (Arundel *et al.*, 2006). The longstanding Community Innovation Survey provides the EU with a useful vehicle for obtaining such measures.

How useful are targets for R&D expenditure?

The target for research and development expenditure set at the Barcelona Council in 2002 has not been met, and is unlikely to be anytime soon. One drawback of the target is that outcomes cannot be controlled directly by member states or the Commission, as they depend mainly on private sector decisions. This raises the question of whether it is sensible to continue to maintain this target. If it cannot be justified, there will be a danger of creating policy distortions, because failure to approach the target could provide impetus for further policy initiatives that may offer limited benefit (van Pottelsberghe, 2008). The European Commission has set up expert groups to evaluate the impact of the target on the policies adopted by the EU and the member states.[4] Member states were initially benchmarked against the EU-wide objective, but more attention is now given to their performance relative to each other (EC, 2009a). It would seem sensible to enhance this analysis by obtaining clearer empirical estimates of some of the key factors that might account for the differences in R&D expenditure across countries. At present differences in particular factors can be observed, but little is known about their relative importance.

Setting an explicit target for publicly-performed R&D has been suggested as an alternative to setting a target for economy-wide R&D (van Pottelsberghe, 2008). This has the advantage of being something directly controlled by government, but would not directly focus attention on the issue of insufficient market led R&D, which is the main source of the R&D investment gap for the EU. In the longer term, a higher level of public R&D should prove favourable for private R&D investment. However, the gains could be slow to arrive, especially if, in the short term, greater public-sector competition for an inelastic supply of researchers were to push up wage costs for the private sector (Jaumotte and Pain, 2005a).

A target for R&D may also be becoming less relevant because of the changing nature of innovation. Increasingly, innovation takes place in service sectors, where R&D is less likely to be undertaken during the innovation process. The connection between innovation inputs, such as R&D, and innovation outputs is thus changing over time. Open innovations (such as open-source software) are also becoming more important, especially in research-intensive fields such as information and communications technologies. More generally, R&D is rapidly becoming more internationalised, with companies undertaking collaborative research efforts across national borders, or sourcing R&D from abroad (OECD, 2008a). In some cases, research activities are being off-shored to take account of expertise available in other economies, including non-OECD economies (OECD, 2008a). In such an environment it may make less sense to focus on the amount of R&D expenditure in a particular location, especially if other locations have a comparative advantage because of size or cost in undertaking research. Scientific and technological co-operation is rising rapidly, both inside the EU and between EU and non-EU agents. Co-publications and co-patents have risen by close to 9% per annum since 2000 (EC, 2008a). The real objective for policy should be to ensure that obstacles to the best use of new knowledge are tackled effectively and that innovation outputs, not just inputs, are stimulated. Thus the skills to utilise new research effectively need to be present, even if comparatively little basic research is undertaken.

The European innovation policy framework

The concept of innovation is extremely broad and encompasses a wide range of diverse activities. An implication of this is that many different policies can affect different stages of the innovation process, and can do so in different ways. The policies, institutions and framework factors that provide the most effective means of supporting innovation need not be the ones that are the most likely to favour the development of new ideas. It is as important for policymakers to focus on obstacles that prevent the diffusion and optimal usage of the existing stock of knowledge as it is to focus on obstacles to the overall expansion of the stock of knowledge. This highlights the challenges involved in designing the optimal policy mix to support innovation (Mohnen and Röller, 2005).

Empirical evidence for OECD countries suggests that economy-wide framework conditions, framework policies and specific science policies and institutions all influence the innovation process, both independently and in interaction with each other (Jaumotte and Pain, 2005a). Policies that raise the absorptive capacity of the economy (the capacity to understand and make use of new knowledge) have dual benefits, not only stimulating new innovative activities, but also helping to maximise the benefits to be gained from the existing stock of knowledge. But, some policies that offer benefits for innovation, such as improved intellectual property protection, also have costs that could adversely affect innovation if applied inappropriately.

The EU-level innovation policy mix is commendably wide-ranging, with initiatives being taken in many different areas. But there is a need for priority setting amongst the initiatives and better quantification of the importance of each in accounting for differences in innovation across countries. The policy initiatives are tied together by the vision of the future European Research Area (ERA) and a broad-based innovation strategy. The decision to create the European Research Area, taken in 2000, reflected a perceived need to tackle national and institutional barriers to the development of a fully integrated and more efficient research area in Europe. At first, the focus was solely on ways of improving the overall efficiency of fragmented research systems. More recently, the vision has been broadened to include the overall level of public investment in research and the need for greater coherence between research and other EU policies. The creation of the ERA has now become a central pillar of the Lisbon Strategy. Education and training are also seen as having a critical role in fostering innovation.

A vision of the European Research Area in 2020 was set out by the European Council in December 2008 (Box 2.2), with the fifth freedom being attained by removing all barriers to the free circulation of researchers, knowledge and technology across the ERA. To achieve this, new policy initiatives will be required to facilitate the establishment and functioning of cross-border markets and networks for research as well as public-private co-operation. These address researchers' careers and mobility, research infrastructure, knowledge sharing (including intellectual property managements), joint programming and international science and technology co-operation. If achieved, such steps should do much to enhance the framework conditions for innovation in the EU. The labour market for researchers and Commission level funding for research are discussed below.

The push towards an integrated research area and the associated policy initiatives can be seen as measures that focus on creating favourable framework conditions for research and the supply-side of innovation. The broad-based innovation strategy, established in 2006, adds to these by placing greater emphasis on demand-driven innovation.

The strategy brings together a range of policy ideas to facilitate the translation of investment in knowledge into new products and services, recognising that the returns to investing in innovation depend on the demand for innovative products and services, the availability of people with sufficient skills to ensure such products and services are delivered

> ## Box 2.2. **The European Research Area**
>
> EU research and innovation policies aim at creating an integrated European Research Area (ERA) which permits the free movement of researchers, knowledge and technology across borders within the EU. The 2020 vision set out by ministers in 2008 highlights the following key factors:
>
> - Greater interactions between individual researchers, companies, funding organisations, universities and research institutions. In particular, all research, education and innovation policies and programmes should be jointly designed among public authorities at all levels, with appropriate involvement of relevant stakeholders.
>
> - Firms should be easily able to engage in research partnerships with a European public science base and benefit from attractive framework conditions, based on pro-active standard-setting and co-ordinated public procurement.
>
> - Firms operating in the ERA should benefit from a single market for innovative goods and services and a single market for knowledge including a well-functioning intellectual property rights framework.
>
> - National and regional research systems, policy objectives, dissemination and support mechanisms and programmes would be developed in a simple and coherent manner.
>
> - A significant share of public funding of research would be provided through ERA-wide open competition between individual scientists and teams based on the quality and relevance of research.
>
> - Cohesion policy and appropriate transnational co-ordination would be used to ensure the optimal regional deployment of science and technology capacities across Europe. Major research infrastructures in the ERA would be co-funded at EU level where appropriate, and offer equitable access to world class modern research facilities and technology demonstrators.
>
> - The interactions of research institutions with business and other actors would be facilitated by an open market for contract research and appropriate guidance for intellectual property management.
>
> - A single labour market should be developed to enhance researchers' mobility between countries and sectors with minimal financial or administrative obstacles.
>
> In a broad sense, these priorities should eventually establish more favourable economy-wide framework conditions for innovation, complementing other developments such as the enhanced competitive pressures that would result from the completion of the single market for goods and services.

to the market and a regulatory framework that enables them to be speedily accepted in the European market. Thus, the innovation strategy is focused more on innovation outputs rather than inputs. The full range of initiatives set out in the innovation strategy, and progress as of the end of 2008, are summarised in Box 2.3. Four key aspects of the strategy – intellectual property policy, tackling obstacles to venture capital provision, fostering demand for innovative products and services and the encouragement of interactions between public research organisations and businesses – are discussed in greater detail below.

The labour market for researchers

The availability of sufficient human resources for science and technology is undoubtedly an important factor for innovative activities to take place, not only because of

Box 2.3. **The broad-based innovation strategy**

The broad-based innovation strategy was first set out by the European Commission in 2006, and modified and approved by the Council in 2007. It aims to improve the framework conditions for innovation by combining supply factors, such as research, education and workforce skills and access to finance with measures strengthening the demand side. The final strategy contains nine strategic priorities for innovation action at the EU level.

- A comprehensive strategy for intellectual property rights.

- Creation of a pro-active standards-setting policy. The Commission is to become more active in influencing global standard-setting systems and work towards streamlining existing standards within Europe, as multiple standards fragment the internal market and add to the costs of introducing new products, technologies and services.

- A pro-active public procurement policy. Innovation can be encouraged by raising demand for innovative products and services and by raising the quality of public services in markets where the public sector is a major purchaser.

- The development of Joint Technology Initiatives. These would improve the focus of EU-wide research activities, by encouraging collaborative research into developing new technologies.

- Boosting innovation in lead markets through concerted actions to strengthen the demand for new innovations in specific areas of the economy.

- Enhanced co-operation between higher education, research and business. This would facilitate knowledge transfer and include the establishment of a European Institute of Technology.

- Help for innovation in regions, through policies to foster the development of clusters and ensuring that Structural Fund programmes become more research-oriented.

- Development of new policies to encourage innovation in services and non-technological innovation.

- Tackling obstacles to cross-border investment by venture capital funds.

Council recommended that these priorities be integrated into the Community Lisbon Programme, with special emphasis given to the benchmarking of EU-level innovation policies against those used in other countries.

Work has begun in each of these strands, with the Commission releasing an initial progress report in November 2008. Among the key initiatives identified in the progress report are:

- Work has continued on the creation of a Community Patent for Europe, although it has yet to be agreed and approved.

- A Commission communication in March 2008 set out a number of important steps towards a standardisation policy that would be more clearly focused on innovation. A review of standardisation policy in the ICT sector is to be published in 2009.

- New guidelines for pre-commercial procurement by the public sector were adopted by Council in May 2008.

- New joint technology initiatives have been launched by the Commission, with calls for proposals in five main areas covering innovative medicines, computing systems and nano-electronics.

- A Lead Market Initiative was introduced in December 2007 and approved by Council in 2008.

- A European Institute of Innovation and Technology was established in 2008, with a specific remit to help establish Knowledge and Innovation Communities in particular areas of research. The first of these are to be selected in early 2010.

Box 2.3. **The broad-based innovation strategy** *(cont.)*

- The Commission has introduced a new policy framework to raise the levels of excellence and openness of clusters in EU countries.

- Work has begun to improve understanding of innovation in services and the ways in which it may differ from that in industrial sectors. A European Innovation Platform for knowledge-intensive services was established in 2008.

- The Commission is continuing to push for mutual recognition of national frameworks for venture capital funds and has begun exploratory work on identifying cross-border obstacles to venture capital provision.

their importance for the development of new innovations, but also because they raise the capacity to understand and utilise ideas developed elsewhere (Jaumotte and Pain, 2005a). Meeting the current targets for significant increases in national R&D expenditure in EU member states will be possible only if there is sufficient growth in scientific and workforce skills. This may take some time to materialise, especially given the expected spate of retirements from the science and engineering workforce over the next two decades. The supply of newly-trained scientists is relatively inelastic in the short run, reflecting the time required to acquire the necessary human capital. Although it is possible to alleviate shortages through the international migration of academics and specialist workers, or through international sourcing, there are obvious limits to the extent to which this can be done simultaneously in all economies.

Public policies designed to support innovative activities thus need to consider the constraints that may arise from a relatively inelastic short-term supply of science and technology workers. Consideration should also be given to the wider range of educational and labour market policies that can help to alleviate supply constraints and encourage the diffusion of scientific knowledge. The Commission is already taking actions in these areas, *via* the New Skills for New Jobs initiative and Education and Training work programme.

Education and training policies clearly have important long-run effects on innovation, in particular through efforts to raise the long-term supply of human resources for science and technology. But, increasing the supply of scientists and engineers available to work in R&D occupations cannot be done by education policies alone. Science and engineering graduates need not choose to work in the country in which they graduate, or in science and engineering occupations. Policy coherence also matters, with well-functioning labour markets and attractive career opportunities also being important for firms and public research organisations hoping to be able to attract and make full use of researchers.

The need for adequate human resources for R&D has been identified as a key challenge since the launch of the Lisbon Strategy (Sheehan and Wyckoff, 2003). However, the number of researchers remains lower in Europe than in other major economies, with the difference especially large in the business sector (Figure 2.4). Business-sector researchers represented 79% of all researchers in the United States in 2005 and 68% in Japan. In comparison, they represented only one-half in the EU27 (OECD, 2008c).

Increasing the numbers of new graduates in science and technology is also particularly important if the supply of scientists and engineers is to rise. Progress has been mixed in Europe. The numbers of students graduating in science and engineering has risen in most EU countries since 2000, but less rapidly than the overall rise in graduate numbers.

Figure 2.4. **Business enterprise researchers**
Per thousand employment in industry

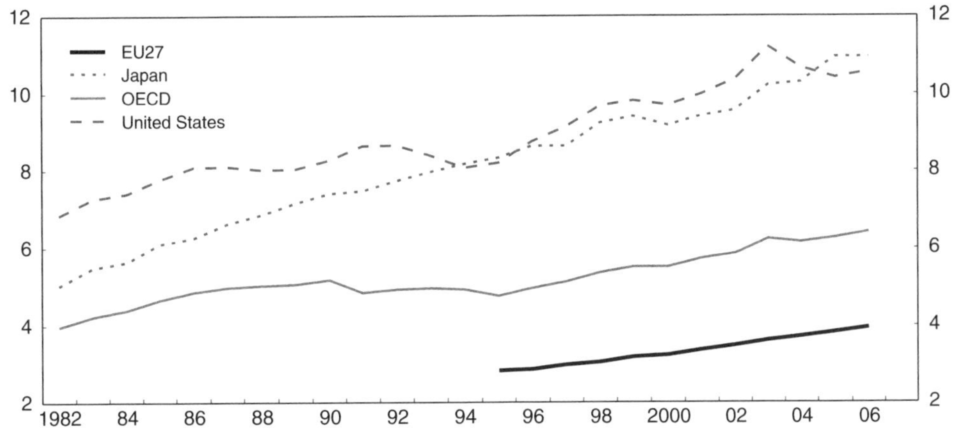

Source: OECD (2008), *Main Science and Technology Indicators*, Vol. 2008/2.

StatLink http://dx.doi.org/10.1787/712288715533

A significant share of university graduates, doctorate recipients and postdoctoral students graduating in Europe also migrate to work elsewhere. For instance, in 2003, there were over 100 000 European-born doctorate holders resident in the United States (Auriol, 2007). However, there are also many non-European-born doctorate holders who work and reside within the European Union (EC, 2008a). The international orientation of researchers should, in principle, enhance knowledge flows to the EU economy. However, steps need to be taken to enhance the circulation of EU and non-EU researchers. Two possible solutions for European policymakers are to attract additional skilled workers and researchers from outside the EU, or to enhance the attractiveness of research careers within the EU. To facilitate this, the creation of a single open market for researchers is essential.

Evidence from surveys suggests that the most important reasons keeping EU-born scientists and engineers abroad relate to work quality. A better position, better opportunities for research funding, a broader mix of professional activities and improved access to leading technologies and centres of excellence are among the most frequently cited factors for decisions to work abroad (Hansen, 2004). Particular obstacles within Europe identified by the Commission include the widespread use of seniority-based promotion systems in universities, the frequent use of short-term contracts, especially for junior researchers, the difficulties of accessing research funding and the limited transferability of supplementary pension rights.

One key consequence of a greater labour mobility of skilled researchers is its contribution to the creation and diffusion of knowledge. In general, it might be expected to help to diffuse codified and tacit knowledge about innovations, especially when researchers closely involved in the development of a new innovation moves from the public sector into the business sector. Enhanced labour mobility can also lead to the development of science networks with expertise that can be drawn on to solve particular research problems (Mason *et al.*, 2004).

Following the launch of the Lisbon Strategy, the Commission introduced a series of measures to increase the mobility of researchers in Europe, but progress was generally slow, not least because the measures were voluntary for member states. The Commission has recently upgraded efforts to improve mobility by launching the European Partnership for Researchers in 2008, with action by member states and the Commission proposed in four key areas.[5] These actions are meant to be implemented by the end of 2010. Most of the areas covered – recruitment, employment and working conditions for researchers, social security and supplementary pension rights and the need to enhance the skills of researchers through stronger linkages between academia and business – are largely dependent on actions at member state level, although the Commission also has an important supporting role. However, the Commission can give a lead by ensuring that the required actions are also reflected in existing Community research funding programmes, as discussed below.

A competitive market in job recruitment is a key requirement of an open labour market for researchers. Here, the Commission and member states should act to ensure that publicly-funded research positions are publicly advertised and fully open to all qualified European nationals. An important step in this process will be to ensure the full functioning of the European Qualifications Framework (EQF) adopted by the Council in 2008. The EQF encourages the mutual recognition of academic and professional qualifications from different countries by relating these qualifications to a common European reference framework. Member states are required to relate their qualification systems to the EQF by 2010 and to ensure that all new national qualifications issued from 2012 include a reference to the equivalent EQF level.

A second key requirement for a European-wide labour market is to ensure that all publicly-funded research grants are open to nationals of all member states and non-EU countries. This is only one aspect of the broader internal market agenda to ensure that national public procurement activities are open to tender from individuals and businesses outside the country concerned. The mobility of researchers is also enhanced if researchers are freer to take individual research grants with them to other locations and institutions. In some member states this is already possible because of the "money follows the researcher" scheme agreed by the association of the European Heads of Research Councils (EUROHORCs). As of 2008, 24 publicly-funded national research organisations covering 14 EU member states were participating in this scheme, allowing researchers to transfer their grants between posts in these member states, subject to the agreement of the funding organisation. The European Commission could usefully augment this initiative by seeking to identify remaining obstacles to research grant portability in other member states and in Commission-run funding programmes.

A third key requirement for an integrated labour market for researchers is that national pension and social security schemes are responsive to the needs of mobile workers who often work on short-term contracts or secondments. Areas for possible action identified by the European Commission include increasing the current possibility for researchers to remain affiliated to a home country social security scheme while working abroad, and the development of pan-EU pension schemes by pension providers. The Commission should continue to assess the need for these changes and consider what steps can be taken to remove obstacles to the development of such schemes.

Migration of highly-skilled workers

Potential barriers that limit the inward migration of skilled workers from other countries should also be tackled. A higher level of skilled immigration would benefit the European economy directly, with population ageing set to begin in many economies and the demand for skilled labour continuing to rise. Tackling possible barriers to mobility has also become increasingly urgent in Europe because of the rising global competition for talent (OECD, 2008d).

Direct comparisons of the mobility of highly-skilled workers across countries are hampered by the difficulties of obtaining comparable data. Nonetheless, it does appear that the European Union attracts far fewer internationally mobile scientists and engineers than the United States. As of 2006, 9.7% of all European human resources in science and technology were born outside their country of residence, with around a third of these coming from non-EU countries (Meri, 2007).[6] In contrast, as of 2003, 18.9% of all university-educated scientists and engineers in the United States were foreign-born; foreign-born individuals also represented one-quarter of those employed in science and engineering occupations (NSF, 2008).

The Commission is attempting to co-ordinate national efforts to attract highly-skilled migrants through the introduction of the Blue Card scheme. The aim of this scheme is to create a single application procedure for highly-skilled non-EU workers to live and work in the EU, provided that they have relevant professional experience and a job offer of at least one year. In contrast to the Green Card in the United States, the Blue Card would be valid for only up to three years, rather than granting permanent residency, but it would be renewable. After discussions in the European Parliament, eligible highly-skilled workers are now required to have at least five years experience in the sector concerned and to have a job offer with a salary 1.7 times the national average wage in the applicant country, somewhat higher than originally proposed. The Competitiveness Council has asked that the Blue Card scheme be adopted by June 2009.

The scheme is a welcome step forward and should help to reduce barriers to inward migration for highly-skilled workers, and thus bring benefits, but it is far from clear whether such benefits will be sizable (Guild, 2007). Employers and potential immigrants will still often face considerable search costs, because application for the Card requires an explicit offer of employment. Moreover, member states will retain their right to determine the overall volume of migration by non-EU nationals on their territories, so there is no guarantee of obtaining a Blue Card on qualifications and job offers alone. After the Blue Card is introduced, it is important that the Commission monitors the impact of the scheme on mobility and continues to explore possible extensions to the scheme, such as the granting of residency rights for a longer time period.

Education and skills

In addition to enhancing labour market conditions for researchers, the EU must identify and foster those skills that can make innovation happen. Education systems have a broad role to play in supporting innovation and developing creativity, reflecting the marked shift in demand towards skilled jobs, and a widening in the skills and competencies that are needed for innovation. In this respect, the European Framework for Key Competences can help to embed these competencies in education systems at all levels. Similarly, management, leadership, marketing, sales and distribution skills are a central part of the innovation process, with organisational innovations becoming increasingly important. The Bologna process, initiated in 1999, aims at creating a European Higher Education Area by 2010. In conjunction with the Copenhagen process regarding vocational education and training, this should help to provide students with a wider choice of courses, enhanced quality assurance and a better recognition of qualifications and periods of study, under the European Qualifications Framework for lifelong learning. The success of these initiatives will partially determine the capacity of the EU to develop and integrate all the necessary skills required to foster successful innovations, and will reinforce the initiatives now underway in the EU broad-based innovation strategy and the steps envisaged in the creation of the European Research Area.

The EU member states and the Commission have worked together on many of these issues through the Education and Training 2010 work programme, introduced in 2001. Reforms to enhance education and training systems have been stimulated by use of the "open method of co-ordination". An important part of the overall process has been the development of a list of key competences for lifelong learning (EC, 2006). If achieved, these should also help to promote innovation. The Commission has recently put forward an updated strategic framework, explicitly recognising the need to enhance the skills required for innovation and creativity, including entrepreneurship, at all levels of education. This is likely to prove one of the key issues for education and training policies in the years ahead.

The European patent system

In almost all countries the general tendency of intellectual property (IP) policy is to offer ever greater protection for the rights of IP holders. This is especially so for patents. Legislative changes have been complemented by moves to encourage greater use of intellectual property rights by universities and other public research organisations. Each of these factors can have different economic effects. For example, strengthening enforcement rights during the lifetime of the patent can affect the chances of follow-on innovations in a different way than lengthening the term of the patent.

Enhanced protection of intellectual property rights (IPRs) involves costs as well as benefits. Patents provide incentives to undertake research and disclose information. They may also provide incentives to invest in production and marketing efforts, potentially increasing the speed with which new ideas are introduced into the market. However, this is at the cost of a potential reduction in the spread of inventions during the lifetime of the patent, unless licences are granted. Disclosure of information about new research is beneficial, not least because it may prevent unnecessary duplication of research efforts. Inventions that might otherwise be kept secret enter the public domain when placed under the protection of patents, but in such a way that they could impede future commercial research, even if exemptions are available for pure scientific research. Stronger patent protection also raises administrative costs, as it increases the burden placed on patent examiners, who have to establish whether applications in new subject areas should be accepted. On the other hand, high quality patent rights that have undergone a rigorous examination create greater legal certainty, both for the patent holder and for third parties.

The design of intellectual property systems becomes particularly difficult once allowance is made for the possibility of cumulative innovation (Scotchmer, 1991). Excessively strong patent rights for first generation innovators could easily be counterproductive if they act to limit access for potential entrants, especially new firms or junior researchers, and possibly even prevent the subsequent development of product and process enhancements. The difficulties of predicting the sources of new ideas mean that they are best encouraged when the costs of entry into the innovation process are kept to a minimum.

The European patent system, and hence the cross-border market for technology, is currently fragmented. At present, it is possible for patent protection to be obtained in multiple European countries by receiving a "European patent" from the European Patent

Office (EPO). The benefits of this are however limited by the need to have such a patent translated into the national language of each country in which it is to be enforced and validated by national patent offices. As a result, the costs of obtaining and maintaining a patent in Europe are often considerably higher than in either the United States or Japan. The gap is also increased by the fact that patenting and maintenance fees are reduced by up to one-half for SMEs in the United States, Japan, Canada and South Korea, but not in Europe. A first attempt to tackle the issue of translation costs was made in the London Agreement in 2000, which was a voluntary agreement which has now been signed by just under half of the 35 EPO member states. Estimates suggest that this will reduce the cost of patenting in multiple European jurisdictions by between 20-30%. But, even after this, the cost of a European patent validated in multiple countries will still be 5 to 7 times higher than in the United States (van Pottelsberghe and Mejer, 2008). This difference accounts for some of the observed difference in the propensity to patent in Europe and elsewhere. De Rassenfosse and van Pottelsberghe (2008) estimate that each 10% reduction in patent costs should raise the number of patents by around 4%.

A possible way forward would involve the creation of a single Community Patent which, when granted, would automatically be valid across the European Union, reducing the costs of patenting. The idea of such a patent has been around for many years, but progress has been slow, in part because of difficulties over the related issue of patent enforcement. Since the Commission issued a communication on enhancing the patent system in Europe in 2007, greater progress has been made, but final agreement has not yet been reached between member states.

Patent costs arise also from the need to enforce patent rights. Again, this can be more costly in Europe than elsewhere. European patents are currently subject to litigation in the national courts of the country in which an infringement occurs, even if the patent is granted by the EPO. Differences in procedural laws and other aspects of enforcement mean that the outcome can be uncertain, costly and, potentially, different across countries. The costs vary according to the complexity of the case. Although single country litigation costs in continental Europe and, to a lesser extent, the United Kingdom, are lower than in the United States, multiple litigation in several European countries need not be (Mejer and van Pottelsberghe, 2009). The existing system fragments the internal market and can result in so-called "forum shopping" with companies pursuing actions in particular countries only because of a particular feature of their legal system. It also poses particular problems for small and medium-sized companies.

One potential solution could be the introduction of a centralised patent court in Europe which would have exclusive jurisdiction in cases dealing with the infringement or potential revocation of patents granted by the European Patent Office. Such a court might resemble the Court of Appeal of the Federal Circuit in the United States, established in 1982, which resulted in prompter settlements of patent infringement disputes in the United States (Galasso and Schankerman, 2008). Estimates by the EPO suggest that a centralised court in Europe could reduce European litigation costs by 10 to 40% (EPO, 2006).

Inconclusive discussions about a European Patent Litigation Agreement and a European Patent Court have taken place between member states of the EPO for several years. Although the Court would be outside the auspices of the EU, because the EPO has a broader membership than the EU, the European Commission is necessarily involved in the discussions, as it covers areas for which the Community has exclusive competence to conclude agreements with third countries.

Separately, the European Parliament and the Council adopted a Directive in 2004 setting minimum requirements for national enforcement procedures, but significant national differences remain (Mejer and van Pottelsberghe, 2009). In December 2003, the Commission also proposed to confer jurisdiction over community patents to the European Court of Justice, which would establish a Unified Community Patent Court with decisions being subject to appeal at the Court of First Instance.

The EPO and the 2003 Commission proposals are both intended to simplify litigation procedures. However, there is a need to find a compromise between the two proposals. One option is to establish a unified patent litigation system, covering both European and future Community patents, which would be open to non-EU Members of the EPO. The Commission adopted a Recommendation to the Council to open negotiations to conclude such an agreement in March 2009. An open issue is whether this type of compromise agreement is compatible with the EC Treaty in light of the involvement of the European Court of Justice in cases concerning European as well as Community Patents. The Council referred this question to the European Court of Justice in June 2009.

The Commission has a central role in the discussions about the Community Patent and the associated patent court, and should continue to work towards finding a solution acceptable to all parties. In the absence of such a solution, the benefits of a Community Patent are likely to be less than would otherwise be the case. This is especially so for SMEs, who do not have the capacity to handle multiple lawsuits in different countries.

Moving towards a simplified intellectual property system would also enhance the evidence base for policy decisions by allowing clearer comparisons to be made between innovative activities inside and outside the EU. It would also facilitate the cross-border transfer of knowledge within a European Research Area. However, there may be limits to what can be achieved. Additional patenting can also bring new costs as well as benefits, especially for incremental innovations which might involve the need to draw on multiple patents, or for areas in which open innovation might otherwise flourish.

Patenting is not the only means of intellectual property protection for organisations and individuals. The Community Innovation Survey shows that innovative companies register design and trademarks as frequently as they patent. Other innovative companies may simply choose to maintain trade secrets. Innovative service sector companies typically make less use of intellectual property protection than those in manufacturing, perhaps because some of the knowledge they generate, such as business methods, is not eligible for such protection. As the nature of innovation shifts towards innovation in services and non-technological innovation, it will be important for the Commission to continue to consider the costs and benefits of different forms of intellectual property protection, such as protection for designs and trademarks, and potential market failures.

Venture capital

The depth of financial markets can have an important impact on long-run economic growth. In particular, it can help to ease internal funding constraints facing firms which want to make uncertain long-term investments. Yet, raising external finance for new innovation projects can be difficult, as the likelihood of asymmetric information between prospective borrowers and lenders is high. Because of this, external investors will typically require a premium to compensate for the agency costs arising from the risks of adverse selection and moral hazard. The difficulties are magnified for young innovative companies, since they are often new entrants into the research process with no history of successful research, only limited collateral and new business proposals that investors may find difficult to evaluate. Thus the market for high-risk capital, such as private equity and venture capital, plays an important role in the financing of innovation. An important strand of the innovation policy mix is to tackle obstacles that may hold back the provision of such capital. This is recognised in the broad-based innovation strategy, with the Commission now taking action to remove obstacles to cross-border investments by venture capital funds.

Although it is difficult to obtain timely, internationally comparable statistics, the provision of venture capital investments appears to be relatively small in most European countries as compared with North America, with the United Kingdom and the Netherlands being two exceptions (OECD, 2006). Survey evidence also indicates that the availability of venture capital in Europe lags well behind that in the United States, although not Japan (WEF, 2008).

Empirical evidence using European CIS data (CIS3) has shown that cross-country differences in the provision of venture capital are significantly negatively correlated with the proportion of firms citing finance as an obstacle to innovation (Jaumotte and Pain, 2005b). The CIS data also show that small firms are much more likely to be constrained in their access to finance than large firms. Just under a quarter of all SMEs report financial constraints and only 2% of them use venture capital (ECB, 2009). This suggests that steps to facilitate greater provision of venture capital could prove beneficial for the commercial development of innovative products.

Differences in the availability and/or use of venture capital across countries may to some extent be rooted in different attitudes towards entrepreneurship and risk taking. But, they also reflect policies that discourage risk-taking and the supply of risk capital. A key issue for the EU is to achieve the mutual recognition of national frameworks for venture capital funds. European venture capital funds invest outside national borders (Bottazzi and Da Rin, 2002), but each home country has different regulatory constraints, resulting in a fragmented venture capital market, with smaller funds tending to remain within their home jurisdiction. Differences in national taxation systems also matter, and can give rise to double taxation on cross-border venture capital operations (EC, 2007a). Prudential regulations can also restrict the growth of venture capital funds. In particular, national constraints on the investment activities of pension and insurance companies still act to limit investment in private equity and venture capital in some countries (ECB, 2009).

It is important that the Commission follows through on the proposed measures to tackle the obstacles to venture capital provision. In identifying the importance of particular obstacles, and planning specific policy initiatives, it will be necessary to recognise that the size of the venture capital industry may be endogenous to other innovation policies. For instance, the supply of venture capital funds is higher in countries with a higher knowledge stock (Romain and van Pottelsberghe, 2004). Evidence for Europe also suggests that firms who eventually receive venture capital funding register more patents than comparable non-funded firms before they receive funding, but not after they do so (Engel and Keilbach, 2007). Policies that tackle obstacles to patenting for SMEs may thus also facilitate venture capital. Estimates of such potential synergies across innovation-related policies have not been published in current Commission policy initiatives.

Even if obstacles to venture capital are successfully tackled, however, the immediate benefits are unlikely to be large, especially given the current turmoil in financial markets. Thus the Commission and other Community-level bodies have taken steps to ensure that financing of SMEs is maintained through the European Economic Recovery Plan. In particular, the European Investment Bank (EIB) has raised the funds available for SME lending by EUR 15 billion in 2009 and 2010. The Commission has also introduced new plans to strengthen the Late Payments Directive to give SMEs greater powers to combat late payment, especially by public administrations. The Commission should likewise reduce its own payment times to businesses. Member states have also been urged to press ahead with prompt implementation of the measures in the Small Business Act, introduced in 2008, which should reduce costs for SMEs.

Research funding by the European Union

Most public funding for research in Europe comes from national and regional administrations. But the European Union also funds a small proportion of EU research directly. Around 2% of all innovating enterprises in 2002-04 received funding from the European Union (EC, 2008a). Three main EU schemes fund research, but a large number of others offer funding for some form for innovation-related activities (EC, 2008c).[7] The rationale for EU support is that it can encourage research activities that might not be central to the work of national funding agencies.[8] In particular, EU funding can facilitate the development of cross-border networks and clusters of researchers and institutions, as well as the development of pan-European research infrastructures. Such funding schemes need careful design and frequent evaluation to ensure that they are not unduly complex or have unexploited synergies that make them less effective than they could be.

Other possible rationales for EU-level funding are that it could help to support research into global challenges, such as climate change (EC, 2008d), or help to reduce unnecessary duplication of research efforts in member states. While this latter argument has some merit concerning funding for large technology projects, it has less merit for smaller-scale research projects. In many areas, innovation occurs incrementally, building on the independent findings of others; verification of innovative research results by independent groups is also necessary.

The three principal EU funding schemes cover different phases and actors in the innovation process. The 7th Research Framework Programme (FP7), with a budget of over EUR 50 billion for the years 2007-13, is mainly disbursed to collaborative research, investigator driven frontier research, researchers' training, mobility and career development and activities to enhance research and innovation capacities. These programmes are not aiming, by definition, to produce commercial outputs. Funding is also available for SMEs and for measures that strengthen the wider European Research Area. This funding is complemented by the much smaller Competitiveness and Innovation Framework Programme (CIP), with a budget of EUR 3.6 billion for the years 2007-13. The CIP provides support for the commercial use and take-up of innovations. The third main source is support for regional research and innovation capacity provided by the Structural Funds. Planned expenditure for the period 2007-13 is EUR 86 billion. It is important that the Commission continues to monitor funding programmes to ensure that the appropriate balance is maintained between funding for commercial implementation of innovation and basic research.

There is potential for the Commission to improve the effectiveness of innovation policy design and delivery by tackling overlaps between the different EU schemes that fund research and innovation activities and by looking for unexploited synergies (Reid *et al.*, 2008). This has already begun to be addressed by the Commission (EC, 2007a and EC, 2008a). One example is the potential for funding regional infrastructures from both FP7 and the Structural Funds. Support for research infrastructures in FP7 focuses on promoting scientific excellence, with Structural Funds support focusing on cohesion objectives (convergence and competitiveness). If the distinct policy aims of the two instruments are to be met, then the different funding programmes may need to be sequenced, with Structural Funds, along with the regions-oriented parts of FP7 and national measures initially being used to specifically develop regional capabilities. This would then enable regional actors to subsequently participate in infrastructure projects supported by the Framework Programme. Progress made in this direction needs to be closely monitored by the Commission to ensure that the objectives of the two funding instruments are clearly understood by stakeholders and that potential synergies are optimised.

A further issue concerns the administrative costs that arise from the complexity of research grant applications to the European Commission. Although the Commission has taken steps to simplify application procedures, the administrative burden placed on applicants remains considerable and limits the overall effectiveness of the funding programmes (Marimon and de Graça Carvalho, 2008; Rietschel *et al.*, 2009). For the FP6 programme (the predecessor to FP7 over 2004-06) only half of all contracts awarded were signed within a year of the deadline for submitting proposals (EC, 2009a). Several Directorate-Generals have administrative responsibility for the disbursement of the FP funding and, despite considerable efforts to harmonise application, evaluation and selection procedures, some differences remain. One option would be to consider enhanced usage of two-stage application procedures, with outline applications being submitted at an initial stage and, if accepted, more detailed proposals would be presented thereafter. This offers potential savings for unsuccessful applicants, but could delay funding for accepted projects. A second option would be to expand usage of executive agencies to evaluate and manage projects using a common procedure, subject to budget and programme specifications laid down by the Commission. An example is provided by the European Research Council Executive Agency, set up by the Commission to oversee applications for frontier research.

The average annual budget for FP7 is considerably higher than for the previous Framework Programmes. This increases the need for effective evaluation of the funds distributed by the Commission. Although evaluations of such funding programmes have always been undertaken, areas for improvement remain. A report by the European Court of Auditors on past evaluation exercises suggested that "poorly defined programme objectives and weak performance management undermined effective monitoring and evaluation" (Court of Auditors, 2007). Particular problems highlighted included differences in evaluation methods across separate Directorate-Generals and the lack of data on longer term research outputs available to the panels of high-level experts who were involved in evaluation decisions.

The Expert Group report on FP6 *ex post* evaluation concluded that the programme had produced substantial net benefits for the European Research Area, but had been only partially successful (Rietschel *et al.*, 2009). The programme had succeeded in supporting high quality projects and researchers, but scope remained for improving programme design and implementation and for further strengthening of the links with industrial sectors.

The Commission is currently taking measures to improve the administration and evaluation of the funding programmes, with a move towards systematic annual monitoring of the entire range of activities financed by FP7. Preliminary figures suggest that the average time taken for funded projects to be agreed has fallen markedly from that for FP6 (EC, 2009b). Other initiatives underway seek to improve the research evaluations by the Commission by augmenting existing evaluation evidence with a study of long-term research impacts, and by strengthening the relationship with evaluation experts in member states .The Court of Auditors (2007) recommended setting up a specialised office or agency for the evaluation of all projects financed from EU research funding programmes. Such an office could facilitate the development and use of best practice evaluation methodologies and techniques, building on examples of effective evaluations in member states. However, the Commission, whilst recognising the need to foster good evaluation practices, has pointed to several practical difficulties with this proposal. Nonetheless, it remains essential that the Commission should take further steps to improve the development and use of common evaluation methodologies and techniques for all innovation programmes.

University-industry linkages

Basic research performed in universities and other public research organisations (PROs) has long been an important source of significant scientific and technological advances and an important input into the private sector research process. Such research is often undertaken with little or no idea of the potential commercial applications, or the length of time that might be required for commercialisation, making it necessary for it to be supported by public funding. Universities also have a central role in ensuring the supply of human resources for science and technology. Empirical evidence indicates that expanding research activities in public research organisations helps to support business sector research activities in the longer term, especially if such expansion is funded directly by the private sector (Jaumotte and Pain, 2005a and 2005b).[9]

Industry funding is only a small fraction of the total funding for higher education R&D in all OECD economies, although the share is higher in the EU than in either the United States or Japan.[10] Despite this, the extent of collaboration between businesses and universities is judged to be weaker in the EU than in Japan or, especially, the United States (WEF, 2008; OECD, 2008e).[11] European innovation surveys also reveal that universities and public research laboratories are a key information source for only a relatively small number of firms. In 2002-04 (CIS4), only 10% of innovative enterprises co-operated with other companies and public sector institutions, with the latter being among the least frequently used co-operation partners. This may simply be because there are relatively few basic innovations for which there is an immediate commercial application. But it could also reflect obstacles preventing firms from either being aware of the work undertaken in publicly-funded research organisations (PROs) or from accessing it, as well as a lack of capacity in the private sector to absorb the full potential benefits of fundamental research.

Many countries have undertaken policy initiatives to stimulate research partnerships between industry and PROs. The ultimate objective of such policies is to generate greater economic benefits from publicly-funded R&D. Research partnerships might be expected to increase the rate of utilisation and transfer of academic knowledge to the private sector. Examples include funding policies, such as the EU Framework Programmes, that aim to increase the number of research joint ventures across borders and measures to encourage the commercialisation of university intellectual property. In Europe, a particular emphasis has often been to provide universities with more control over the IP generated by individual researchers.[12] Patenting by the universities in Europe continues to lag behind that in the United States. In the EU, just under 3% of patents were owned by the university sector over 2003-05, less than half the rate of ownership in the United States (OECD, 2008e).

The benefits of university research for the private sector in Europe appear to vary by sector, by firm and by project size. Firms with an already high research intensity are more likely either to source, or to access, university knowledge; firms also appear more likely to collaborate with universities if they make use of other external sources of knowledge as well (Laursen and Salter, 2004). Thus the gains from encouraging enhanced research collaboration may offer only limited benefits to firms that undertake little innovation.

Collaboration between organisations in different sectors and different countries has become an increasingly important requirement for applications to public funding programmes in Europe. One rationale for this is that it facilitates research co-operation that might not otherwise take place. Co-operation is more likely to occur across borders if firms access EU funds than if they access only national funding (Segarra-Blasco and Arauzo-Carod, 2008). Highly innovative firms – the ones introducing innovations new to the market – appear the most likely to receive significant benefits from co-operation with universities located elsewhere in Europe (Monjon and Waelbroeck, 2003). Such findings provide support for the design of policies to encourage research co-operation across national borders, as well as for the decision to support the development of regional clusters as part of the Commission's innovation strategy.

The Commission produced a set of voluntary guidelines for universities and research institutions to improve their links with European companies in 2007 and adopted in 2008 a Recommendation on the management of intellectual property in knowledge transfer activities and a Code of practice for universities and other public research organisations (EC, 2008e).[13] It is intended that the upgraded EU Forum for University-Business Dialogue will facilitate the exchange of good practice and also provide countries and institutions with practical help in developing closer university-business co-operation. This should help to facilitate the flow of knowledge within the European Research Area. The rules for participation in Community-level research funding programmes should be extended to ensure that all applicants have to submit plans for the dissemination of research findings as part of their research project proposals.

Traditionally, universities and other non-profit PROs could be seen as producers of knowledge, a public good that was disseminated *via* means such as journal publications and conference presentations. Greater use of patents also provides a means by which information is made available publicly, but is likely to raise the lag before it can be disseminated. The Commission should ensure that placing increasing emphasis on university-business linkages in funding programmes does not come at the expense of assisting basic research with few immediate commercial or policy spin-offs. It will also be necessary for the Commission, as well as member states, to ensure that greater use of intellectual property management in PROs increases the visibility of research information to a broader range of interests and does not disrupt the flow of research information received by the private sector.

Fostering demand for innovation

The broad-based innovation strategy contains a number of measures that aim to strengthen the demand for innovative goods and services. The rationale for such initiatives is that the commercial development of some forms of innovation may be hampered by uncertainty over market demand for products and services or, for smaller enterprises, the difficulties of breaking into markets dominated by established suppliers. Between 10 and 15% of all innovative enterprises cite such factors as constraints on their innovation activities (CIS4).

The Commission has launched a Lead Markets Initiative as part of the broad-based innovation strategy. Following consultations with stakeholders, six separate markets – eHealth, protective textiles, sustainable construction, recycling, bio-based products and renewable energies – have been chosen as the focus of the initiative. All these markets are judged to be highly innovative, with a strong existing technological and industrial base in Europe, and to be dependent on the creation of favourable framework conditions through public policy measures, so that potential market failures might prove costly if not overcome. An action plan for each market has been formulated for the next 3-5 years. The eventual goal of policy is stated as helping to turn innovations into world-wide leading products or services in markets that are projected to grow rapidly over the next decade.

The Commission may have a role to play in some areas of the development of the European markets for innovations, as it has in developing the European market for existing products. Taking action to facilitate the mutual acceptance of national standards for innovative goods and services is one example, as is already the case in the internal market programme. Ensuring adequate levels of protection for consumers of such goods and services is another. Government procurement, including direct procurement by the Commission, can also support existing markets for emerging technologies if this is cost effective. The Commission also has competence for many important areas of regulation that affect the markets and incentives for innovation.

The initial set of markets chosen are also ones that are consistent with broader goals, such as environmental needs, and ones which, a priori, appear likely to expand in the future. However, considerable care will be needed in the design of policies under this initiative to ensure that the Commission and member states avoid "picking winners" or creating new markets where none exist. Long-term projections of market size should not be used as the only means of selecting areas to support, given the inherent uncertainties around such projections. It will also be important to ensure that the initiative does not result in attempts to subsidise "infant industries" or protect them from (external) competition. Ongoing assessments of the market and policy failures that hold back the commercial implementation and diffusion of particular innovations in the lead markets will be necessary as the markets evolve, building on the work undertaken for the initial preparatory papers.

Finally, if the initiative is enlarged to include other markets, the Commission and member states will need to ensure policy coherence. Greater focus on the policy actions necessary to foster emerging innovations must be combined with internal market policies to raise competition and, in effect, expand the European market for existing innovations. Continued efforts to improve European-wide framework conditions for innovation will also need to be maintained; without these the supply of new innovative goods and services will be limited.

Concluding comments

Innovation policy is a complex area. Many of the policy objectives are difficult to measure in a timely fashion and the time taken to change the overall level of innovative activities is likely to be lengthy. The inherent difficulties of predicting the sources of new ideas and uncertainties about their commercial applications at the time of discovery suggest that policies should be directed, as far as possible, to tackling barriers to a favourable research environment and obstacles to the successful commercial application of new ideas.

Recognition of the barriers to innovation has improved in recent years, and the Commission has made welcome progress in starting to address these and creating more favourable framework conditions for innovation. But much remains to be done. The measurement of innovation needs to be broadened and become more timely, market failures need to be identified more clearly and policy evaluation can be improved. At present there are many separate initiatives to support innovation, but little sense of priority between them. Benchmarking, which is widely used by the Commission, helps to identify differences across countries, but does not indicate how important each of these are. The main recommendations on innovation are outlined in Box 2.4.

Box 2.4. **Recommendations concerning innovation**

- Improve the statistical information available about innovative and creative activities in the European Union. Make greater use of output-based measures of innovation in policy guidelines to member states.

- Broaden the evidence base concerning the key policy influences on innovative activities. Consider the relative importance of improving economy-wide framework conditions, such as the single market, and the European Research Area, as well as specific science and innovation policies and different types of skills.

- Enhance evaluation of the impact and effectiveness of measures being introduced in the Innovation Strategy. Take further steps to improve the development and use of common evaluation methodologies and techniques for all EU innovation programmes.

- Pursue the introduction of a Community Patent and a centralised Patent Court to reduce the costs of patenting in Europe.

- Simplify the cost of research grant applications to the Commission and consider possible synergies between the existing schemes that offer funding for innovation. Ensure that all national research grants are open to all EU nationals.

- Further encourage research co-operation across national borders and between universities, research institutes and businesses. Ensure that all research grant applicants to EU research funding programmes submit plans for dissemination of research findings as part of their research projects.

- Improve the supply and cross-border mobility of skilled researchers by developing the European Partnership for Researchers and the European Blue Card scheme. Ensure that all national research grants are open to all EU nationals.

- Follow-through on tackling obstacles to cross-border venture capital provision in Europe.

Notes

1. These are a specific type of patent family, covering patents that have been applied for at the European Patent Office and Japanese Patent Office and applied for and granted at the United States Patent and Trademark Office (OECD, 2008a).

2. Direct comparisons across countries can be distorted by differences in the number of separate claims included in individual patent applications.

3. In CIS4, companies undertaking only organisational innovations are not included in the count of innovating companies. So there are some non-innovating companies who still have expenditure on innovation activities.

4. Each member state has a separate objective for their R&D intensity, with the targets set reflecting national structures and institutions. National objectives for investment in R&D by 2010 range from 0.75% (Malta) to 4% (Sweden and Finland) (EC, 2008a).

5. This initiative was originally going to be termed "the researchers' passport".

6. Human resources in science and technology include individuals with a tertiary level degree in a science and technology subject and/or those working in a science and technology occupation as professionals or technicians.

7. Nine additional programmes with funding for innovation-related activities are mentioned in EC (2008c).

8. If there are informational asymmetries, public funding for innovative research can also act as a mark of quality for private investors, providing one means of reducing the marginal cost of external funds for innovators who would otherwise be hampered by financial constraints.

9. The benefits of enhancing public sector research efforts can be mitigated in the short term if the supply of researchers is relatively inelastic, since an expansion of public sector research pushes up the wage costs of researchers in the business sector.

10. In 2006, the business sector funded 6.6% of higher education R&D expenditure in the European Union, compared to 5.4% in the United States and 2.1% in Japan (OECD, 2008c).

11. On a scale of 1 (low) to 7 (high) of collaboration in R&D between the business community and local universities, executives give an average score of 5.8 to the United States, 4.6 to Japan and, using a GDP weighted average, 4.4 to the OECD economies that are members of the European Union (WEF, 2008, Data Table 12.04).

12. The US Bayh-Dole Act of 1980, which allowed universities to retain the intellectual property rights (IPRs) on research results obtained using public funds, was subsequently followed by a sharp rise in the number of patents granted to US academic institutions. This has helped to encourage the consideration of related legislation in other countries.

13. A working group of member state representatives will monitor the implementation of the Recommendation and exchange information on national policies. A knowledge transfer forum for stakeholders has been also been created to discuss practical implementation of the Code of Practice.

Bibliography

Aghion, P. et al. (2005), "Competition and Innovation: An Inverted U Relationship", Quarterly Journal of Economics, Vol. 120.

Arundel, A. et al. (2006), "The Organisation of Work and Innovative Performance: A Comparison of the EU-15", DRUID Working Paper, No. 06-14.

Auriol, L. (2007), "Labour Market Characteristics and International Mobility of Doctorate Holders", STI Working Paper, No. 2007/2, OECD, Paris.

Bauwens, L., G. Mion and J.-F. Thisse (2007), "The Resistable Decline of European Science", CORE Discussion Paper, No. 2007/92.

Bottazzi, L. and M. Da Rin (2002), "Venture Capital in Europe and the Financing of Innovative Companies", Economic Policy, Vol. 17.

Court of Auditors (2007), "Evaluating the EU Research and Technological (RTD) Framework Programmes – Could the Commission's Approach be Improved?", EuropeanCourt of Auditors Special Report, No. 9/2007.

de Rassenfosse, G. and B. van Pottelsberghe (2008), "On the Price Elasticity of Demand for Patents", ECARES Working Paper, No. 2008_031.

DTI (2005), "Creativity, Design and Business Performance", DTI Economics Paper, No. 15, Department of Trade and Industry, London.

EC (2006), Key Competences for Lifelong Learning: European Reference Framework, European Commission, Brussels.

EC (2007a), "Competitive European Regions through Research and Innovation", *European Commission Communication*, COM(2007)474.

EC (2007b), "Removing Obstacles to Cross-Border Investments by Venture Capital Funds", *European Commission communication*, COM(2007)853.

EC (2008a), "A More Research Intensive and Integrated European Research Area", *Science, Technology and Competitiveness Key Figures Report 2008/09*, European Commission, Brussels.

EC (2008b), *European Competitiveness Report 2008*, European Commission, Brussels.

EC (2008c), *Practical Guide to EU Funding Opportunities for Research and Innovation*, European Commission, Brussels. *www.cordis.europa.eu/eu_funding_guide/home_en.html*.

EC (2008d), *Challenging Europe's Research: Rationales for the European Research Area*, report of the ERA Expert Group, European Commission, Brussels.

EC (2008e), "Recommendation on the Management of Intellectual Property in Knowledge Transfer Activities and Code of Practice for Universities and Other Public Research Organisations", European Commission, COM(2008)1329.

EC (2009a), "European Innovation Scoreboard 2008 – Comparative Analysis of Innovation Performance", Pro-Inno Europe, Brussels.

EC (2009b), *First FP7 Monitoring Report*, European Commission, Brussels.

ECB (2009), "Financing of Small and Medium-sized Enterprises and Young Innovative Companies in Europe", *Financial Integration in Europe*, April, European Central Bank.

Engel, D. and M. Keilbach (2007), "Firm Level Implications of Early Stage Venture Capital Investment – An Empirical Investigation", *Journal of Empirical Finance*, Vol. 14.

EPO (2006), *Assessment of the Impact of the European Patent Litigation Agreement (EPLA) on Litigation of European Patents*, European Patent Office, February.

Eurostat (2008), *Science, Technology and Innovation in Europe*, Eurostat, Brussels.

Galasso, A. and M. Schankerman (2008), "Patent Thickets and the Market for Innovation: Evidence from Settlement of Patent Disputes", *CEPR Discussion Paper*, No. 6946.

Guellec, D. and F. Sachwald (2008), "Research and Entrepreneurship: A New Innovation Strategy for Europe", paper presented at Knowledge Intensive Growth conference of the French Presidency of the European Union, Toulouse, 7-9 July.

Guild, E. (2007), "EU Policy on Labour Migration: A First Look at the Commission's Blue Card Initiative", *CEPS Policy Brief*, No. 145, November.

Hansen, W. (2004), "EU-25 Scientists and Engineers International Mobility", presented at Productivity, Innovation and Value Creation Conference, Amsterdam, June.

Hölzl, K. (2006), "Creative Industries in Europe and Austria: Definition and Potential", KMU Forschung Austria, Vienna.

Jaumotte, F. and N. Pain (2005a), "Innovation in the Business Sector", *OECD Economics Department Working Paper*, No. 459, OECD, Paris.

Jaumotte, F. and N. Pain (2005b), "From Development to Implementation: Evidence on Innovation Determinants from the Community Innovation Survey", *OECD Economics Department Working Paper*, No. 458, OECD, Paris.

Laursen, K. and A. Salter (2004), "Searching High and Low: What Types of Firms use Universities as a Source of Innovation?", *Research Policy*, Vol. 33.

Marimon, R. and M. de Graça Carvalho (2008), "An Open Integrated and Competitive European Research Area Requires Policy and Institutional Reforms and Better Governance and Coordination of S&T Policies", *Knowledge Economists Policy Brief*, No. 3, Knowledge for Growth Expert Group.

Mason, G., J.P. Beltramo and J.J. Paul (2004), "External Knowledge Sourcing in Different National Settings: A Comparison of Electronics Establishments in Britain and France", *Research Policy*, Vol. 33.

Mejer, M. and B. van Pottelsberghe (2009), "Economic Incongruities in the European Patent System", *CEPR Discussion Paper*, No. 7142.

Meri, T. (2007), "How Mobile Are Highly Qualified Human Resources in Science and Technology?", *Statistics in Focus*, No. 75/2007, Eurostat.

Mohnen, P. and L.H. Röller (2005), "Complementarities in Innovation Policy", *European Economic Review*, Vol. 49.

Monjon, S. and P. Waelbroeck (2003), "Assessing Spillovers from Universities to Firms: Evidence from French Firm-Level Data", *International Journal of Industrial Organisation*, Vol. 21.

NSF (2008), *Science and Engineering Indicators 2008*, National Science Board, Arlington VA.

OECD (2006), *Going For Growth*, OECD, Paris.

OECD (2008a), *OECD Science Technology and Industry Outlook*, OECD, Paris.

OECD (2008b), *Statistics on International Trade and Services, Volume I*, OECD, Paris.

OECD (2008c), *Main Science and Technology Indicators*, OECD, Paris.

OECD (2008d), *The Global Competition for Talent: Mobility of the Highly Skilled*, OECD, Paris.

OECD (2008e), *Compendium of Patent Statistics*, OECD, Paris.

Reid, A., E. Denekamp and P. Galvao (2008), "Synergies Between EU Instruments Supporting Innovation", *Pro-Inno Europe Report*, June.

Rietschel, E.T. *et al.* (2009), *Evaluation of the Sixth Framework Programmes for Research and Technological Development:* Report of the Expert Group.

Romain, A. and B. van Pottelsberghe (2004), "The Determinants of Venture Capital: Further Evidence", *Economic Research Centre Discussion Paper*, No. 19/2004, Deutsche Bundesbank.

Scotchmer, S. (1991), "Standing on the Shoulders of Giants: Cumulative Research and the Patent Law", *Journal of Economic Perspectives*, Vol. 5, No. 1.

Segarra-Blasco, A. and J.-M. Arauzo-Carod (2008), "Sources of Innovation and Industry-University Interaction: Evidence from Spanish Firms", *Research Policy*, Vol. 37.

Sheehan, J. and A. Wyckoff (2003), "Targeting R&D: Economic and Policy Implications of Increasing R&D Spending", *STI Working Paper* No. 2003/8, OECD, Paris.

van Pottelsberghe, B. (2008), "Europe's R&D: Missing the Wrong Target?", *Bruegel Policy Brief*, No. 2008/03.

van Pottelsberghe, B. and M. Mejer (2008), "The London Agreement and the Cost of Patenting in Europe", *CEPR Discussion Paper*, No. 7033.

WEF (2008), *The Global Competitiveness Report 2008-09*, World Economic Forum, Geneva.

Chapter 3

Deepening the single market

The single market programme has been important in promoting integration in Europe and has improved longer term growth prospects. But much more can be done to raise living standards further, particularly by reforming service sectors and some network industries. OECD product market regulation indicators show that existing regulations remain relatively stringent and that competition is less intense than it should be. There also continue to be substantial delays in the full implementation of some directives by member states, especially in the areas of financial services, energy and transport. The Services Directive should bring further improvement provided it is implemented in a timely and effective fashion, as intended, by the end of 2009. Looking ahead, the Commission should continue efforts to raise competition and reduce administrative burdens by identifying and tackling obstacles to integration and by pursuing the Better Regulation agenda.

The single market programme, now in place for well over two decades, has already delivered many benefits to the European economy.[1] However, completion of the market is progressing at an uneven pace and much more remains to be done, especially in service sectors and some network industries. A detailed overview of the single market legislative programme was provided in the previous *Economic Survey of the European Union* (OECD, 2007). This chapter concentrates on discussing developments since that point, focusing both on the need to implement past product market reforms fully as well as steps that can be taken to further deepen the single market and follow up the Single Market Review programme set out by the Commission in 2007 (EC, 2007a).

In the near term, the challenges arising from the severe economic recession also need to be tackled by the Commission and member states in ways that avoid long-lasting setbacks to the single market programme. It is essential to ensure that national policies to support local jobs and businesses do not endanger the European single market or hamper external access to the European Economic Area. The European Economic Recovery Plan has set out a series of principles to guide the design of recovery measures in a way that is intended to create positive synergies and avoid distortions to the Single Market. As permitted within the existing State Aid provisions of the EC Treaty in the event of a serious economic downturn, there has been a temporary relaxation of the State Aid rules for 2009-10, allowing member states, under certain conditions, to provide greater assistance to their economies. The Commission has already intervened promptly against temporary measures proposed by member states that would favour selected subgroups of companies and violate single market principles, and must continue to do so.

The current state of the single market

The single market programme is extremely wide-ranging and ambitious, requiring continuous updating as industrial structure and technology evolve. Considerable progress has been made over the past two decades, but further structural reforms are needed to increase competition in product markets, especially by reducing entry barriers in network industries and liberalising services markets. European Commission estimates suggest that the first two decades of reforms have generated a permanent rise of around 2 per cent in the level of EU GDP and have boosted employment by just under 1½ per cent (Ilzkovitz *et al.*, 2007). These benefits, though significant, are less than half of what could be possible if the single market was to be completed more fully. The gains so far reflect the impact of stronger competition on price-cost mark-ups along with improvements in innovation and productivity brought about by market integration in manufacturing; the opening up of competition in electricity and telecommunications markets; and the enlargement of the EU.

OECD product market regulation indicators show that regulations remain relatively stringent in EU countries, suggesting that competitive pressures are lower than they could be (Figure 3.1). Over time, there has nevertheless been considerable progress in easing regulations in the EU, especially in network industries. Many countries have moved to

Figure 3.1. **Product market regulation**

Index scale of 0-6 from least to most restrictive[1]

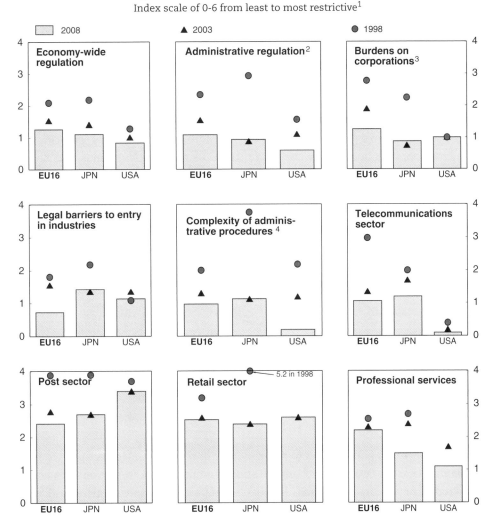

1. Aggregate EU16 (excluding Greece, Ireland and the Slovak Republic due to data unavailability in 2008) has been calculated using 2003 GDP weights.
2. Covers regulatory and administrative opacity and the administrative burdens on business start-ups.
3. Administrative burdens on corporations and sole proprietor start-ups.
4. Covers complexity of government communication of rules and procedures, as well as of licences and permit systems.

Source: OECD, Product Market Regulation database and OECD Economic Outlook database.

StatLink ⟶ http://dx.doi.org/10.1787/712345844104

regulated third party access to networks, have unbundled networks from production and distribution and have reduced the share of public ownership considerably. However, progress has generally slowed over the past five years, and regulations often remain more stringent than in Japan and the United States, both at the economy-wide level and in many specific industries. The average level of barriers remains relatively high in many service sectors, although this is common to non-EU countries as well, reflecting the difficulties in tackling anti-competitive regulations in these sectors.[2]

The general picture provided by the OECD indicators is mirrored in the most recent Doing Business survey of the World Bank, covering the period 2007-08. This provides a survey-based assessment of various forms of national business regulations and their enforcement. All EU member states are judged to be less business-friendly than the United

States and, with three exceptions (Denmark, the United Kingdom and Ireland), less business-friendly than Japan (World Bank, 2009).

There are other signs that the rate of integration is slowing and that more could be done. The intra-EU trade to GDP ratio increased markedly in the late 1990s, but this pace has not been maintained, although the trade ratio does continue to rise. Nonetheless, intra-state goods trade in the United States is still considerably higher than cross-border trade in the EU (Ilzkovitz *et al.*, 2007). Cross-border trade in services in the EU is only about a quarter of that for goods, again indicating that remaining product market regulations hamper competition in many service sectors (Figure 3.2). Greater harmonisation of such regulations could increase cross-border trade of services within the EU significantly (Nordas and Kox, 2009) and, more generally, add to competitive pressures in many service sectors.

Figure 3.2. **Trade integration inside the EU27**[1]

In per cent of GDP

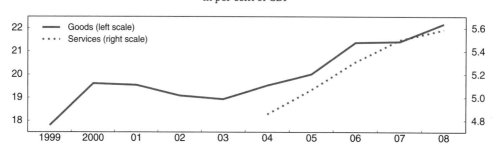

1. Defined as exports of goods or services to other EU27 countries, as a percentage of GDP.
Source: Eurostat.

StatLink 🔗 http://dx.doi.org/10.1787/712360108136

Weak competition and barriers to market entry and exit can also hamper productivity growth and necessary sectoral and organisational adjustments in response to economic shocks. Productivity growth in the EU has been comparatively poor relative to that in the United States since the mid-1990s in almost all sectors of the economy (Figure 3.3),

Figure 3.3. **EU15 labour productivity growth relative to the United States**

Output per hour worked, average annual growth rates

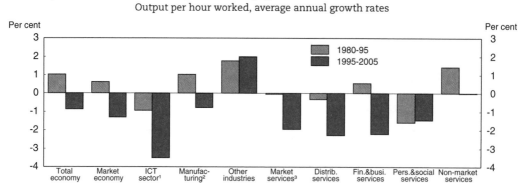

1. Electrical machinery production, post and communication services.
2. Excluding electrical machinery production.
3. Excluding post and telecommunications.

Source: EU KLEMS database, March 2008, see Timmer, M., M. O'Mahony and B. van Ark, *The EU KLEMS Growth and Productivity Accounts: An Overview,* University of Groningen and University of Birmingham; downloadable at www.euklems.net.

StatLink 🔗 http://dx.doi.org/10.1787/712423122140

although there are some signs that the gap may have begun to close in the immediate past (OECD, 2009a). The gap between labour productivity growth in the EU and that in the United States is especially large in many market service sectors. More detailed accounting exercises for a subset of countries suggest that this is mirrored in differences in total factor productivity growth (Timmer *et al.*, 2007), suggesting that more could be done to increase competitive pressures and reduce inefficiencies in these sectors in Europe.

The potential productivity gains from regulatory reforms are substantial. Simulations undertaken in Arnold *et al.* (2009) illustrate the effects of aligning the product market indicator for each non-manufacturing sector in each EU country that is an OECD member to international best practice. Such an exercise would be ambitious, as it would imply a lower average level of regulation than currently observed in any of the OECD countries individually, but it is a target worth aiming at and illustrates the potential importance of such a move. The potential benefits vary markedly across countries. In certain new member states, such as Hungary and Poland, such reforms could boost labour productivity by close to 20% over a decade. For larger EU member countries like France, Germany, and Italy the gains would be around half of this, while there would be only limited gains in Sweden and the United Kingdom, reflecting the low initial level of regulatory barriers in these countries. Cross-country differences in the potential benefits from reforms also reflect differences in industrial structure, and the relative economic importance of sectors that are heavily regulated.

Tackling anti-competitive regulations would have both direct and indirect effects on productivity growth. First, easing restrictive regulations would augment productivity growth in ICT-producing and using sectors, where there are clear differences between the EU and the United States. Catching up to best practice would also be much easier in countries where regulation promotes competition than it would be in poorly regulated ones. Furthermore, as countries or sectors with a low productivity level have the largest potential for catch up, the reform dividend of abolishing inappropriate regulations is largest for the countries that are furthest away from the world productivity frontier.

Ensuring proper implementation of Single Market rules

In addition to introducing new reforms to deepen the single market, there is a continued need to ensure that existing rules are implemented effectively. Improved enforcement of policies is one of the key factors stressed in the 2007 Single Market Review (EC, 2007a). There continue to be delays in the transposition of single market legislation by the due date. An interim target of 1½ per cent for the transposition deficit (the share of directives yet to be implemented by each member state) was set by the European Council in 2001. This has proved an effective means of persuading some member states to improve the rate of transposition, with the transposition deficit having declined to 1% by the end of 2008. This interim target has been reduced to 1%, with effect from 2009. However, the improvement in transposition disguises the large number of directives that have yet to be fully transposed by all member states by the due date. As of the end of 2008, there were 92 directives (6% of the outstanding total) still awaiting full transposition (Figure 3.4), with a quarter of these being more than two years overdue (EC, 2008a).[3] Thus, many aspects of the internal market remain incomplete. Most incomplete directives cover aspects of financial services, energy and transport markets. There are no estimates of the overall economic importance of the directives that remain outstanding, but it is clear that the Commission must continue to instigate infringement procedures promptly to encourage compliance. As suggested in the previous *European Union Survey* (OECD, 2007), the

Figure 3.4. **Fragmentation of the internal market**[1]

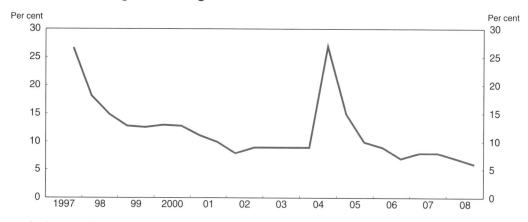

1. The fragmentation factor is the number of directives that have not yet been transposed by all member states, as a percentage of all internal market directives, the 2004 spike being due to the initial effects of enlargement.

Source: European Commission, *Internal Market Scoreboard*, various issues, *http://ec.europa.eu/internal_market/score/index_en.htm.*

StatLink http://dx.doi.org/10.1787/712467554037

Commission should also continue to encourage member states to make it easier for private individuals to challenge transposition infringements.

Additional problems arise from incorrect transpositions and applications of single market directives by member states. This also prevents the single market from working efficiently. To ensure compliance with Community law, the Commission is required to launch infringement proceedings against member states. Little action has been taken by the majority of member states to reduce the number of open infringement proceedings in recent years and, as of the end of November 2008, there were more than 1 200 open infringement cases (EC, 2008a). Infringements occur most frequently over environmental issues, taxation and customs union, and energy and transport. Member states are also often slow to comply with judgements from the European Court of Justice, with the average delay until action is taken to comply with rulings being over 18 months. These problems cannot be tackled by the Commission alone. However, the Commission should continue to ensure that infringement proceedings are managed as efficiently as possible.

Some complaints against the violation of single market legislation by member states can be solved by other means. An online problem-solving network to deal with misapplications of internal market law by public authorities, known as SOLVIT, was created by the Commission and member states in 2002. Since then, its workload has grown steadily, with over 1 000 cases submitted in 2008. For the first time, the number of cases tackled through the SOLVIT network exceeded the number of new infringement cases launched by the Commission. Two-thirds of the SOLVIT cases were in the areas of social security, residence rights and the recognition of professional qualifications. Overall, the network is proving to be an efficient source of fast-track dispute resolution, with resolution rates of over 80%. This is helping to reduce the costs of challenging obstacles to the single market. Increasingly SOLVIT centres are also pursuing cases that require changes in national law, in addition to those that arise from a misapplication of correctly transcribed legislation.

Deepening the single market

Overall, the single market in goods is reasonably complete. Integration is not perfect, but the key remaining barriers are well-entrenched and will be difficult to overcome quickly. Factors such as tax differentials, differences in transport costs, language problems and differences in national consumer preferences will all continue to slow integration even if other regulatory and administrative barriers can be removed successfully. This is also true of services and many network industries, although much more can be done in these cases to deepen the single market. Competition has gradually been encouraged in these sectors, but many areas of comparatively poor performance remain. The Services Directive, postal services, telecommunications and port services are each discussed in detail below. The steps necessary to complete the single market in energy are discussed in Chapter 4. Obstacles to cross-border trade in retail financial services were set out in the recent *Survey of the euro area* (OECD, 2009b).

The Services Directive

Services account for over two-thirds of value added and employment in the EU. Yet, regulatory barriers often make it hard to provide services across borders and hamper entry into national markets. Some laws amount to non-tariff barriers to trade, while differences in regulations across countries make it more difficult to sell services to all European citizens. They also increase business costs significantly, especially for small firms. Cross-border transactions in services frequently require the presence of the service provider in both countries, resulting in an exposure to two different regulatory systems, with a consequent duplication of regulatory burdens.

The Services Directive, introduced in 2006, is intended to reduce such regulatory obstacles. Member states are due to implement the directive by the end of 2009. The scope of the Directive, as well as its potential limitations, were discussed in detail in OECD (2007). Implementation of the Services Directive is a demanding task for member states, as it necessitates changes in national legislation, many administrative simplifications and the introduction of several new large-scale projects, notably the requirement to give service providers the possibility of completing all necessary administrative procedures through so-called "points of single contact". Electronic procedures have also to be set up to allow all service providers (national and from other member states) to complete administrative formalities on-line, and also to facilitate administrative co-operation between member states.

The Commission is actively providing guidance and assistance to member states during the ongoing implementation process. Some indications on the overall progress made by member states towards implementing the Services Directive are available from surveys undertaken by business organisations. The Confederation of European Business released a survey in November 2008 (BusinessEurope, 2008) and the European Association of Chambers of Commerce released a survey in February 2009 (Eurochambers, 2009). The general message provided by these surveys is that the implementation process appears to be proceeding well in many member states, but is lagging behind considerably in a handful of others. A renewed and determined effort is needed on the part of these member states to ensure that the Services Directive will be implemented on schedule. The Eurochambers study estimates that implementation will be achieved fully by the due date in only three-quarters of the member states. Assessments of the state of transposition could be helped by the development of a centralised Web site with timely information on measures adopted by member states.

In most member states, the necessary steps towards adoption of the "points of single contact" are now well underway. There appears to be a marked diversity in the structures and models that are being adopted, including the degree of regional decentralisation. Most countries have opted for a mix of electronic and physical points of single contact. Five member states had yet to decide on the model to be adopted, as of January 2009 (Eurochambers, 2009). Another source for concern amongst businesses is the potential for language barriers to cause difficulties; rapid and efficient translation mechanisms have to be established to solve this problem. As of the end of 2008, 10 member states had not yet developed plans for the use of foreign languages by users of the single point of contact (BusinessEurope, 2008).

The Services Directive requires member states to undertake a thorough screening process of their legislation relating to services activities and to either simplify or abolish unnecessary legislation. Member states have to report to the Commission by the end of 2009 on the results of their reviews. Almost all member states have started the screening process, but progress is slow and fragmented, in spite of the advice and assistance being provided by the Commission. Business federations expect a reduction in administrative burdens in only 17 of the EU member states (BusinessEurope, 2008). Some countries are close to completing the screening process, but others are experiencing significant delays (Eurochambers, 2009).

The area of greatest concern for business federations is the progress made towards setting up integrated national electronic systems and procedures, and the interoperability of the frameworks across member states. All countries have plans to implement electronic procedures, but there are indications that the solutions adopted may differ across countries, in part because of differences in their authentication tools.[4] If so, it is less likely that the different structures chosen for the points of single contact will be fully interoperable, or function smoothly, reducing the benefits to businesses. The Commission and member states are working on some facilitation measures to allow the cross-border use of e-procedures through the points of single contact.

The Services Directive also sets out a legal obligation for member states to provide mutual assistance to one another. To implement this obligation, the Commission has developed in co-operation with member states an electronic system that allows direct contact between competent authorities and an easy exchange of information. A specific application of the Internal Market Information System (IMI) shall support administrative co-operation under the Services Directive. A pilot project was launched in mid-January 2009 and will be tested intensively until the end of 2009.

Despite the active involvement of the Commission in the implementation phase, a minority of member states appear to be experiencing implementation delays. The Commission will need to act decisively if member states do not meet the transposition deadline. Plans have already been drawn up to ensure further progress through a "mutual evaluation exercise" that will begin with member states as of January 2010. This exercise is designed to promote the exchange of best practices across member states. It will also provide a means of seeing where further progress will be needed.

Postal services

Postal services account for approximately 1% of GDP in the EU, and the creation of an integrated postal market is an important element of overall single market policy. A series of Commission directives since 1997 have progressively opened the postal market by reducing the segments of national markets that could be legally reserved for incumbent operators.[5] But competition has been slow to develop, in part because the reserved areas (post below 20 grams) represent the bulk of postal transactions. The market share of the incumbent provider still exceeds four-fifths in most member states.

The Third Postal Directive, adopted in early 2008, has removed the most important entry barrier to the postal market by ending the reserved area for incumbents. The majority of member states (representing 95% of the EU market volume) are required to implement the directive by the end of 2010, with the others required to do so by the end of 2012. A number of member states have already opened up their market to full competition or have firm plans to do so before the 2010 target date. It will be important for the Commission and member states to ensure that the Directive is implemented on time.

Even after implementation, further actions may be needed to tackle remaining entry barriers to ensure that competitors can enter national markets. One outstanding issue is the question of access to the existing postal infrastructure, such as letterboxes, and the wider postal supply chain. National regulatory authorities will have an important role in ensuring that such factors are not used as an obstacle to market entry even after the abolition of legal monopolies. At present, member states have different policies on whether market dominant operators (incumbents) should be obliged to provide access to third parties, and also have different tariff regulations (EC, 2008b). The Postal Directive does not impose specific access rules, although it does allow Parliament and the Council, acting on a proposal from the Commission, to harmonise access rights to the public postal network, if necessary. The Commission should continue to actively assess potential barriers to entry and take action where needed. Member states should ensure that national regulators are given sufficient powers and resources to fulfil their obligation under the postal directive, and the Commission should also continue to promote and facilitate the exchange of best practices pursued by national regulators.

Telecommunications

Competition has steadily increased in the EU telecom market. This has helped telecommunications prices to fall rapidly, with national call charges (for a 3 minute call) having declined by almost two-thirds over the past decade (EC, 2009a). Regulatory barriers to entry have also gradually decreased. On average, however, they remain much higher in the EU than in the United States (Figure 3.1), but lower than in Japan. The potential gains from opening markets further are considerable (Martin et al., 2005; OECD, 2007) and the wide disparity in performance and outcomes across national telecommunications markets in the EU suggests that further progress could be made in removing barriers to entry and reducing the market power of incumbent operators.

In November 2007, the Commission proposed a series of reforms to address these issues and complete the internal market for telecommunications. These proposals have now entered the final stage of the negotiation process between the European Parliament and the Council. Key features of the reform include strengthening the independence of national regulatory authorities and the establishment of a Body of European Regulators. The latter will advise the Commission on the development of the internal market in the telecommunications sector and provide an interface between national regulators and the Commission. This will provide the Commission with more control on regulatory remedies, so as to ensure better regulatory consistency across the EU and the most efficient use of radio spectrum throughout the Community.

In addition, the European Council and European Parliament have recently adopted a regulatory initiative to reduce the costs of roaming calls in Europe, with effect from July 2009. A Roaming Regulation was introduced in 2007, setting out a series of declining retail price caps up to 2010 for the costs of receiving and making mobile phone calls whilst abroad. Wholesale prices (the prices operators charge to each other) were also capped. This is estimated to have led to a reduction in roaming prices of around 70%, as of 2009 (EC, 2009a). A follow-up review of the Roaming Regulation has resulted in an extension of price caps to the years beyond 2010. Furthermore, a new retail price cap of 11 cents on the cost of text messages has been introduced as of July 2009, with additional actions to limit data roaming fees at the wholesale level and enhance price transparency for consumers.

The price caps imposed by the Commission need to be carefully judged. If set too high, they may allow some of the more efficient operators to earn rents by maintaining higher prices than would otherwise be the case in a more competitive market. Indeed, one reason for extending the declining retail price cap beyond 2010 was that the follow-up review of the Roaming Regulation found that most operators were charging a price close to the price cap, suggesting competitive pressures remained weaker than they could be. A continual annual step decline in the price caps is built into the legislation, but the Commission and national regulatory authorities should continue to monitor and report on the impact of the price caps on competitive pressures.

In May 2009, the Commission adopted a Recommendation setting out the costing principles that national regulatory authorities should adopt when determining the level of fixed and mobile termination rates. The objective of the recommended costing approach is to ensure that operators are aware of the true costs associated with providing and purchasing a wholesale call termination. Adopting a common approach across countries should help to foster a more stable and effective regulatory environment for future investments and enhance competition, which should ultimately benefit consumers. National regulators have until the end of 2012 to implement the recommended methodology.

Continued efforts are needed to adjust regulatory barriers to reflect the rapid changes in the business environment as new technologies develop and enter the marketplace. In particular, structural factors that impede the development of a fully integrated pan-European market for mobile services need to be tackled. An important step towards this would be to make open access to mobile networks compulsory. As discussed in the previous Survey (OECD, 2007), full integration of the mobile market would also require changes in the spectrum allocation system (currently under the responsibility of the EU member states). This is also one of the key features of the reform proposals made by the Commission in 2007 and which are about to be adopted by the European Parliament and the Council, with the Commission being requested to propose pluri-annual policy programmes on spectrum.

The Commission will also need to carefully monitor potential impediments to the roll-out of broadband in the EU, where take-up and usage levels remain very different across member states. The decision of the Commission to increase the funds available for broadband infrastructure investments in order to provide high-speed internet coverage to all citizens (part of the European Economic Recovery Plan), is welcome. Such investments are essential to support future growth prospects. The Commission also needs to ensure that the so-called "digital dividend" from the transition to digital terrestrial broadcasting (envisioned at the latest by 2012) will be used in the most efficient way in order to stimulate growth and competition in the European telecom market.

New regulatory issues also arise from the convergence of previously distinct applications (data, telephone, fixed and mobile phone services) into single applications being delivered over "next generation" networks (OECD, 2008). A particularly important issue for national regulators, and also the Commission, is to ensure that new barriers to competition and investment do not develop. In particular, there is a need to ensure that new entrants are able to offer services over existing networks and that there are no unnecessary obstacles that prevent market entry and investments in new facilities (such as difficulties in accessing the existing infrastructures of incumbent operators).[6] The Commission is currently working on a Recommendation about the appropriate regulatory approach to adopt for next generation access networks.

Port services

The development of containerisation, the reduction in the extent to which shipping lines are dependent on individual ports and the increasing overlap in the hinterlands of ports have all raised competitive pressures on ports, especially those in the same region (JTRC, 2008). But ports are not perfect substitutes, and congestion in port access or hinterland infrastructure, as well as national administrative barriers, can mute competitive pressures. Market concentration has increased somewhat in recent years in Europe. In 2007, the largest 15 ports handled two-thirds of container throughputs in Europe, up from three-fifths in 1985 (Notteboom, 2008). This increase of concentration raises issues regarding the degree of competition present in ports and whether ports are being operated as efficiently as they could be. As noted in the previous *Survey* (OECD, 2007), evidence suggests that while some European ports are efficient and competitive, others are well behind the productivity frontier.

The Commission has considered impediments to competition in port services and issued a communication on European ports policy in 2007. This is the latest attempt to improve competition in this sector after almost two decades of failed attempts (OECD, 2007), illustrating the difficulties of making progress in this area. The 2007 communication emphasised the extent to which administrative barriers and regulations were holding back the development of a single market for maritime transport, noting that a ship travelling between two EU ports faces more costly administrative procedures than inland modes of transport between these ports. The Commission has proposed the creation of a paperless environment for customs and trade, including a single window for the submission of data. Steps were also outlined to improve the available evidence base about the extent and impact of such obstacles.

A ten-year strategy plan for the EU maritime sector was published by the Commission in January 2009 (EC, 2009b). The strategy emphasised the need for full implementation of the ports policy communication issued in 2007, with a particular emphasis on prioritising modernisation and expansion of port and hinterland connection infrastructure projects to overcome congestion problems. New guidelines are also to be issued on the role of environmental assessments of port expansion projects.

More generally, the strategy plan is intended to enhance the competitiveness of European shipping and related maritime industries in world markets. The plan also aims to create a maritime transport space without barriers in Europe, by tackling administrative obstacles, such as customs procedures, that hamper the development of intra-EU shipping trade. In addition to the economic benefits that this will offer, if developed effectively, it could also result in environmental benefits by reducing artificial barriers that push traffic away from the maritime sector towards alternative modes of transport, such as road transport, that sometimes have higher environmental costs. The Commission and member states should keep trying to increase efficiency of ports as part of a broader transport strategy.

Market monitoring and screening procedures

Market monitoring is a new tool for evidence-based policy making which was developed as part of the 2007 Single Market Review (Box 3.1). The market monitoring approach should facilitate more comprehensive assessments of the sources of market failure. Previously, policies had concentrated primarily on removing barriers to cross-border trade in Europe. Clearly more remains to be done in this area, especially in sectors such as retail financial services (OECD, 2009a), but other factors may also hamper the development of the internal market.

Box 3.1. **The Market Monitoring Process**

The Commission has developed a new two-stage procedure for product market and sector monitoring, designed to make single market policies more impact-driven and derived from a consistent methodology across all sectors of the economy (EC, 2007b).

The first stage is an initial screening process of all sectors in order to identify those in which there may be the greatest economic gains from in-depth monitoring and eventual policy initiatives. Three criteria are used in the screening process:

- The economic importance of the (two-digit) sector, in terms of its contribution to EU value added and employment and its projected importance for future economic growth.

- The importance of the sector for the adjustment capacity of the EU economy. The criteria used include: inter-linkages with other parts of the economy (measured using input-output tables); the importance of the sector for the introduction and diffusion of new technologies; and the extent to which the sector has a relatively high degree of price stickiness.

- The presence of signs of market malfunctioning in the sector such as a poor productivity performance relative to that of the United States or evidence of consumer satisfaction.

The initial screening is accompanied by a robustness check of the sector selection, to test whether there are broader signs of market malfunctioning in the sector. The robustness check draws on evidence about factors such as the extent of cross-border market integration and the degree of competition and innovation in the sector.

In the second stage, which more closely resembles the previous single market policy process, the selected sectors are examined in greater detail to identify the possible factors associated with market malfunctioning and the possible approaches that can be adopted to deal with these.

Overall, this approach facilitates the development of horizontal policy initiatives, as underperformance in any sector may reflect not only barriers to market entry but also other structural problems requiring different policy instruments.

Market monitoring is a two-stage exercise; with an initial screening process being complemented by subsequent in-depth analyses of the problems identified in particular sectors. As of the end of 2008, 24 sectors had been selected as a result of the initial screening process, representing one-half of EU value added and employment (EC, 2008c). Half of these were manufacturing sectors. A further indicator-based analysis was then undertaken of the possible causes of market malfunctioning, focusing on excessive regulation, a lack of competition, an absence of integration and an unsatisfactory innovation performance (Ilzkovitz *et al.*, 2008). All of the sectors were found to have problems in at least one of these areas, with half having problems in all of them. Poor innovation performance was the most frequently found problem.

The second stage is an in-depth analysis of sectors identified in the first stage. The Commission has already completed an in-depth market monitoring exercise covering the food supply chain, and has launched exercises on electrical engineering (flat screen televisions and household refrigerators), retail services and the pharmaceutical sector. In two of these sectors – electrical engineering and retail trade – productivity growth in the EU has lagged well behind that in the United States since the mid-1990s. The results of these exercises should be concrete findings that can feed directly into policy making and also provide the basis for actions such as tackling barriers to competition (EC, 2008c). It is important that the Commission follows through on such findings by taking decisive action where necessary. In addition, decisions need to be made about the timing and extent of in-depth investigations into the other sectors identified in the screening exercise. The economic importance of the sectors identified again suggests that the single market is far from complete. Evaluation of the policies introduced would be aided by clear quantitative estimates of the market failures and inefficiencies that currently exist and their impact on market size and productivity growth.

The European Company Statute

Companies who wish to operate on a European-wide basis have the option, in place since 2004, of setting up a European Company [a "Societas Europaea" (SE)] instead of a network of subsidiary companies. An SE is governed by a single set of Community rules while still being subject to different national laws in some areas. The intention of the European Company Statute is to reduce administrative and legal costs for companies and to facilitate restructuring in the single market.

The initial take-up of the SE option was limited. In part, this might reflect the failure of member states to agree on common EU rules on all issues, so that national differences still persist. Winding-up, liquidation and insolvency procedures, along with taxation, are still largely determined by the national law of the country in which the headquarters of the SE are located. Employment contracts and pensions are also not covered by the Directive.

More recently, the total number of SEs has risen more sharply. As of October 2008 there were 284 SEs, with around 100 of these having been set up in the preceding six months (Kelemen, 2008). But, whilst the number of companies has grown, it is less clear that many of these offer clear economic benefits. Fewer than 60 of the companies are thought to be normal operating companies. Of these, over half are established in Germany. Over 100 of the SEs appear to have been set up for special purposes, having either no employees or no assets. Three-quarters of these are registered in the Czech Republic and Germany. At the sector level, the largest number of companies is in financial services, followed by the metal industry. There are clearly some grounds for concern that the SE statute is being misused. A study is currently being undertaken for the Commission on the reasons for the marked disparity across member states in the number and scope of SEs and the nature of their operations. The Commission is due to decide at the end of 2009 whether the SE directive should be reviewed.

The Small Business Act, proposed by the Commission in 2008, includes a proposal to allow SMEs to establish a European Private Company (SPE). The aims of this proposal are similar to those behind the European Company Statute, but it is adapted to meet the specific needs of

SMEs. Many of these wish to operate across national borders without merging with another foreign company or setting up subsidiaries. But in doing so, they can face a higher administrative burden because of the potential need to comply with different national regulatory and legal requirements. The SPE Statute is intended to simplify the legal framework for SMEs and facilitate their access to cross-border markets. The March 2009 Competitiveness Council called for the work on the European Private Company Statute to be pursued actively, as part of the wider range of initiatives to support small businesses during the current recession. In doing so, it will be important for member states and the Commission to monitor and evaluate take-up of the scheme to ensure that it is being used for its intended purposes.

The Better Regulation agenda

The body of European law is vast, with a concomitant regulatory burden; the existing body of Community legislation (the "*acquis*") runs to several thousands of legal acts. Inevitably, this can result in some degree of regulatory overlap, excessive complexity and some regulations becoming outdated. The Commission embarked on an ambitious "Better Regulation" programme in 2002, designed to screen the acquis in its entirety and simplify and improve the overall regulatory environment for consumers and businesses and public authorities. This programme has two important strands – a thorough re-examination of existing legislation and improvements in the quality of new policy initiatives.

Considerable progress has been made on the Better Regulation agenda since 2005, with the drive to simplify regulation now a key part of policy revisions across all policy areas, coupled with an overall objective of reducing administrative burdens by 25% by 2012. The economic impact of such a reduction is difficult to assess *ex ante*, since it depends on which regulations are simplified, but has been estimated to be worth around 1¼ per cent of EU GDP (OECD, 2007). Possible simplifications have now been identified in over 180 different areas for the period 2005-09, with the Commission already having tabled simplification proposals in over 130 of them. Of these, around 50 are pending, as of March 2009, before the Council and Parliament. There are also ongoing efforts to withdraw pending proposals that are no longer relevant, to codify and consolidate pieces of legislation and all of their amendments as well as to repeal obsolete legislation. In all, the actions taken since 2005 are estimated to have resulted in a reduction of almost 10% in the existing body of Community legislation. An additional 33 simplification initiatives are to be tabled by the Commission in 2009. Further ahead, another 81 areas have been identified for possible action (EC, 2009c).

There has also been welcome progress in improving the assessments of new initiatives. Impact assessment is now compulsory for all major policy proposals by the Commission and relevant stakeholders are involved more fully in the assessment process. Since 2002, over 400 impact assessments have been completed. An independent Impact Assessment Board (IAB) has been set up by the Commission to support the quality of impact assessments undertaken by individual directorates. In 2008, the IAB examined 135 draft impact assessments carried out by the Commission and asked for a resubmission of almost a third of them. This suggests that there is scope for further improving the quality of impact assessments. To this end, new Impact Assessment guidelines have been in place since the start of 2009; it will be important to monitor the improvements that these generate.

Some scope remains for improving the EU-level assessments of new policy proposals. In particular, the assessment process could incorporate more thorough assessments of the costs and benefits of possible alternatives to the specific policy being assessed (Jacobzone *et al.*, 2007). More could be done to follow up initial impact assessments to take account of revisions made by Parliament and the Council during the legislative process. This is currently rarely done. A common approach to impact assessment was, however, agreed between the three EU institutions in 2005. A mid-term review is currently taking place and it will be important to monitor the improvements that this may generate. Impact assessments of Commission proposals are always made, but are rarely revisited after amendments are made by the European Parliament and the European Council. This complicates effective evaluation of the final policies introduced. Evaluations could also be improved through a more systematic inclusion in the legal text of specific requirements for subsequent monitoring and evaluation when new legislation is proposed.

Concluding comments

Some slowing in the pace of integration of the single market was only to be expected over time, as remaining barriers are typically much harder to tackle. But there is still much to be done, to improve the implementation of past reforms and to also deepen the single market further. The Commission is making commendable progress in some areas, notably the Better Regulation agenda, but is facing considerable obstacles in others. Structural reforms remain essential to strengthen the longer term growth prospects of the European economy and it is vital that the momentum of single market policy is maintained. The key recommendations concerning single market policy are set out in Box 3.2.

Box 3.2. **Recommendations concerning the single market**

- Take effective action to ensure the proper and timely implementation of single market rules.
- Ensure the timely and full implementation of the Services Directive by the end of 2009 and the third Postal Directive by the end of 2012.
- Develop a centralised Web site with timely information on the measures adopted by member states in transposing new Directives.
- Continue to tackle the remaining administrative and regulatory barriers to cross-border competition in network industries. In particular, if competition law alone does not suffice, take action to ensure adequate access to the distribution networks of incumbent operators with significant market power in postal services and telecommunications.
- Further strengthen the evidence base for single market initiatives and build on the market monitoring exercises to identify the overall importance of specific barriers on market size and productivity growth.
- Continue the simplification of administrative burdens *via* the Better Regulation agenda and further improve the impact assessment of new initiatives.

Notes

1. All relevant Community single market legislation applies throughout the European Economic Area.

2. There is a considerable divergence in national regulatory policies that are not revealed by the aggregate indicators for the EU (Arnold *et al.*, 2009; OECD, 2009a). Three country groups can be distinguished. Sweden and the United Kingdom have very competition-friendly regimes. Many other European countries cluster around a middle range of the indicators. And regulations are more stringent in Belgium, the Czech Republic, Hungary, Poland and Portugal.

3. The fragmentation ratio shown in Figure 3.4 spiked up markedly at the end of 2004 because of the accession of the new member states. Since then, they have made rapid progress in transposing the single market directives.

4. Authentication tools that may be required include electronic signatures and electronic certificates.

5. The initial legislation reserved the markets for incumbent operators to mail under 350 grams. This was amended to 100 grams in 2002 and reduced further to 50 grams in 2006.

6. Example of such "passive" infrastructures include, rights of ways, ducts and poles (OECD, 2008).

Bibliography

Arnold, J., P. Hoeller, M. Morgan and A. Wörgötter (2009), "Structural Reforms and the Benefits of the Enlarged EU Internal Market: Much Achieved and Much to Do", *OECD Economics Department Working Paper*, No. 694, OECD, Paris.

Business Europe (2008), *Ready, Steady, Service!*, Report on the Transposition of the Services Directive, BusinessEurope, Brussels.

EC (2007a), "A Single Market for 21st Century Europe", *European Commission Communication*, COM(2007) 724 final.

EC (2007b), "Implementing the New Methodology for Product Market and Sector Monitoring: Results of a First Sector Screening", *Commission Staff Working Document*, SEC (2007) 1517.

EC (2008a), *Internal Market Scoreboard*, No. 18, December, European Commission, Brussels.

EC (2008b), "Report from the Commission to the European Parliament and the Council on the Application of the Postal Directive", *European Commission Staff Working Document*, COM(2008) 884 final.

EC (2008c), "Market Monitoring: State of Play and Envisaged Follow-Up", *European Commission Staff Working Document*, SEC(2008) 3074.

EC (2008d), "A More Research Intensive and Integrated European Research Area", *Science, Technology and Competitiveness Key Figures Report 2008/09*, European Commission, Brussels.

EC (2009a), "Progress Report on the Single European Electronic Communications Market 2008", *European Commission Communication*, COM(2009) 140 final.

EC (2009b), "Strategic Goals and Recommendations for the European Union's Maritime Transport Policy 2009-2018", *European Commission Communication*, COM(2009) 8.

EC (2009c), "Third Strategic Review of Better Regulation in the European Union", *European Commission Communication*, COM(2009) 15 final.

Eurochambers (2009), *Eurochambers Policy Survey*, January, European Chamber of Commerce, Brussels.

Ilzkovitz, F., A. Dierx, V. Kovacs and N. Sousa (2007), "Steps Towards a Deeper Economic Integration: The Internal Market in the 21st Century", *European Economy Economic Papers*, No. 271.

Ilzkovitz, F., A. Dierx, and N. Sousa (2008), "An Analysis of the Possible Causes of Product Market Malfunctioning in the EU".

Jacobzone, S., C.-W. Choi and C. Miguet (2007), "Indicators of Regulatory Management Systems", *OECD Working Papers on Public Governance*, No. 2007/4, OECD, Paris.

JTRC (2008), "Port Competition and Hinterland Connections", 2008-19, *JTRC OECD/ITF Discussion Paper*.

Kelemen, M. (2008), "Recent Developments on New and Established SEs", European Trade Union Institute, Brussels.

Martin, R., M. Roma and I. Van Steenkiste (2005), "Regulatory Reforms in Selected EU Network Industries", *ECB Occasional Paper*, No. 28.

Nordas, H.K. and H. Kox (2009), "Quantifying Regulatory Barriers to Services Trade", *OECD Trade Policy Working Paper*, No. 85, OECD, Paris.

Notteboom, T. (2008), "The Relationship between Seaports and the Intermodal Hinterland in Light of Global Supply Chains. European Challenges", *JTRC OECD/ITF Discussion Paper*.

OECD (2007), *OECD Economic Surveys: European Union*, OECD, Paris.

OECD (2008), *OECD Policy Guidance on Convergence and Next Generation Networks*, OECD, Paris.

OECD (2009a), *Going For Growth*, OECD, Paris.

OECD (2009b), *OECD Economic Surveys: Euro Area*, OECD, Paris.

Timmer, M., M. O'Mahony and B. van Ark (2007), "EU KLEMS Growth and Productivity Accounts: Overview November 2007 Release".

World Bank (2009), *Doing Business 2009: Comparing Regulation in 181 Economies*, World Bank Group, Washington DC.

Chapter 4

Energy policy and the transition to a low-carbon economy

European energy policy faces a number of interrelated challenges, including making the transition to a low-carbon economy, increasing cross-border competition in electricity and gas markets and diversifying Europe's energy supply. The EU has developed a comprehensive strategy in all of these areas, encapsulated in 2020 targets for reducing greenhouse gas emissions, raising renewable energy and increasing energy efficiency. These targets are underpinned by an Emissions Trading Scheme, legally binding reduction commitments by member states for the emissions not covered by the trading scheme, the third energy liberalisation package and the Energy Security and Solidarity Plan. The EU should be applauded for the significant steps it has taken; the EU's environmental actions and targets are very ambitious and will increase the likelihood of a global climate agreement later in 2009. But there is also room for improvement. To ensure that the transition to a low-carbon economy is achieved at a low cost, the EU should seriously consider including all transport sectors in the Emissions Trading Scheme when practical and appropriate, and ensure that only sectors rigorously identified as being at genuine risk of carbon leakage should continue to receive free allowances until 2020. Consideration should be given to making use of an EU-wide market instrument to deliver the EU's renewable energy target, and it will be important to ensure that the 10% renewable transport fuel target efficiently achieves its objectives of sustainability and security of supply given the high cost of many renewable transport fuels. Measures to raise energy efficiency will have to be designed carefully so that the overall cost of mitigation is not raised. The Commission's third energy market liberalisation package should be strengthened by requiring full ownership unbundling of transmission service operators and ensuring the powers of the proposed Agency for Co-operation of Energy Regulators are broad enough to contribute effectively to a truly single European energy market.

European energy policymakers face a number of complex challenges, as well as significant opportunities. Europe must make the transition to a low-carbon economy as part of a co-ordinated global approach to mitigating greenhouse gas emissions and avoiding irreversible damage of climate change. Cross-border competition in electricity and gas markets must increase markedly so that the goal of a single European energy market is finally realised. Energy security must be strengthened so that Europe is less vulnerable to supply disruptions that originate in other countries. These challenges are of course interrelated. Reducing European greenhouse gas emissions will be more costly if segmentation in energy markets dulls the price signals from emissions trading. And without more competition in energy markets, necessary investments in cross-border transmission networks will be delayed, thereby inhibiting European energy security.

Perhaps the most significant of these challenges is climate change. Climate change represents a global market failure. The social cost of consuming and producing greenhouse gas-intensive goods and services and the atmospheric concentration of greenhouse gases is higher than the private cost (Box 4.1). To meet the energy and climate challenges, the European Commission will need to work closely with member states as well as countries outside the Union, and make use of a comprehensive set of instruments that address all the market failures that plague energy and climate change policy. In addition to addressing the wedge between the social and private cost of greenhouse gas emissions, policy will also have to overcome other market failures, including capital market imperfections, externalities in R&D, lack of sufficient information, monitoring and enforcement costs, the market power of incumbent firms and the incentives for free-riding. Recognising this, the EU has developed a comprehensive energy and climate policy strategy. To contribute to climate change mitigation, the EU has set a target for reducing its greenhouse gas emissions by 20% below 1990 levels by 2020 and increasing the share of renewable sources in gross final energy consumption to 20% by 2020. To internalise the social cost of greenhouse gas emissions and send a long-term price signal in favour of investment in low-emission technologies, the EU has introduced an Emissions Trading Scheme (ETS). To improve the efficiency with which households and firms use energy, the EU has set an indicative target for reducing energy consumption by 20% by 2020 and upgrading efficiency standards applying to new buildings, passenger cars and appliances. A third liberalisation package has been agreed to increase competition in electricity and gas markets, raise the effectiveness of price signals from the ETS and stimulate investment in grids that can absorb new renewable energy capacity.

However, it is essential that the instruments to reach these targets are as efficient as possible, correct only genuine market failures and are flexible enough to cope with future scientific, economic and technological changes. In the short and medium term, policies to mitigate climate change will slow potential GDP growth as the higher cost of carbon-intensive goods and services reduces the productivity of the existing capital stock, and lower cost technologies are substituted for higher cost technologies. To minimise the impact on growth, the EU should avoid policies that unnecessarily raise the cost of carbon

Box 4.1. **Greenhouse gas emissions and climate change**

Since 1970, global greenhouse gas (GHG) emissions have doubled and the concentration of greenhouse gases in the atmosphere has increased to just over 380 parts per million (ppm) of carbon dioxide equivalent (CO_2^e) (National Oceanic and Atmospheric Administration Earth System Research Laboratory, 2008).[*] Without further policy initiatives, global GHG emissions could nearly double again by 2050 and the atmospheric concentration of greenhouse gases increase to 650 ppm CO_2^e (Figure 4.1) (*IIASA GGI Scenario Database*, 2008). According to the Intergovernmental Panel on Climate Change (IPCC), the increase in the atmospheric concentration of greenhouse gases since the industrial revolution has contributed to global warming of around 0.7 °C over the past 100 years (IPCC, 2007).

Figure 4.1. **World GHG emission trends by country/region**[1]
As a share of world total emissions

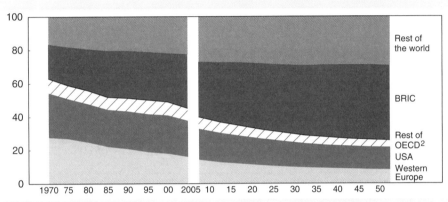

1. Data exclude emissions from land use, land-use change and forestry. Break in series in 2005 due to different sources.
2. The rest of the OECD does not include Korea, Mexico and Turkey which are aggregated in rest of the world.
Source: OECD (2008), *OECD Environmental Outlook* and OECD ENV-Linkages model.

StatLink http://dx.doi.org/10.1787/712468263377

If emissions growth continues on its current trajectory, global temperatures are likely to increase by between 2 °C and 6 °C this century (Figure 4.2), and contribute to rising sea levels and more frequent, extreme weather events (IPCC, 2007). Climate change is likely to imply declining global agricultural yields, reductions in biodiversity, reduced availability of fresh water, and higher rates of diseases. Although there is uncertainty about the social cost of greenhouse gas emissions, estimates suggest that the net present value could be as high as USD 85 per ton of CO_2 (Figure 4.3) (Tol, 2005). Reducing the probability of extreme and irreversible climate change will require very large emission reductions in the course of the century, though there is considerable debate in the scientific and economic literature over the optimal magnitude and timing of emission reductions.

[*] The six major greenhouse gases are carbon dioxide, methane, nitrous oxide, hydrofluorocarbons, perfluorocarbons and sulphur hexafluoride.

Box 4.1. **Greenhouse gas emissions and climate change** *(cont.)*

Figure 4.2. **Projected temperature increases under OECD baseline scenario**[1]

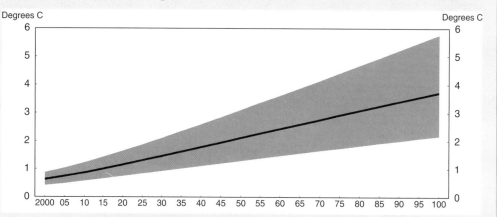

1. Lower and upper bounds correspond to lower and upper values of the climate sensitivity parameter.

Source: Burniaux *et al.* (2008), "The Economics of Climate Change Mitigation: Policies and Options for the Future", *OECD Economics Department Working Paper*, No. 658.

StatLink http://dx.doi.org/10.1787/712560842547

Figure 4.3. **The probability distribution of the social cost of carbon**[1]

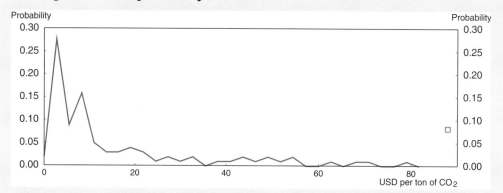

1. The social cost of carbon is the net present value (over the simulation horizon) of the climate change impact of one additional ton of CO_2 emitted in the atmosphere today. The observation on the right hand side is the cumulative probability of social cost of carbon in excess of USD 85/tCO_2.

Source: Burniaux *et al.* (2008), "The Economics of Climate Change Mitigation: Policies and Options for the Future", *OECD Economics Department Working Paper*, No. 658.

StatLink http://dx.doi.org/10.1787/712565843202

abatement, potentially lock-in inefficient technologies and overlap too much with other, more efficient policies. This chapter assesses the EU's policy strategy in this light.

A snapshot of the energy sector

The EU is heavily dependent on energy imports. In 2005, imports represented about 50% of total EU energy supply, with import dependence most acute for oil and gas. Between 1990 and 2005 energy consumption increased by 10%, compared to a 35% increase in GDP, implying an average annual drop of 1.4% in the energy intensity of the economy (IEA, 2008a). Fossil fuels dominate energy supply; in 2005 oil, gas and coal together accounted for 78% of the total, compared to just 7% for renewables. Within fossil fuels there has been some substitution from coal to gas, though the share of fossil fuels is only slightly lower than it was in 1990. The share of nuclear energy was 14% in 2005, up from 12% in 1990.

Although the energy mix has been fairly stable over the past two decades, this masks considerable variation across sectors as well as member states. Overall, the industrial and transport sectors account for the largest shares of final energy consumption (each around 30%), followed by the residential sector at just over 20% (Figure 4.4). Not surprisingly, oil is the predominant energy source for the transport sector, while electricity dominates the industrial and residential sectors. At the member state level there is considerable variation in the energy used to produce electricity (Figure 4.5). For example, France has the highest share of nuclear, while Sweden makes proportionally more use of renewable energy (largely hydropower) and the Eastern European countries are the heaviest consumers of

Figure 4.4. **Sectoral final energy consumption by source**
Share of each country's total final consumption[1]

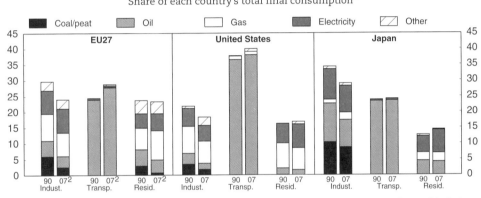

1. The three sectors shown (industry, transport and residential) don't add up to the total as the total includes other sectors such as agriculture.
2. 2006 data.

Source: IEA (2009), *Energy Balances of OECD Countries* and *Energy Balances of non-OECD Countries.*

StatLink http://dx.doi.org/10.1787/712676132854

Figure 4.5. **Total primary energy supply**
Per cent of total, 2008[1]

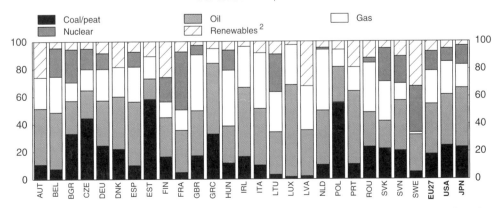

1. The total excludes electricity and heat. 2006 data for Bulgaria, Estonia, Lithuania, Latvia, Romania, Slovenia and the EU27.
2. Hydro, geothermal, combustible renewables and waste and solar, wind and other.

Source: IEA (2009), *Energy Balances of OECD Countries* and *Energy Balances of non-OECD Countries.*

StatLink http://dx.doi.org/10.1787/712700441414

coal. The difference in the energy mix across countries reflects a number of factors, including available national resources, policy choices and R&D priorities.

There is also considerable variation in energy prices. For example, electricity prices for industry in 2008 ranged from EUR 40 per megawatt hour in France to about EUR 200 per megawatt hour in Italy (Figure 4.6). These differences reflect differences in the cost of generating electricity, together with the lack of competition and integration in the EU electricity market which hampers electricity being exported from low-cost countries to high-cost countries. Differences in taxation also have an impact. The introduction of the EU Emissions Trading Scheme (ETS) in 2005 is having an impact on absolute and relative energy prices. The spot price of emission allowances has so far averaged EUR 16 per tonne of carbon dioxide equivalent (CO_2e) during the second phase of the ETS, which had only a small effect on average retail electricity prices. The variation in the use of energy sources across member states, combined with the different carbon intensities of those energy sources (coal is most carbon intensive per unit of energy produced, and nuclear and renewable least), means that the ETS is having a differential impact on overall energy prices across countries.

Figure 4.6. **Electricity prices for industry**
EUR per thousand kilowatt hours, 2008[1]

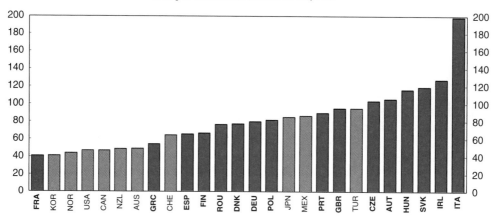

1. Or latest available data.

Source: IEA (2009), *Energy Prices and Taxes*, 2nd Quarter 2009.

StatLink http://dx.doi.org/10.1787/712723170413

Greenhouse gas emissions in the EU27 fell by 7.9% between 1990 and 2005, while emissions fell by 2% in the EU15. Overall, the carbon intensity of the EU economy has fallen by 0.8% per annum since 1990. The reduction in carbon intensity predominantly reflects the substitution in the energy mix from coal to gas, and the restructuring of the eastern European economies after the fall of their Communist regimes (IEA, 2008a). Under the Kyoto Protocol, the EU15 is obliged to reduce its greenhouse gas emissions by 8% from 1990 levels by 2008-12 in aggregate, though obligations vary from country to country and some countries are making better progress toward their targets than others. Per capita greenhouse gas emissions vary considerably because EU countries vary both in their relative use of carbon-intensive energy sources and the efficiency with which they use those energy sources (Figure 4.7). Although poorer EU countries tend to have lower per capita emissions, they also tend to be more carbon intensive per unit of GDP. Overall,

Figure 4.7. **Per capita GHG emissions**
tCO$_2$-equivalent, 2006[1]

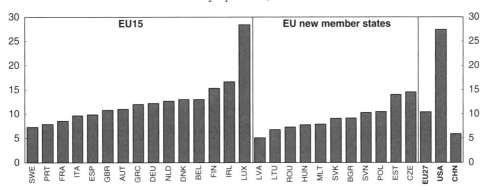

1. 2005 data for the United States and China.

Source: EEA (2008), *Greenhouse Gas Emission Trends and Projections in Europe 2008*, and Burniaux *et al.* (2008), "The Economics of Climate Change Mitigation: Policies and Options for the Future", *OECD Economics Department Working Paper*, No. 658.

StatLink ⟨⟨⟨⟩⟩⟩ http://dx.doi.org/10.1787/712732208160

per capita emissions in both the EU15 and EU27 are considerably lower than in the United States and Japan, though above those of most developing countries.[1]

The energy policy framework

To get energy policy right, policymakers must have a good sense of the factors that will shape energy demand and supply over the coming decades and plan ahead accordingly. Energy policies enacted today can have long-lasting impacts because the economic life of the energy capital stock is often very long (Table 4.1). This is complicated by the uncertainty that surrounds future economic developments, the state of scientific knowledge about climate change, potential breakthroughs in low-emission energy technologies and the elasticity of such breakthroughs with respect to carbon prices, and the energy policies of other countries.

Table 4.1. **Typical service life for selected investments**

Type of asset	Typical service life (years)
Household appliances	8-12
Automobiles	10-20
Industrial equipment/machinery	10-70
Aircraft	30-40
Electricity generators	50-70
Commercial/industrial buildings	40-80
Residential buildings	60-100

Source: Jaffe, A., R. Newell and R. Stavins (1999), "Energy-Efficient Technologies and Climate Change Policies: Issues and Evidence", *Resources for the Future Climate Issue Brief*, No. 19, Resources for the Future, Washington DC.

Recognising the importance of a forward-looking, comprehensive energy strategy, the EU has agreed to the EU energy and climate change policy in 2007. Key elements of the strategy are:

● Reducing greenhouse gas emissions by 20% below 1990 levels by 2020. The main instruments to achieve this target are the ETS and other measures targeted at sectors not covered by the ETS.[2] To achieve the overall reduction of 20% relative to 1990 levels, the EU needs to cut its greenhouse gas emissions by 14.5% relative to 2005 levels. This will be achieved by capping emissions for all installations across the EU covered by the ETS at 21% below 2005 levels and through individual member state targets for emissions reductions in all sectors outside the EU ETS, which add up to a reduction of 10% relative to 2005 levels.

- Involving non-EU countries in an international agreement to reduce global greenhouse gas emissions through the United Nations Framework Convention on Climate Change process. The EU is willing to go further and sign up to a 30% reduction target in the context of an ambitious and comprehensive international agreement if there are comparable reductions by other developed countries and appropriate contributions by the economically more advanced developing countries based on their responsibilities and capabilities.

- Raising the share of renewable energy to 20% of total EU gross final energy consumption by 2020. In addition to subsidies for renewable energy generation, the EU proposes to step up R&D spending on renewable energy technologies.

- Increasing the use of renewables in transport fuels to 10% in each member state.

- Reducing EU energy consumption by 20% by 2020, compared to baseline developments. Measures include introducing EU-wide vehicle efficiency standards for new passenger cars, a building efficiency code, and updated, comprehensive performance standards for electrical appliances.

- Developing a fully integrated single market for electricity and gas, through the effective unbundling of transmission system operators, strengthening and enhancing co-operation amongst energy regulators, increasing investment in infrastructure to facilitate cross-border trade in electricity and gas, and rapid growth in renewable energy.

- Establishing a legal framework on carbon capture and storage (CCS) and using a dedicated part of the proceeds from the ETS to finance a number of CCS demonstration plants and innovative renewables.

- Enhancing energy security through the development of a European energy grid and diversifying the energy mix. Pricing carbon and the move to a single market for electricity and gas will be critical for achieving these goals.

This is an ambitious programme along a number of dimensions. In absolute terms, Europe's current emissions reduction targets are larger than for other comparable regions. A balance will have to be struck between spreading the cost of reducing emissions widely across the economy and avoiding carbon leakage. It is critical that the ETS delivers a long-term price signal that encourages firms to substitute high-emission production processes for low-emission processes, encourages households and firms to use energy more efficiently, and encourages R&D on low-emission technologies. Some of the technologies such as carbon capture and storage that will be necessary to deliver even greater emission reductions in the future have yet to be commercially developed and face high costs. To achieve the binding 20% renewable energy target will require more than doubling the share of renewables over the next decade. Raising energy security is an important goal, but even under the latest EU initiatives, the share of imports in primary energy supply will increase further over the next decade (IEA, 2008a). Achieving an effective, single energy market will be a challenge, particularly as some member states may have to defer national priorities, but this will be critical for reaching the EU's environmental targets.

The economic costs of delivering the climate-related elements of the energy and climate change policy are very uncertain and will depend on many variables, among other overall economic development, energy price development on the international market, the further development of the global carbon market (Box 4.2), the instruments chosen to

Box 4.2. **Sharing the global burden of climate change mitigation policies**

Because climate change is a global market failure with severe environmental, social and economic costs, mitigation requires co-ordinated global action to reduce global greenhouse gas emissions. However, there is still no agreement amongst all countries by how much global emissions should be reduced and how the burden of reducing greenhouse gas emissions should be distributed across countries, creating incentives for countries to free ride on the actions of others. This makes effective global mitigation actions less effective.

Some developing countries argue that as climate change is largely due to earlier emissions by developed countries, it would be unfair for them to bear much of the cost of abatement, particularly as their living standards are still comparatively low. On the other hand, because developing countries now account for over half of GHG emissions, and their share is rising over time, climate mitigation will be unsuccessful without an important contribution by developing countries, and poor countries have the most to lose from climate change (Stern, 2007).

A variety of suggestions have been made to secure binding political support for mitigation across all countries. These include:

- Allocating emission allowances to countries on the basis of historical emissions.
- Allocating emission allowances on the basis of long-term equalisation of per capita emissions.
- Implementing a globally-agreed carbon tax without explicit country-specific emission targets.
- Country-specific targets differentiated according to a country's ability to abate.
- Burden sharing, whereby developed countries agree to immediate abatement while abatement in developing countries is delayed until they reach higher per capita income levels.
- Dynamic targets taking into account historic and projected future emissions, per capita income and population (Bosetti *et al.*, 2008).

By requiring binding emission reductions of only developed (Annex 1) countries by 2012, the Kyoto Protocol took the burden-sharing approach. However, because of the rapidly growing share of developing countries in global emissions, an agreement that does not require at least some binding emission reductions below their business-as-usual path from large developing countries such as China and India appears unlikely.

In January 2009, the European Commission unveiled its proposals for achieving a global agreement at the next UN climate conference in Copenhagen in December 2009. The Commission has called for collective 30% emission cuts for the group of developed countries by 2020 below 1990 levels and has proposed 15-30% cuts below current baseline trajectories for developed countries as a group. The Commission called on OECD members to set up their own Emissions Trading Scheme (ETS) by 2013 and will reach out to developing nations such as China, India and Brazil to encourage them to join an international carbon trading system by 2020. The Commission has also advocated substantial funding for developing countries to help them reduce their emissions and help secure their participation.

While the EU's example from its own mitigation policies, together with its international leadership in forging an effective global agreement, are laudable, it remains to be seen whether these proposals will be adequate to secure that agreement. Some developed countries have already signaled that a 30% reduction in absolute emissions by 2020 would be more than they would be willing to agree to, and it is unclear whether developing countries will agree to binding emission reductions below baseline levels without ambitious action by developed countries.

encourage emission reductions, how quickly the cost of low-emission technologies falls over time, and whether a single market for energy is achieved. The Commission's impact assessment projects the cost of reaching its climate mitigation and renewable energy goals, including access to project-based mechanisms, to be 0.45% of EU GDP in 2020. This would require a carbon price of EUR 30 per tonne of CO_2 (2005 prices) and a renewable energy incentive of EUR 49 per MWh. Oil and gas imports would fall by EUR 41 billion by 2020, while electricity prices are likely to increase by 10-15%.

Overall, this leads to an energy intensity improvement of approximately 30% between 2005 and 2020. Results of OECD modelling suggest that if Europe acts in concert with other countries to stabilise the atmospheric concentration of GHG at 550 ppm, GDP in 2050 would be just over 2% below its baseline level (Burniaux et al., 2008) (Figure 4.8). The costs for the EU are considerably smaller than those for many other countries, largely because countries in Europe are less fossil fuel intensive (Figure 4.9). However, this assumes that there is a global carbon tax and that there is no burden sharing between the EU and developing countries. The 550 ppm stabilisation target used in the modelling is also higher than the 450 ppm being pursued by the EU in international negotiations.

Figure 4.8. **Costs of stabilising GHG concentrations at 550 ppm**[1]
Deviations from baseline, in percentage points of GDP

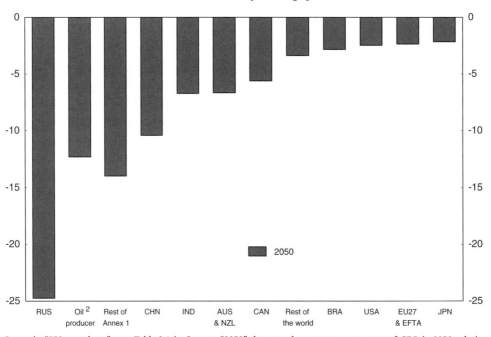

1. Scenario "550 ppm-base", see Table 3.1 in Source. "2050" denotes the cost as a per cent of GDP in 2050 relative to baseline.
2. The region includes the Middle East, Algeria-Libya-Egypt, Indonesia and Venezuela.

Source: Burniaux et al. (2008), "The Economics of Climate Change Mitigation: Policies and Options for the Future", OECD Economics Department Working Paper, No. 658.

StatLink ⟶ http://dx.doi.org/10.1787/712734885021

If inefficient instruments are chosen to reduce emissions, abatement costs will be higher and output will be lower. If R&D leads to only incremental improvements in energy efficiency, mitigation costs will be reduced little. If, however, R&D leads to major technological breakthroughs, especially in the transport and industry sectors where marginal abatement

Figure 4.9. **Projected fossil fuel intensities**
Under baseline and 550 ppm GHG concentration stabilisation scenarios[1]

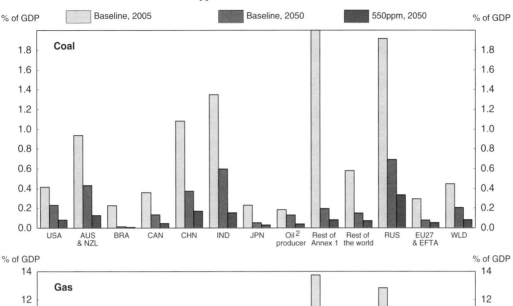

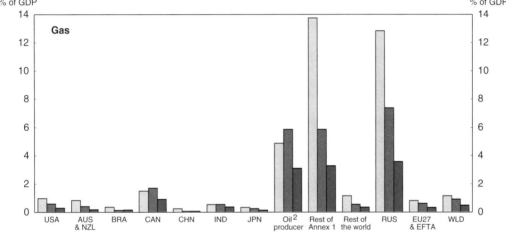

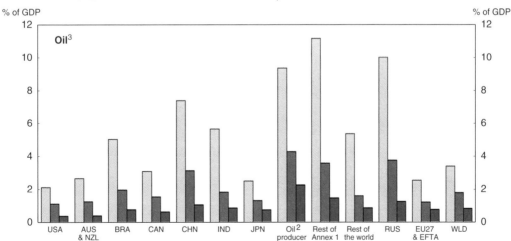

1. Energy intensity, defined as domestic demand as a percentage of GDP in 2050.
2. The region includes the Middle East, Algeria-Libya-Egypt, Indonesia and Venezuela.
3. Refined oil only.

Source: Burniaux *et al.* (2008), "The Economics of Climate Change Mitigation: Policies and Options for the Future", *OECD Economics Department Working Paper*, No. 658.

StatLink 🖉📊 http://dx.doi.org/10.1787/712755088156

costs are highest, mitigation costs could fall significantly. If Europe does not move promptly toward a single energy market, the price signals from the ETS will be blunted, convergence in energy prices will not take place, and it will be more difficult to absorb low-emission energy sources into energy grids (Bosetti *et al.*, 2008). The rest of the chapter considers the EU's battery of energy and climate change mitigation policies in more detail.

Emissions Trading Schemes

The most important instrument for delivering the goal of reducing greenhouse gas emissions is the European Emissions Trading Scheme (EU ETS). The rationale for the policy is simple (Duval, 2008). In fossil fuel intensive sectors of the economy, a by-product is the emission of greenhouse gases which also has a social cost. The energy price will not include the social costs of climate change and emissions will be larger than is socially optimal. The main market mechanisms for internalising the social cost of carbon emissions are "cap and trade" emissions trading schemes and carbon taxes. Under "cap and trade" total emissions are capped in each period and allowances to emit allocated to firms either free or through an auction. Firms can then trade their allowances depending on whether it is profitable to emit more or less than their allocation. Because the quantity of allowances in the market is fixed, the price of allowances, and hence the price of carbon, adjusts according to demand and supply in the allowance market. In contrast, under a carbon tax, the price of carbon is set by the government, with the quantity of emissions determined by households and firms reacting to the change in relative prices (Box 4.3).

The European Union chose a cap-and-trade ETS because it will credibly deliver its emissions-reduction targets for covered sectors; it could be linked with emerging national schemes in countries like the United States, Australia and New Zealand, provided that the schemes are compatible with the EU ETS; it is more likely to sustain the political coalition required for the long-term credibility of climate mitigation policy; and it enables firms to manage carbon risk through the secondary market for emission allowances. When setting up an ETS, a number of important design issues need to be considered, including:

- The sectoral coverage of the scheme. The efficiency and fairness of an ETS will be enhanced if the scheme includes as many sectors as is practical. Broad coverage ensures that low-cost abatement opportunities will be implemented and distributes the social burden more equitably (Duval, 2008; Garnaut, 2008). Governments also need to decide where in the supply chain the point of obligation for surrendering allowances should be. The implementation of schemes can be different for different sectors, and for some sectors it may be easier to implement schemes at upstream points (*e.g.* oil importing companies rather than individual emissions sources) due to lower compliance and administrative costs, while for others (*e.g.* energy utilities) implementing schemes downstream, *i.e.* at the point source of emissions, is more practicable and likely to ensure necessary compliance.[3]

- A mechanism for allocating emission allowances. Allowances to emit greenhouse gases can be allocated to firms through auctioning and/or free allocation based on likely losses in asset value, historic emissions (grandfathering) and industry benchmarks. When allocating allowances, governments need to consider equity and the need to encourage abatement and promote market efficiency. Emissions trading *per se* ensures static efficiency because it generates a uniform price signal that allocates mitigation efforts across firms depending on their own marginal abatement costs. In addition to that,

Box 4.3. **Emissions trading compared with other carbon pricing mechanisms**

Cap and trade emissions trading and carbon taxes should result in the same price and quantity of emissions when there is no uncertainty about current and future costs and benefits of greenhouse gas abatement; the policymaker would set the tax or cap on emissions to equalise the benefits and costs of abatement. However, because there is uncertainty about the impact of climate change and the costs of abatement, in practice the two instruments are not equivalent (Weitzman, 1974; Stern, 2007). Determining the optimal scale and timing of greenhouse gas abatement is further complicated by the fact that policymakers have to weigh the welfare of current and future generations because the costs of policies to reduce climate change accrue mostly to the current generation, while the benefits accrue mostly to future generations.

Any welfare advantages of carbon taxes are most likely to exist in the short run, where abatement costs are arguably relatively high because production reflects the low relative prices of fossil fuels and the capital stock is fixed, while the short-run benefits of abatement may be relatively low because emissions in any one year have little impact on the stock of greenhouse gases in the atmosphere (Weitzman, 1974; Stern, 2007; McKibbin and Wilcoxen, 2006). In this case, if policymakers believe that the cost of abatement is lower than it actually is, a carbon tax will be more efficient than an emissions cap because the cap has to be met by firms regardless of the cost. The price of carbon will also be more volatile under a cap if the costs of abatement shift with the state of the economy. However, given the broad uncertainty about likely environmental damages and the fatness of the tails in the distribution of possible damage costs, the benefits of price-based instruments in the short run may be overstated (Jamet and Corfee-Morlot, 2009).

In the long run, when the costs of abatement are likely to be lower because production has adapted to the higher relative prices of fossil fuels and the benefits of abatement are greater because the costs of climate change increase sharply as cumulative emissions increase, welfare is likely to be higher under a cap (Weitzman, 1974; Stern, 2007). Here, if the policymaker believes that the cost of abatement is lower than it actually is, a relatively low tax would result in less abatement than is socially optimal. Hence, if a carbon tax was in place, its level would need to be updated when new information about long-run costs and the *ex post* quantity of emissions became available.

However, even in the short term a quota scheme such as an ETS can be adapted to mimic the short-run benefits of carbon taxes. Flexibility mechanisms such as emission fees, banking and borrowing can all help to contain the short-run costs of abatement, while secondary markets for emission allowances help firms to hedge their carbon risk. It may also be more difficult to build long-term political coalitions around carbon taxes, which could undermine the credibility of climate mitigation policies. On the other hand, transaction and administrative costs of permit trading are likely to be higher than for carbon taxes, caps potentially offer more opportunities for rent seeking by interest groups and it may be difficult to implement a truly international permit trading system because of monitoring problems in poor countries (Nordhaus, 2004). Hybrid approaches have also been advocated that explicitly combine the short-term benefits of a fixed carbon price, with the advantages of tradable long-term permits (Mckibbin and Wilcoxen, 2006).

auctioning maximises dynamic efficiency through incentivising long-term technological change. Moreover, auctions deliver revenue to governments that allows other taxes to be reduced and greater support for research and development of low-emission technologies. Auctions can also promote equity by transferring income from firms that can pass on the cost of allowances to those that are most affected by carbon pricing. One argument for the free allocation of allowances to firms is that it is a transparent way of compensating firms for the loss of value of their existing assets that still preserves the price signal from the ETS. However, Stern (2007) argues that free allocation (especially if based on grandfathering) can reward the worst polluters, delay investment in low-emission technologies and can deter competition if new entrants in a polluting industry do not receive any free allowances. Free allocation may also generate windfall profits for firms that are over-allocated allowances and are able to pass the opportunity cost of holding allowances to households and firms downstream. Free allocation is more likely to be appropriate for firms operating in energy-intensive, trade-exposed industries that cannot pass on the cost of allowances as a way of combating carbon leakage to countries that have not imposed a price on carbon (Reinaud, 2008). However, assistance should only be given to firms that are genuinely at risk of relocating offshore or losing market share; assistance should be strictly transitional, and allocated on the basis of industry best practice.

- Measures to increase the flexibility of the scheme. The short-run costs and uncertainty from complying with an ETS can be alleviated by allowing the use of carbon offsets that come at a cheaper price than allowances for compliance purposes. Offsets can be created outside or within a country with an ETS by investing in projects that reduce greenhouse gases already in the atmosphere (carbon sinks) or by capturing and storing gases at the point of emissions (carbon sequestration). Investors in offsets can be credited with allowances that can be sold to emitters with allowance shortfalls. Flexibility can also be enhanced by allowing allowances that are not used within an allocation period to be banked and used to acquit emissions in future periods. Borrowing allows emitters to use allowances allocated to them for use in future periods to meet current period emissions. By allowing emissions to be transferred between periods, borrowing and banking may imply that the profile of emission reductions may vary from the trajectory chosen by the government. This should not affect the integrity of the scheme as long as the long-term emission reduction target is achieved. However, because emitters have an incentive to bank allowances for future use and pay the emission penalty when they expect the future price of allowances to increase above the level of the penalty, it is necessary to limit the amount of allowances that can be banked in a scheme with a fee, or at least raise the fee in real terms over time (Duval, 2008). Borrowing can create shortages of future allowances, increasing the cost of the scheme, undermining the credibility of the scheme and pressuring governments to relax emission caps. For this reason borrowing should only occur within one trading period, thus not jeopardising the envisaged emissions trajectory.

- Penalties can be charged for non-compliance to firms whose emissions exceed the amount of allowances they hold (IEA, 2009). Schemes can also levy fees designed to cap the short-term cost of the scheme. Capping prices below the potential market price of allowances comes at the expense of losing short-run control over aggregate emissions, although authorities can maintain longer term control by including a make-good provision that requires any short fall in emission reductions to be made up in future periods.

- A process for setting long-term emission reduction trajectories. In setting a long-term trajectory for emissions reductions, governments provide firms greater predictability. But they must balance firms' desire for certainty over future emission constraints with the need to retain flexibility to react to new information and future international agreements on emissions reductions.

- Emission trading schemes in different regions can be linked, by acquitting allowances created in one region against emissions in another. Linking can reduce the cost of global emission reductions, enhance liquidity in the market and thus avoid volatility of carbon prices stimulating the development of a global carbon market (Garnaut, 2008). Different emission penalties for non-compliance or fees may be one of the main barriers to linking schemes in case the fee set in one system is below the current market price. In this case emitters in the market with the lowest fees will have an incentive to sell their allowances in the markets where the price is above the domestic market price and meet their domestic obligations by paying the fee in their domestic market. This arbitrage will drive carbon prices across linked markets towards the lowest carbon price.[4] Different rules governing banking, borrowing and allowable offsets can also make it more difficult to link schemes.

The European Emissions Trading Scheme

The EU ETS has distinct trading phases. Phase I (2005-07) was the initial learning period which primarily did not aim to reduce emissions but set up the institutions and to create a carbon market. Phase II (2008-12) coincided with the Kyoto Protocol commitment period which requires the EU15 to reduce its annual emissions to 8% below the 1990 level. It cut down the EU's emissions 6.5% below 2005 emissions, achieving more than 40% of the EU's Kyoto obligation. Phase III will cover the period from 2013 to 2020 and aims to reduce emissions in the ETS by at least 21% below 2005 figures. Key features of the EU ETS in Phase I included:

- The coverage of the scheme was limited to the stationary energy sector, production and processing of ferrous metals, parts of the mineral industry, and pulp, paper and board activities. In total, some 12 000 installations were covered, representing some 50% of total CO_2 emissions and 40% of total greenhouse gas emissions. The point of obligation was set at the point of emission, meaning for example that electricity generators had the obligation of surrendering allowances.

- Emitters were allocated free, grandfathered, multi-year allowances, known as EU allowances, which were used to acquit their actual emissions. Although the Commission was responsible for the overall governance of the scheme, allowance allocations were undertaken by member states. Member states submitted a National Allocation Plan to the Commission for approval, including overviews of action in sectors not covered by the scheme.

- An emitter with a shortfall in allowances must pay a fine of EUR 40 per tonne of CO_2, but must nevertheless purchase the missing allowances. No banking or borrowing was allowed.

- The scheme was internationally linked through the Kyoto Clean Development Mechanism (see below).

Phase I of the ETS contained successes and failures that have paved the way for reform in subsequent phases of the scheme. The most important success was the demonstration that carbon trading could work and the institution building, including the gathering of a robust data base to build on for future targets. Another was the development of a range of financial derivatives of European Emission Allowances (EUAs) that have allowed emitters to transfer some of their carbon risk to others for a price and thereby helping to prevent the volatility in EUA spot prices from affecting investment decisions. There is also some evidence that limited abatement occurred in Phase I (Ellerman and Buchner, 2007).

The biggest failure of Phase I was the collapse in EUA prices in April 2006 when it was revealed that actual emissions, and expected emissions during the rest of Phase I, would be lower than the total cap. Prices collapsed because Phase I allowances were in oversupply and could not be banked for later phases (Figure 4.10). There are two explanations for the excess supply in the allowance market. First, member countries over-allocated allowances to emitters by, in many cases, basing allocations on what emitters claimed their emissions were rather than on rigorously measured actual emissions, as such emission data were not available at that time. Second, traders in the EUA market may have over-estimated the cost of abatement, a fact only revealed when 2005 emissions came in below expectation (IEA, 2008a). There are other criticisms of Phase I: emitters may have expected the grandfathering of allowances to continue, reducing incentives to abate (Neuhoff et al., 2006); the allocation of free allowances to new entrants may have created incentives to set up new fossil fuel fired electricity generation plants; national methods for allocating allowances varied significantly across member countries, undermining competition in the internal market; free allocation of allowances to firms that could pass on the opportunity cost of allowances may have generated windfall profits for some emitters; too many small installations were included, resulting in compliance costs for small installations that were disproportionate to their emissions; and by making the ETS a point of emission scheme, it has made it more difficult to broaden its coverage to include other sectors such as road transport. Some of these flaws have been addressed for Phases II and III of the scheme.

Figure 4.10. **EUA prices in Phase I and Phase II of the EU emissions trading scheme**
EUR/tCO_2

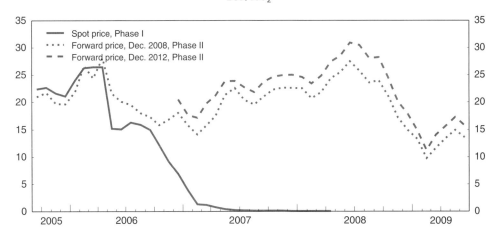

Source: Point Carbon and Caisse des Dépôts (2009), Tendances Carbone, No. 38, July.

StatLink ⟨⟩ http://dx.doi.org/10.1787/712760525002

An important change for the ETS in Phase II was to allow EUAs to be banked for later phases, making it unlikely that prices would fall to zero. Limited auctioning by member countries of up to 10% of allowances is also allowed to recover the cost of setting up and running the scheme but so far few countries have taken up this opportunity. The allowance fine has been increased to EUR 100/t. National Allocation Plans (NAP) for Phase II will result in an average cut in emissions of around 6.5% below 2005 levels (Figure 4.11). The magnitude of the cuts varies across EU member states according to their individual obligations under the Kyoto Protocol. The European Commission approved the original National Allocation Plans only conditionally for all member states except Denmark, France,

Figure 4.11. **Greenhouse gas emission targets for 2008-12**
Percentage variation relative to 2005 level

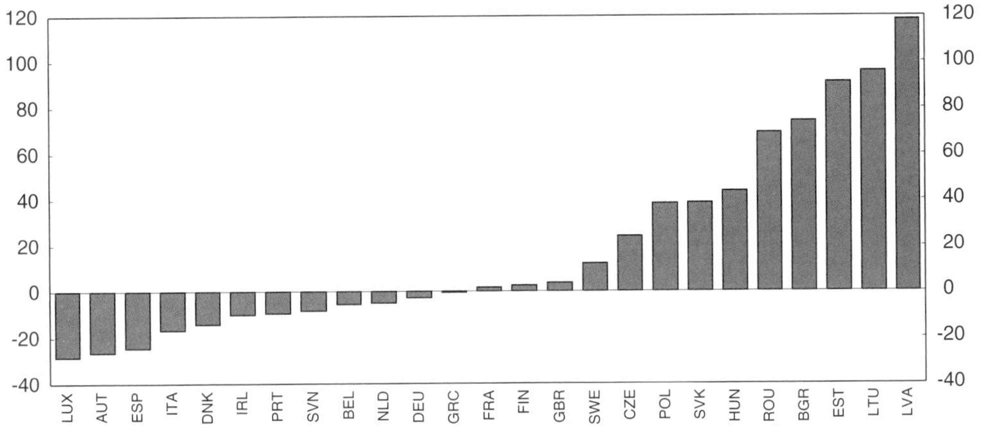

Source: EEA (2007), Greenhouse Gas Emission Trends and Projections in Europe 2007.

StatLink ⟨⟨⟨ http://dx.doi.org/10.1787/712783561730

Slovenia and the United Kingdom, because various shortcomings of member states' NAPs, including the outer limit of allowances that member states wanted to allocate to their industries which did not comply with criteria as set out in European legislation, in parts also because the planned reductions were not strict enough to be consistent with some member states' Kyoto commitments. The Commission also commenced infringement proceedings against some countries for failing to submit National Allocation Plans on time.

The global financial crisis and associated recession have been a pivotal event during Phase II of the ETS. Before the collapse of Lehman Brothers on 15 September 2008, the December 2009 EUA contract price was trading around EUR 25. Subsequently, the contract price fell significantly and at end-August was trading around EUR 15 as the economy in the EU appeared to be stabilising. In one sense, the fall in allowance prices was to be expected; the recession, together with expectations for only a weak recovery, have left many emitters with an excess supply of allowances, which they sold. The fall in allowance prices also provides a small amount of counter-cyclical support to the economy during the downturn. However, the magnitude of the fall seems a little surprising given that allowances can be banked for future use. There are a few potential explanations. The first is that the price genuinely reflects the bearishness of investors about future energy growth. Another is that amidst the financial crisis emitters and speculators are dumping allowances to raise liquidity. Whatever the explanation, because forward permit prices are quite low there is a concern that the price signal coming from the ETS will be insufficient to drive enough investment in low-emission technologies.

Phase II of the EU ETS worked within the existing Kyoto framework. However, with no international agreement in place for the period beyond the expiry of the Kyoto commitment period in 2012, the EU decided to push ahead unilaterally by announcing that it would reduce GHG emissions by 20% from 1990 levels by 2020 and 30% if an effective international agreement is achieved. The Commission's original proposed changes to the ETS for Phase III were far-reaching and included:

- A single EU-wide cap on emissions instead of 27 separate national caps. The annual cap will decrease by a linear factor of 1.74% *per annum* compared to the average annual total quantity of allowances for the period 2008 to 2012 and extend beyond 2020, and be equivalent to a further 21% reduction from 2005 levels by 2020. The 1.74 percentage point linear factor implies that by 2050 EU emissions will be around 70% below their 2005 levels, an amount that the Commission sees as consistent with Europe's share of the obligation of stabilising the concentration of GHG in the atmosphere at 450 ppm and possibly limiting temperature increases to 2 °C above pre-industrial levels.

- Because it is cheaper and easier to reduce emissions in the sectors covered by the ETS, there will be a 21% reduction in ETS sector emissions and a 10% reduction for sectors not covered by the scheme, with 2005 as benchmark year.

- Around two-thirds of total allowances would be auctioned from 2013, and 100% of allowances for the stationary energy sector.[5] The proportion would increase toward 100% by 2020.

- All allowances allocated for free for the industry sector would be distributed according to EU-wide rules ensuring that allocation mechanisms are harmonised across the EU. Any free allocation would be benchmarked so as not to reward the least energy-efficient producers.

- If a sector is deemed to be exposed to risk of carbon leakage, the sector will have its benchmark multiplied by 100% when calculating the amount of free allowances to a facility in the sector. For other sectors the benchmark will be multiplied by a discount factor that will start at 80% and decline annually to reach 30% in 2020.

- Coverage would be extended to CO_2 emissions from petrochemicals, ammonia and aluminium, as well as N_2O emissions from the production of nitric, adipic and glyoxylic acid production and perfluorocarbons from the aluminium sector. The capture, transport and geological storage of all GHGs will also be covered.

- Member states will be allowed to remove small installations with emission of less than 25 000 tonnes of CO_2 and where they carry out combustion activities, have a rated thermal input below 35 MW from the scheme if other measures are put in place to achieve equivalent reductions. Around 4 200 installations (0.7% of total ETS emissions) could opt out under these provisions.

- The net impact of the changes will be to increase coverage by around 7 percentage points of overall GHG emissions to 46%.

- Generally, the use of credits under the Kyoto Clean Development Mechanism (CDM) and Joint Implementation (JI) initiatives from 2008 to 2020 will be limited to credits granted by member states for 2008 and 2012, or to an amount which shall not be set below 11% of their allocation during the period 2008 to 2012, whichever is higher. For the existing sectors EU member states may allow the use of credits from CDM and JI by their operators up to 50% of the reductions achieved below 2005 levels under the ETS over the period 2008-20. In the context of an international agreement, the limit on the use of such credits would be increased, depending on the respective additional reduction effort necessary. It will not be possible to use credits from carbon sinks such as forests.

The originally proposed reforms for Phase III aimed at increasing the overall efficiency and equity of the scheme, especially by moving toward allocation based predominantly on auctioning emission allowances. However, from an efficiency perspective the watering down of the original Commission proposals for auctioning allowances was disappointing, but probably necessary to secure an agreement. The original proposals were for 100% auctioning for all power companies, industrial firms not exposed to international competition were to move to 100% auctioning by 2020, and there was to be a rigorous framework for determining the criteria governing which trade-exposed firms would receive free allocations. However, at the December 2008 meeting of the European Council it was agreed that subject to a number of criteria, installations for electricity production in certain member states may receive transitional free allocation until 2020. In addition, industrial firms not exposed to international competition will still receive 30% of the benchmarks by 2020, with no free allowances as from 2027. However, the total amount of free allocation to industry is limited (to the share of these industries' emissions in 2005-07) and will decline annually in line with the emissions cap. The absolute amount of free allowances will be determined by the benchmarks. If adding up all the benchmarks would lead to exceeding the maximum amount for free allocation, a correction factor will be applied. Finally, the basic criteria for allocating free allowances to industries at risk of carbon leakage were determined without a Commission impact assessment, although the final list of sectors will be subject to rigorous quantitative and qualitative assessments based on the criteria set in the directive. These decisions may somewhat reduce the efficiency and equity of the ETS compared to the Commission proposal, but it is important to note that the overall cap and the annual reductions were not modified by the Council. The environmental outcome was thus ensured. Reducing the scope of auctioning for non-trade-exposed firms will reduce the amount of revenue available that could be used for public investment in low-emission sectors and technologies and cuts in other distortive taxes. It also represents a transfer of wealth from taxpayers to industry compared to the original proposal. Countries with a lower than EU average GDP per capita were already set to benefit from a redistribution of 10% of allowances for auctioning.

The issues surrounding carbon leakage and free allowance allocation to trade-exposed firms is more vexed as carbon leakage is a genuine possibility when all firms in a global industry are not exposed to the same carbon price (Burniaux *et al.*, 2008; Garnaut, 2008; Reinaud, 2008). Carbon leakage arises through two channels:

- A competitiveness channel whereby carbon-intensive industries in participating countries lose market share or relocate capital to non-participating countries.
- A fossil fuel price channel whereby emission reductions in participating countries reduce fossil fuel demand and global price falls that encourage more use in other countries.

OECD (2008) simulations suggest that if the EU acted alone in cutting emissions by 50% by 2050, 20% of the reduction would leak to other countries. However, if all Annex I countries acted in unison, leakage would drop to just 9%.[6] These results underline the importance of securing an effective international agreement to reduce GHG emissions.

However, carbon leakage is more complicated than is sometimes made out. In addition to relative input costs, firm location decisions are based on criteria such as the quality of local infrastructure, political stability, the rule of law, and access to skilled labour. Recent research by the IEA suggests that there has been little carbon leakage from the ETS so far, in contrast to the predictions of theoretical models prior to the introduction of the scheme (Reinaud, 2008).[7] Moreover, other research suggests that investment in countries with credible GHG pricing schemes could attract greater investment because of enhanced certainty about future carbon prices.

There are a number of options to respond directly to leakage, including border adjustments (tariffs on imported goods from countries that do not impose carbon prices on domestic firms), sectoral agreements and free allowances to trade-exposed sectors (Duval,

2008). Although border adjustments may reduce leakage, they may not reduce overall output losses because they raise the cost of energy imports, raise the price of non-energy inputs and raise the carbon price necessary to meet emission reduction targets. Border adjustments should, if they ever were to be introduced, be designed in a way consistent with WTO rules. Global agreements between all firms active in particular energy-intensive industries are an alternative option but reaching agreement could be complicated and it will be important to implement effective caps on emissions in any agreements.

Allocating free allowances to energy-intensive trade-exposed firms is the approach that has been adopted. At the December 2008 European Council, EU leaders agreed that a sector would be deemed to be at significant risk of carbon leakage if:

- The sum of direct and indirect additional costs induced by the implementation of the EU ETS would lead to an increase in production costs exceeding 5% of its gross value added and if the total value of its exports and imports divided by the total value of its turnover and imports exceeds 10%.

- The sum of the direct and indirect additional costs would lead to an increase in production costs exceeding 30% of its gross value added, or if the total value of its exports and imports divided by the total value of its turnover and imports exceeds 30%.

- The list may be further supplemented after completion of a qualitative assessment based on criteria set out in the Directive.

It is of concern that these criteria were determined without rigorous counterfactual analysis of what the most appropriate thresholds for assistance should be. Although free allocation still largely preserves incentives to abate because there is an opportunity cost to holding allowances, the criteria risk being seen as arbitrary and transfers to industries that do not need support will raise the overall cost of abatement. It is welcome that the free allocation will be based on ambitious benchmarks, but it would be better if all firms received only partial free allocations.

It is also the case that, as the world moves toward a global carbon price and the world price of fossil-fuel intensive goods and services increases to reflect their social cost, production in those sectors will be lower than their baseline levels. Arguably, transfers to prevent carbon leakage today should take into account the longer run adjustments that will occur in a carbon constrained world, but short-term transition issues have to be effectively dealt with. For this reason, Garnaut (2008) has argued that transfers to trade-exposed firms should be relative to the expected uplift in world product prices that would occur if all countries had imposed a carbon price, not relative to a world where no countries have imposed a carbon price. Such a framework would increase the incentives for trade-exposed firms to adjust to the coming carbon constraint, and contribute to overall abatement efforts. In practice however, the modelling requirements for calculating assistance in this way would be complicated and the results could therefore also appear arbitrary.[8] A more radical option that would avoid the need for governments to determine optimal compensation criteria would be for governments to simply reduce the overall tax burden on households and businesses. Pricing carbon effectively introduces a new tax to the economy. Governments could therefore use carbon pricing as an opportunity to lower other more distorting taxes, thereby offsetting some of the impact of the ETS on potential output. However, such decisions on fiscal policy are a matter for individual member states. Indeed, this highlights the dilemma that plagues coherent EU-wide energy and climate change policies. Although EU institutions can shape a consensus-based area-wide strategy, member states must do the work of actual policy implementation.

Complex issues need to be addressed regarding how EU countries allow firms to use credits generated by emission-saving projects undertaken in third countries. Under the EU ETS, member states may allow their companies to use credits generated by emission-saving projects undertaken in third countries to cover their emissions in the same way as ETS allowances. These projects must be officially recognised under the Kyoto Protocol's Joint Implementation (JI) mechanism (covering projects carried out in countries with an emission reduction target under the Protocol) or Clean Development Mechanism (CDM) (for projects undertaken in developing countries). Credits from JI projects are known as Emission Reduction Units while those from CDM projects are called Certified Emission Reductions (CER). The Commission has set proposals for the use of CDM/JI credits depending on whether or not there is a satisfactory agreement to combat climate change post-2012. In the absence of a satisfactory international agreement, the limit on the use of JI/CDM credits has been calibrated to ensure that no more than half of the emission reductions required between 2008 and 2020 could be achieved through this mechanism.

The use of CDM/JI credits in the EU ETS must be monitored carefully. Forthcoming OECD analysis suggests that the current CDM raises a number of concerns that, if not addressed, could undermine its ability to deliver the expected benefits in terms of actual emission reductions. For example, there are doubts whether all the emission reductions credited under the CDM reflect cuts that would not have occurred otherwise, implying that many CERs are simply income transfers to countries outside the EU and thereby generating carbon leakage. Recent estimates suggest that 40 to 50% of CDM projects may not reflect actual emission reductions (Schneider, 2007; Wara and Victor, 2008). CDM projects may create incentives to raise investment and output in carbon-intensive projects in the first stage of projects, to obtain emission credits for reducing emissions in a second stage, especially when the gap between the market price of CERs and abatement costs are large. They may also reduce the willingness of developing countries to sign up to binding emission reduction commitments. For all of these reasons the EU ETS may not be contributing to as much global emission reductions as policymakers assume, and the EU should therefore take a lead role in working toward reform of the CDM within any future international emission reduction agreements.

An important principle of emissions trading is that coverage should be as broad as practicable (Duval, 2008). This helps to align price signals across sectors, ensures that emission reductions occur in those sectors for which it is most efficient to do so, market liquidity is maximised and the costs of the scheme are broadly distributed. An obvious way to broaden the ETS is to include the road transport sector, which accounts for around 20% of GHG emissions, but the inclusion of road transport is complicated by the already high excise duties on transport fuels in all EU countries.[9] Although these taxes were not originally put in place to price the carbon externality, they deliver an effective carbon price in this sector of well over EUR 100/t CO_2 in all EU countries, which is more than five times higher than the current price of EUAs.

An option that would allow road transport to be included in the ETS without further increasing the taxation bias against transport fuels would be for member states to reduce their excise rates periodically in line with the changing incentives provided by an expanded ETS. This is the course of action being pursued in Australia. Eventually, this option would make it possible to align the price signal to the road transport sector with the signal being sent to other sectors of the economy. However, the very high current level of excise duties in many countries means that such an alignment could take decades and reduces the urgency of road transport's inclusion. In addition to the complex interaction with existing energy taxes, there are other practical barriers to including road transport in the ETS. The point of obligation for the EU ETS is at the point of emission, which in road transport means individual vehicles. This would entail excessive administrative costs and is not in line with the better regulation principles. An alternative would be to shift the point of obligation upstream to producers of transport fuel and fuel suppliers.

However, some question whether such a change would have a significant effect on the incentives perceived by drivers. Such a change would mean that the price of allowances would be incorporated into final prices without any possibility for the consumer to detect whether a price change comes from a variation in the cost of oil, in the price of allowances, in the level of taxation or simply in the commercial policy of fuel producers. This could also mean that any advantages in terms of visibility of the carbon price at the point of emission would be lost and could add considerable complexity as member states would have to grapple with determining how regularly to update their excise rates, and fuel producers and suppliers would face an additional regulatory burden. On the other hand, it should be remembered that in the stationary energy sector final consumers also have no simple way of separating the relative effect of these factors on retail energy prices.

Given all of these difficult issues, the Commission and member states should continue to reassess the most appropriate way to deal with GHG emissions in the road transport sector, and in particular how to ensure that in the longer term abatement incentives provided by the ETS are consistent with the incentives to abate provided by existing energy taxes. It would also be useful to pursue the exercise of internalisation of external costs so that prices take into account non-carbon externalities such as local pollution, traffic congestion, accidents and noise. The Commission should also take care that mandatory emission standards for passenger vehicles only counteract market failures associated with innovation and do not further increase the implicit shadow cost of abatement for the road transport sector.

The 20% renewable energy target and low-emission technologies

The primary aim of the target to lift the share of renewable energy in gross final energy consumption to 20% by 2020 is to complement the EU ETS in reducing GHG emissions and to improve energy security. The EU has also fixed a target for energy from renewable sources in transport to be 10% of overall transport fuels. Recognising that member states have different capacities to deploy renewable energy, national targets will be allowed to vary according to the existing share of renewable energy, and the level of GDP per capita to reflect fairness and cohesion, though all member states will be required to reach the transport renewable energy target. Each country will have to submit a national action plan showing how their targets will be met. Because the cost of exploiting renewable energy varies across countries, member states will be allowed to make their contributions through statistical transfers and joint projects between member states and with third countries that will sit alongside existing national renewable energy support schemes. This flexibility should help to reduce the cost of meeting the target. The scheme to boost the use of biofuels in transport will include sustainability criteria in relation to a number of environmental impacts including the GHG performance of biofuels, biodiversity and land use changes and information about impacts on soil, water, air and social issues. The

European Commission will soon analyse possible ways to extend the biofuels sustainability scheme to the whole biomass area.

The rationale for the target is that pricing carbon through the ETS may not be sufficient to overcome a variety of market failures that limit the use of renewable energy (Duval, 2008). For example:

- Learning effects imply that large deployment costs may be incurred before renewable energy technologies can become competitive.
- Network effects can make it difficult to displace carbon-intensive technologies.
- The homogeneity of energy infrastructures may keep the demand for renewables low until they are price competitive.
- Carbon-intensive energy technologies may be locked into energy systems without deployment subsidies.

In short, deployment subsidies and other policies to boost the use of renewable energy raise the short-term cost of emissions abatement, but by smoothing the transition to a low-carbon economy, may reduce the long-run cost of abatement.

Meeting these targets will be a significant challenge. In 2007, renewable energy represented 8.5% of final energy consumption in the EU, 3 percentage points higher than in 1990 (IEA, 2008a). Biofuels represented just under 3% of petrol and diesel consumption. Renewables are most heavily used in the electricity sector, accounting for around 15% of total production. To meet the 20% target by 2020 will require a dramatic increase in renewable electricity production to as much as 35% and require major upgrades to electricity grids (IEA, 2008a). Reaching the EU-wide target will also be complicated by the fact that energy policy is a shared competency between the Community and member states.

A number of separate initiatives will contribute to reaching the renewable target. The EU ETS will reduce the relative price of renewable energy, encouraging substitution in production processes and investment in low-emission R&D. More directly, many member states already offer substantial deployment subsidies to renewable energy producers in the form of feed-in-tariffs and tradable renewable energy certificates. At the Community level, in addition to providing a new legislative framework, the most important policies to directly support the development for the renewable sector are EU funds (including European Regional Development Funds, Cohesion Fund), the Intelligent Energy Europe programme (part of the Competitiveness and Innovation programme, which strongly supports the market introduction of renewables) and two further programmes to support additional funding for low-emission technology R&D: the 7th Framework Programme for Research Funding (FP7) and the Strategic Energy Technology Plan (SET). An enabling framework is also provided by the guidelines on state aid for environmental protection.

In addition, a "lead market initiative" (LMI) aims to accelerate the conversion of research findings into commercially valuable innovations and stimulate markets for innovative goods and services. The LMI hopes to generate more rapid returns on investments, encourage more private investment in R&D, and raise productivity, exports, economic growth and employment. Renewables were one of the six lead markets chosen by the EU, in particular because they: are highly innovative; are not dependent on a single product or technology; already have a strong technology and production base in Europe; provide solutions to broad strategic, societal, environmental and economic challenges; have largely demand-driven market potential; and depend on favourable framework conditions. Support for lead markets makes use of demand-side instruments such as innovation-friendly public procurement practices, more consistent technical, performance and product standards, business and innovation support services, training and communication. A mid-term review of the implementation of the LMI is due by late 2009. Although it seems likely that the growth of the renewable energy sector faces demand-side constraints, care should be taken to ensure that the benefits of such policies exceed their costs. For example, public procurement policies that actively favour renewables could increase the cost of providing government goods and services. In addition, the renewables sector already receives effective support through the ETS, public funding for R&D and deployment subsidies in some countries.

The decision to allow statistical transfers and joint projects within Europe is expected to reduce the cost of meeting the 20% renewable target substantially. However, because of concerns about the likely impact of trading on the development of higher cost renewables, the impact on existing support systems in member states, and the possibility that windfall profits will accrue to existing low-cost renewable producers, it will be for member states to manage and control the use of these mechanisms, which will potentially limit trading (IEA, 2008a).

Support for renewable energy deployment raises a number of concerns such as the magnitude of subsidies exceeding the magnitude of externalities or locking in the wrong technologies and thus raising the cost of GHG abatement. Existing subsidies to renewable electricity in some countries exceed EUR 250 per ton of CO_2 abated for wind power and EUR 1 000 for photovoltaics (Burniaux et al., 2008). Price support mechanisms in European countries come in two forms: feed-in-tariffs used in Germany and Spain, which provide a fixed-price per unit of electricity produced over a particular period; and tradable renewable energy certificates used in Italy and the United Kingdom, which require a fixed share of electricity to be generated from renewable sources and force firms to purchase certificates on an open market to make up for shortfalls in production (Duval, 2008). Such schemes have to be designed carefully when they sit alongside an ETS. If they are ramped up too quickly, they can lead to most abatement occurring through the renewable support scheme, rather than the ETS, raise electricity prices beyond what is necessary to meet emission reduction targets, and reduce incentives to invest in other low-emission technologies (Garnaut, 2008). An alternative way of providing support for demonstration and commercialisation of renewables and other low-emission technologies is through matched funding to private firms, financed through the auctioning of emission allowances. Matched funding has the advantage of maintaining firms' risk exposure because they still bear and manage the risks of bringing a new technology to market (Garnaut, 2008).

In the longer term, consideration should be given to harmonising existing national renewable energy support mechanisms and, if appropriate, moving toward a single European support mechanism, a possibility supported by the Commission. This would help to ensure that the European renewable energy target is met at least cost and would also help the development of the single electricity market. One potential model for this would be Australia's mandatory renewable energy target. This scheme requires electricity retailers to purchase a rising proportion of their electricity from renewable generators in the form of tradable renewable energy certificates. The price of a renewable energy certificate is determined in the tradable market and depends on the difference in cost between producing renewable energy and the average wholesale price of electricity. Although the scheme offers an implicit subsidy to renewable energy producers, it is technology neutral within the renewable sector and investment flows to those renewable technologies that can produce electricity most cheaply. To maintain incentives to invest in all low-emission technologies such as carbon capture and storage (Box 4.4), a European mandatory renewable energy target could be expanded to include all low-emission technologies. However, it may be that that there is no single optimal instrument appropriate in all countries, situations and for all technologies. As an alternative pathway, the Commission could encourage member states to replace domestic feed-in tariffs with tradable renewable certificates in those countries, where appropriate. Once renewable energy technologies compete fairly (that is, once all external costs and market failures other than climate change are addressed) in the energy market, consideration should be given to phasing out all price support mechanisms to ensure that the ETS operates as efficiently as possible.

The EU thinks of the 10% target for renewable transport fuels as a way to ensure sustainability, security of supply and competitiveness objectives of the EU energy and climate change policy, particularly by addressing GHG emissions from the transport sector through the sustainability criteria that have been imposed and by replacing some of the fossil fuel use in this sector. Although the 10% target for renewable transport fuels covers all renewable energy and not just biofuels, it is still expected that biofuels will make a very large contribution to meeting the target. The implicit costs of abatement measures in the transport sector are frequently higher than in other sectors. For instance, some ethanol subsidies exceed EUR 250/t of CO_2 avoided, although other types of biofuels may reduce greenhouse gas emissions at costs of as little as EUR 20/t CO_2 avoided. The EU has established the world's first sustainability regime for biofuel use and a monitoring regime whereby companies, member states or the Commission will closely assess land use change consequences as well as social, biodiversity and other possible negative impacts. The Commission is working on how to include indirect land use change in the sustainability criteria for biofuels. On the basis of this monitoring, the regime will be reviewed in 2014. Given the high cost of some biofuel technologies, it will be important to ensure that the 10% renewable transport fuel target efficiently achieves its objectives of sustainability and security of supply. The 38% tariff rate that applies to undenatured ethyl alcohol effectively restricts imports from countries such as Brazil, where biofuels can be produced far more cheaply than in Europe. Biofuel subsidies may also encourage the conversion of land used for food production to land for energy production, contributing to higher food prices (World Bank, 2008). Overall, because it is extremely unclear whether the benefits of the transport fuels target in terms of improved energy security justify its large costs, the EU should consider scrapping the biofuels target altogether. The EU should consider reducing tariffs on biofuels and ensure that production within the EU takes place where it is cheapest to obtain sustainable biofuels.

The nuclear landscape is changing rapidly. Many countries have announced and decided to invest into nuclear energy. If stringent emission targets are to be met governments should ensure that nuclear energy will play an increasing role in the generation mix. Nuclear power is an important component of the solution to climate change, energy security as well as competitiveness. In this context, more EU countries have announced new nuclear programmes. However, even in those countries where nuclear is acceptable, financing new nuclear power plants in liberalised markets is an issue. Government actions to mitigate construction, financial and regulatory risks would be useful to move projects forward. This is especially true for "first-of-a-kind" plants and for new nuclear programmes.

Box 4.4. **Carbon capture and storage**

Coal and gas-fired power stations are the dominant sources of electricity in most countries due to their abundance and low cost relative to other energy sources. The use of coal and gas has also been growing rapidly as countries such as China and India have added significant new capacity to supply energy. Because coal and gas power stations and industrial installations also make a large contribution to global greenhouse gas emissions there is a significant international effort investigating and demonstrating technologies that have the potential to reduce those emissions cost effectively.* This effort falls into the following categories: improving the efficiency of these installations; determining the viability of carbon capture technologies; and determining the viability of carbon storage (sequestration) technologies.

There are a number of technologies for capturing the carbon from coal-fired power stations. Integrated Gasification Combined Cycle plants gasify the coal, allowing the pre-combustion capture of CO_2. Sequestration involves the pumping of liquid CO_2 into suitable geological formations deep underground. The most likely sites for carbon storage are depleted oil or gas fields, deep saline aquifers and deep coal seams. Although the technology for permanently pumping liquid CO_2 underground has been proven for some time, the technology is currently only used commercially in gas and oil fields.

Although there are no full-scale coal or gas-fired power plants in operation that demonstrate all aspects of carbon capture and storage (CCS) technology, a number of full-scale demonstration projects have been proposed in Germany, the Netherlands, Poland, Spain and the United Kingdom (IEA, 2008b).

There are a number of barriers to the commercialisation of CCS technology for coal and gas-fired power stations. The first is cost; current estimates suggest that the cost of CCS per ton of CO_2 avoided could initially range anywhere from EUR 30 to EUR 90, well above current expected allowance prices (IEA, 2008b). Although the cost of CCS technology is likely to fall over time, it is unclear by how much or how quickly. This means that additional private investment in CCS technology is unlikely to be forthcoming without substantial additional financial incentives and mandates from governments. Recognising this, the European Council and the European Parliament agreed on setting aside EUR 1.05 billion to partly fund seven CCS projects in seven countries. Additionally, proceeds from auctioning 300 million allowances from the new entrants reserve under the revised ETS will be used to support up to 12 carbon capture and storage demonstration projects and projects demonstrating innovative renewable energy technologies. There are also public opinion concerns surrounding the safety of the technology with environmental groups expressing concerns about the likelihood of CO_2 leaking from underground, undermining the emission reduction benefits and posing health risks. Investment is also being held back by regulatory uncertainty, including over future carbon prices and long-term public investment (IEA, 2008b).

All of these factors mean that major reductions in EU emissions from CCS technology are unlikely in the short term.

* CCS technologies will not only be important for the power sector. The IEA believes that by 2050 the cement, refining, pulp and paper, iron and steel, and chemicals sectors will need to deliver almost as much greenhouse gas reductions *via* CCS as the power sector.

Key actions to be considered by governments that wish to see investment in new nuclear power plants include:

- Provide clear and sustained policy support for the development of nuclear power. Strong and consistent government support is an essential prerequisite for initiating or expanding any nuclear programme. Given the long time frame involved, a broad-based political consensus is likely to be needed.

- Establish an efficient and effective regulatory system which provides adequate opportunities for public involvement in the decision making process, while also providing potential investors with the certainty they require to plan such a major investment. A one-step licensing process with pre-approval of standardised designs offers clear benefits in this regard.

- Put in place arrangements for the management of radioactive waste and spent fuel, with progress towards a solution for final disposal of waste. For investors in plants, the financial arrangements for paying their share of the costs must be clearly defined. An effective framework for nuclear insurance and liabilities must also be in effect.

- Reduce policy uncertainty over environmental objectives and in particular, where reducing greenhouse gas emissions is to act as an incentive for nuclear investment, the government may need to provide some guarantees that policy measures will keep carbon prices at sufficiently high levels.

- In some cases, provide additional financial support to investors. For countries with one or more large utilities having the financial strength to invest directly in new plants, or where there are well-resourced foreign utilities willing to make such investments, such additional support may not be necessary. But where there are no sufficiently strong established utilities, and/or the government wishes to move ahead rapidly with plant designs which have not already been built elsewhere, more direct financial support is likely to be necessary.

Research and development

Policies to increase public and private funding of R&D of climate-friendly technologies are a key element of Europe's strategy to reduce GHG emissions and support renewable energy production, as well as the Lisbon Strategy for Jobs and Growth. If Europe is to meet its long-term objectives to reduce GHG emissions by 60-80% by 2050, new technologies will be required. In most high-emission activities, low-carbon technologies are currently more expensive than fossil fuel technologies. A moderate carbon price would not change this. Anderson (2006) suggests that a carbon price of USD 80 per tonne is required to make a low-carbon portfolio in electricity, industry, transport and buildings competitive. Most technologies are also relevant to only a narrow range of economic activities – for example, solar and wind are only relevant for electricity generation – implying that a broad portfolio of technology options will need to be employed.

Although a strong price signal is essential to stimulate R&D in low-emission technologies, important market failures prevent private R&D from reaching sufficient scale (Burniaux *et al.*, 2008) because: there is a wedge between the expected social and private returns from R&D; there is uncertainty about the timing and magnitude of clean energy technology markets that are created by carbon regulation; existing infrastructure can create network effects that create barriers to entry; and inadequate competition in energy markets can reduce incentives for firms to undertake R&D. These market failures, combined with long lead times in research, development, demonstration and deployment of low-emission technologies, mean that funding must be ratcheted up over the coming decade. This is especially the case considering that average public energy-related R&D expenditure has declined significantly in Europe since the early 1980s, though there is wide variation across countries (Figure 4.12). European energy firms now spend less than 1% of net sales on clean energy R&D.

Figure 4.12. **Public energy-related R&D budgets in OECD countries**

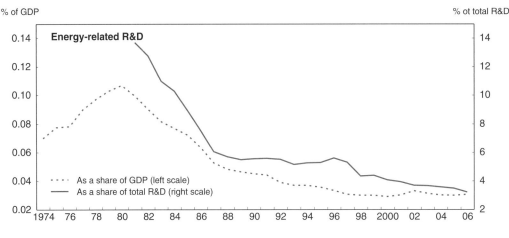

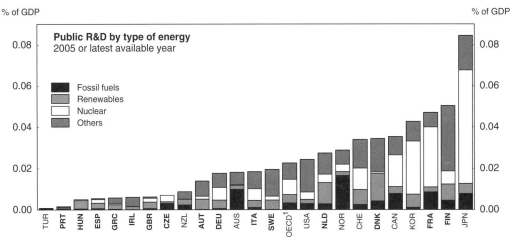

1. Unweighted average of OECD countries less non-IEA member countries (Iceland, Mexico, Poland and Slovak Republic). Due to lack of data, Belgium and Luxembourg are also excluded.

Source: Burniaux et al. (2008), "The Economics of Climate Change Mitigation: Policies and Options for the Future", OECD Economics Department Working Paper, No. 658.

StatLink ᵃᵍ⁵ᵖ http://dx.doi.org/10.1787/712786234464

Much of the EU budget for energy research is allocated through the Research Framework (FP) Programme (Chapter 2). European Technology Platforms bring together stakeholders to establish long-term strategic research agendas and contribute directly to work plans to ensure that EU-funded R&D is relevant for users. FP7, which runs from 2007 to 2013, outlines a number of areas for energy research: hydrogen and fuel cells; renewable electricity generation; renewable fuel production; renewables for heating and cooling; carbon capture and storage technologies for zero-emission power generation; clean coal and other technologies; smart energy networks; energy efficiency and savings. A shortcoming of FP7 is that insufficient funds are allocated to low-carbon technologies because the allocations were determined before accelerating the development of low-carbon technologies became a priority. Of the more than EUR 5 billion allocated to energy under FP7, just EUR 2.35 billion was allocated to non-nuclear research.

To overcome this funding shortfall, the European Strategic Energy Technology Plan (SET) was adopted in 2007. The plan aims to mobilise private funding for a broad technology portfolio that should avoid locking in inefficient technologies. European Industrial Initiatives are being created that aim to strengthen energy research and innovation by bringing together resources and actors in a particular industrial sector. They will have measurable objectives in terms of cost reduction or improved performance, and will bring together the efforts of the EU level, member states and industry. A European Energy Research Alliance will also be created to enable greater co-operation across Europe of the research work going on in universities, research institutes and specialised centres. The priorities under the plan include:

- Making second generation biofuels competitive alternatives to fossil fuels, while respecting the sustainability of their production.

- Enabling commercial use of CCS.

- Doubling the power generation capacity of the largest wind turbines.

- Demonstrating the commercial readiness of large-scale photovoltaics.

- Developing a single smart European electricity grid able to accommodate the integration of renewable and decentralised energy sources.

- Bring to mass market more efficient energy conversion and end-use devices and systems, in buildings, transport and industry, such as poly-generation and fuel cells.

- Maintain competitiveness in fission technologies.

However, as of April 2009, no announcements have been made by the Commission on exactly how greater funding will be mobilised to reach the ambitious objectives of FP7 and the SET Plan. Given the externalities from R&D spending and the difficulty of firms to mobilise funding in the current economic climate, the absence of substantial funding measures and instruments makes achieving the goals of these plans less likely.

The 20% energy savings target

Sitting alongside the 20% GHG emissions reduction target and the 20% renewable energy target is a 20% energy savings target for 2020. Unlike the other targets, the energy savings target is not binding on member states. Although improving energy efficiency is a means of achieving energy savings, the energy savings target is more stringent than an energy efficiency target; an energy efficiency target would allow an increased use of energy overall, whereas the energy saving target requires energy consumption to fall in absolute terms. The primary objective of the energy savings target is to help firms and households cope with the rising relative price of energy. It also aims to raise productivity and economic growth, and improve energy security. The Commission believes that the energy savings target is achievable because there are cost-effective opportunities for improving energy efficiency in all sectors of the economy, particularly in transport. Indeed, it has been argued that many of these opportunities – such as improving building insulation, increasing fuel efficiency of vehicles, making more use of sugarcane biofuels, and improving lighting systems – might raise energy efficiency and reduce GHG emissions at a negative cost of emissions abatement; that is, some options for improving energy efficiency and reducing GHG emissions are profitable for firms and households now, even without a carbon price (Enkvist *et al.*, 2007).

A number of market failures might explain the sub-optimal take-up of energy efficiency measures (Duval, 2008):

- With asymmetric information and adverse selection, efficient investments may not take place. For example, developers and owners may not install efficient lighting and heating systems in buildings because they may not be able to pass on the higher costs to tenants.

- Imperfect competition in energy markets can dull price signals. For example, in many countries, retail electricity prices are regulated and prices faced by users rarely depend on whether consumption occurs during peak periods when it is more expensive to generate.

- Capital market imperfections may make it harder for households and firms to finance the up-front cost of investments in energy efficiency measures.

- Households and firms may apply excessively high discount rates to future savings on energy bills, or inaccurate rules of thumb when making decisions.

- Households and firms may lack the information required to adopt efficient technologies and practices when the information has public goods characteristics that mean it is underprovided by the private sector.

The European Energy Efficiency Action Plan (EEAP) came into effect in 2006, as an instrument to contribute to the 20% energy savings target, endorsed by heads of states and governments in March 2007. The EEAP identified six areas with the highest potential for energy savings: products, buildings and services; transport; energy transformation; financing; energy behaviour and international partnerships. The implementation of the action plan should be completed by 2012 and involves 85 specific actions and measures to be undertaken at the EU and national levels. The Plan will be evaluated in 2009. National Energy Efficiency Action Plans have also been prepared to show how each member state will achieve its energy savings objective. To date the Commission is satisfied with the progress of member states in transposing Community law into national legislation and with the speed with which financial support has been provided. To overcome capital market failures, the Commission is working with international financial institutions to explore avenues to increase funding for investments in energy efficiency.

To ensure that the energy savings target is reached by 2020, the EU has also launched an Energy Efficiency Package with the following elements:

- A proposal to recast the Energy Performance of Buildings Directive (EPBD).

- A proposal to revise the Energy Labelling Directive.

- The already adopted Directive that introduces a labelling scheme for tyres.

- Guidelines clarifying the calculation of the amount of electricity from cogeneration.

- A Communication on Cogeneration arguing that energy can be saved by combining heat and power generation.

In addition to these measures, the EU legislature has adopted mandatory EU-wide fuel efficiency standards for passenger cars, and further action is envisaged for light commercial road transport vehicles.

To overcome information asymmetries and other market failures there may be a role for command and control mechanisms such as labelling, technology and performance standards for some goods and services, to complement emissions trading and deliver an overall lower cost of abatement. Mandatory disclosure through labelling requirements on appliances can be particularly effective because it helps to overcome information barriers and makes it easier to act on the price signal provided by the ETS (Garnaut, 2008). After more than a decade the Commission is currently revising the Energy Labelling Directive. The existing labelling classifications will be upgraded and reviewed regularly following technological developments. The proposal for a recast of the Directive enlarges the scope to products used in the commercial and industrial sectors and to products which do not consume energy but allow for significant energy savings once in use (*e.g.* windows).

Where labelling requirements are insufficient to overcome information problems, minimum energy performance standards can also be cost effective (Duval, 2008). In light of this, the EEAP aims to improve efficiency of equipment and appliances through establishment of mandatory minimum requirements under the Eco-design of Energy-Using Products Directive. Specific measures (daughter directives) are adopted for particular product groups. One horizontal measure was adopted to require stand-by or off-mode electricity consumption of appliances to be near zero. However, because governments also have imperfect information about the factors that shape supply and demand in particular product markets, minimum standards should focus on performance rather than specific technologies, features that do not affect consumers' amenity and removing the least energy efficient products from the market. In combination with the labelling scheme, the level of the efficiency requirements should also be moving, rather than being fixed, over time to ensure ongoing incentives for innovation.

Because residential and commercial buildings are a source of large energy inefficiencies, the Energy Performance of Buildings Directive was adopted in 2003. It provides for:

- A general framework for guiding the calculation of the integrated performance of buildings and the establishment and regular reviews of energy performance standards.
- The requirement for minimum energy efficiency for new buildings.
- The requirement for minimum energy efficiency for the refurbishment of large existing buildings greater than 1 000 m^2.
- Requirement of energy certification of buildings when buildings are constructed, sold or rented.
- Inspection and assessment of heating and cooling installations.

Although the directive was supposed to be transposed by 2006, only five member states had properly done so by 2008. The EU should be commended for establishing mandatory requirements, but there may be room for strengthening the Directive further. For this reason, the Commission presented a proposal for its recast in 2008. Its main elements are the following:

- Removing the 1 000 m^2 limit on building refurbishment requirements.
- The introduction of benchmarking to achieve cost-optimal levels.
- Strengthening the role and the quality of energy performance certificates as well as of inspections for heating and air-conditioning systems.
- Addressing the public sector as a leading example.

These recommendations should be subject to rigorous cost-benefit analyses, and in particular the benefits of abolishing the limit on floor area would have to be weighed against the compliance costs for smaller businesses.

Although energy efficiency in the transport sector has improved over the past two decades, overall emissions in the transport sector have increased by 25% over the same period, largely because of an increase in the number of cars and an increase in the kilometres driven per car. Because the road transport sector is excluded from the ETS, the Commission has proposed emission performance standards for new passenger cars. The Regulation adopted by the Council in April 2009 set out the following:

● Set limits on emissions per kilometre.

● Define a limit value curve of emissions allowed for new vehicles according to the mass of the vehicle so that a fleet average of 130 g CO_2 per km is achieved.

● Include an excess emissions premium if manufacturers' emissions lie above the limit value curve.

These standards will contribute to reducing emissions in the transport sector insofar as they are stringent enough to imply additional efforts to improve vehicle efficiency over and above those already planned by manufacturers. However, as discussed earlier, the pros and cons of including road transport in the EU ETS should be analysed in more depth. Moreover, light vehicles are just one component of the transport sector. It is important that there is further investigation to determine whether it is advisable to pursue a more integrated approach to reducing emissions in the whole transport sector so that a similar price signal would be sent to all segments (road, air, rail and water). A proposal was tabled to require the labelling of tyres (covering also replacement tyres); the labelling covers rolling resistance performance (with direct impact on fuel consumption), wet grip and rolling noise, with the view of optimising the performance of tyres on all parameters.

Overall, the evidence suggests that there is considerable room to improve energy efficiency in the EU and the Commission has a number of well-targeted policies and directives that should help member states to meet their 20% energy savings target. That said, care must be taken to ensure that all command and control measures are carefully designed to address specific market failures and are proportional to the size of those market failures. Moreover, because there is no EU-wide system for harmonised, quantitative monitoring of energy efficiency or energy savings goals at national level, it is extremely difficult to assess aggregate progress toward these goals.[10]

More generally, it is not clear why a separate energy savings target is required. It should also be remembered that energy efficiency is not the same as economic efficiency; if measures that improve energy efficiency require more input of non-energy resources than is saved in energy, economic efficiency is reduced. New Community guidelines for state aid for environmental protection from 2007 proposing continuing state aid for renewable energy and energy efficiency also have the potential to encourage distorting policies. Some believe that there are circumstances where reduced value added tax (VAT) rates to provide for energy-friendly consumption can be beneficial, although the Commission should carefully consider the evidence before lending its support to such proposals. Concerns that current exemptions for electricity and heating fuels bias the tax system in favour of fossil-fuel intensive goods and services might be better addressed by ending those exemptions. In addition, the price signal coming from the EU ETS, together with the proliferation of Commission and member state initiatives supporting renewables and energy efficiency measures should provide opportunities for low-emission and energy-efficient goods and services to increase their market share without an additional tax.

Toward a single and secure electricity and gas market

Further liberalisation of EU electricity and gas markets is critical for delivering a number of the EU's objectives: lower barriers to entry and greater competition will put downward pressure on wholesale and retail electricity and gas prices paid by households and firms and increase incentives to innovate; more integrated and competitive energy markets will increase incentives to invest in new generation and transmission capacity, improving energy security; more competitive energy markets will allow clearer price signals to be sent through the ETS, allowing emission reductions to be achieved at lower cost; and liberalisation in energy markets will facilitate the upgrade of electricity grids so that greater renewable energy capacity can be brought online.

A fully competitive internal market for gas and electricity has been a long-standing goal of the EU. The first liberalisation directives for electricity (1996) and gas (1998) made some progress by allowing large customers to choose their suppliers, but did not require all countries to set up independent regulatory authorities, did not set out a regulated access framework for electricity grids, and did little to reduce the market power of vertically-integrated companies that owned transmission networks and generation plants. The second liberalisation package adopted in 2003 provided, *inter alia*, for full market opening for all customers by July 2007, stricter provisions for the unbundling of transmission networks leaving only legal unbundling and full ownership unbundling, and mandatory establishment of independent regulators. There were also provisions for market-based allocation of available transmission capacity, provisions for the use of congestion rents from auctioning and transparent and non-discriminatory procedures to calculate transmission capacity. In 2006, the Commission responded to concerns that progress on implementation of directives was slow in many countries by launching an energy sector inquiry, the largest ever study of the EU energy markets. The Commission identified serious shortcomings in the electricity and gas markets:

● Electricity markets remained national in scope, with dominant firms inhibiting competition within countries and stifling investment in the transmission and interconnection capacity needed to increase trade and competition between countries.

● Legal unbundling of vertically-integrated firms that owned both generation assets and transmission networks raised barriers to entry and inhibited investment in new capacity.

● Consumer switching at the retail level was above 5% in 2006 in only three European countries, suggesting a lack of competition in retail markets.

● There was a lack of reliable and timely information on markets, inhibiting transparency.

● Price information was not transparent and regulated tariffs discouraged entry.

● Gas markets were highly concentrated, insufficiently integrated, and there was too much vertical integration between suppliers and transmission operators of gas. New large suppliers were often in conflict with the network owners of existing pipelines and upstream supply was largely outside of EU countries' control.

The Commission's third liberalisation package responds to these findings, concentrating mainly on strengthening the requirements and provisions of the second directive. Crucially, it recognises that transmission system operators (TSOs) play a critical role in electricity markets because they have monopoly control of the operation of transmission systems, make investment decisions on new transmission infrastructure, influence the adaptation of transmission networks to new energy sources, and they have information advantages over regulators about the networks they operate. A particular problem in the EU is that, in some countries, vertically-integrated companies own both transmission networks and electricity generation assets, which reduces incentives to treat all players equally and increases incentives to maximise the total value of the company by extracting monopoly rents. Because regulators may be unable to overcome these problems, the Commission recommended that member states move to full ownership unbundling of TSOs. As an alternative, the Commission proposed the unbundling of system operation, with owners of supply interests allowed to keep their transmission grid assets. An Independent System Operator (ISO) would then have control over grids and investment plans.

However, because neither full unbundling, nor the ISO solution was acceptable to all member states, the Commission worked together with the Council to develop a "third way" solution: TSOs will be allowed to remain part of vertically-integrated companies, but detailed rules will govern the autonomy, independence and investment of TSOs. The Commission believes that this Independent Transmission Operator (ITO) option will provide for "effective" unbundling. The TSO will have to be certified by the national regulator, but there will not be any binding oversight from the Commission in the certification procedure. Instead, national regulators are obliged to "take the utmost account of the Commission's position". Every two years, the Commission will submit, as part of the general review required, to the European Parliament and the Council, a detailed specific report outlining the extent to which the unbundling requirements under the ITO option have been successful in ensuring full and effective independence of transmission system operators. Although the Commission does not intend to undertake a new impact assessment of the ITO proposal, a review clause was inserted into the Directive enabling the Commission to assess the efficiency of ITOs after two years. It will be critical that such a review takes place, since if the ITO option does not produce the effective unbundling expected by the Commission the internal energy market will be set back considerably.

An equally important issue in constructing a fully functioning internal energy market is effective cross-border co-operation and regulation. An institution is required to manage cross-border investments and supervise co-operation between national regulators. Although the European group of Regulators for Electricity and Gas has helped the development of the internal market, it does not have binding decision making powers. In light of this, the Commission's proposal for an Agency for the Co-operation of Regulators (ACER) is welcome. For ACER to be effective it will be important that it has binding powers to set common codes on cross-border infrastructure regarding third-party access, operating procedures, new capacity requests and additions, interconnection procedures and standards and transparency. To carry out all of these tasks effectively ACER needs to be adequately staffed (IEA, 2008a). The EU should also give consideration to how EU-wide oversight of the electricity and gas markets can contribute to delivering the renewable energy and energy savings targets. For example, it will be important that distribution companies have incentives to invest in "smart grids" and end-use energy efficiency as a "supply" option within an integrated resource management approach. In the longer run the EU will need to give consideration to extending the powers of ACER so that it has binding regulatory and decision making powers over national regulators. As has been demonstrated recently in financial markets, it is difficult to achieve a fully functioning single market without a strong central authority to oversee and enforce the rules of that market.

The third liberalisation package also contains provisions for strengthening the independence of national regulators. This is necessary to ensure that large national firms do not impede competition within and across borders. The Commission has identified a number of areas in which national regulators require more powers: all aspects of third party access to networks and gas storage; compliance with functional and account unbundling of Distribution Service Operators; cross-border issues; information gathering; and strong sanctions for non-compliance with regulations. Amendments to the original Commission proposals to further strengthen national regulators by requiring them to approve and enforce TSOs annual investment plans, enforce consumer protection measures, monitor restrictive contractual practices, give them greater power to improve competition in supply markets, and provide for autonomous financing of regulators, are especially welcome. Given the slowness with which previous directives pushing for better regulation and integration have been implemented, it will be important for the Commission to closely monitor member states' progress.

Another priority is to significantly increase investment in cross-border transmission networks. Without sufficient interconnection capacity foreign suppliers cannot exert enough competitive pressure on national incumbents. The Commission has begun implementing new network projects through the Regional Initiatives programme, with the support of the European Group of Regulators for Electricity and Gas. The 2007 EU *Survey* (OECD, 2007) argued that the approach of leaving member states to voluntarily develop joint schemes for congestion management had delivered insufficient progress, and that only a small proportion of congestion revenues had been used to build new inter-connectors or reinforce grids. Under the third liberalisation package, operators of the main gas and electricity transportation networks will be obliged to co-operate and co-ordinate the operation of their networks through the European Network of Transmission System Operators. This network should also facilitate the joint implementation of cross-border transmission network projects determined through the European Investment Plan. A good model is NordPool, the integrated Nordic energy market (IEA, 2008a). The Commission will need to monitor cross-border investment and implement additional processes should investment be inadequate. Responsibility for and financing of new interconnections should be defined and facilitated by cross-border regulations.

Regulated energy tariffs inhibit retail competition, distort investment and consumption decisions by firms and households, and weaken the price signals coming through the EU ETS. Although the Commission acknowledges that member states have the right to regulate prices to protect vulnerable citizens, they have affirmed that regulated prices should be the exception rather than the rule. To that end, the Commission has launched infringement action against those states that retain extensively regulated prices. The Commission should be commended for undertaking these infringement actions and should continue to encourage member states to abolish tariff regulation. Member states' concerns about the impact of high or volatile energy prices on the welfare of disadvantaged groups can best be addressed through targeted transfers that do not distort investment and consumption decisions (IEA, 2008a). According to the European Group of Regulators for Electricity and Gas (2009), 15 EU countries have some form of price controls. In those countries where end-user regulated prices still exist in at least one market segment, in general, only a limited number of customers have switched from regulated prices to free market retail prices. For most countries, the share of customers supplied with regulated prices is usually greater than 80% for most market segments.

Legislation has been accompanied by a robust application of the competition law in energy markets. The Commission stepped up its efforts to enforce competition policy. A number of cases have led to decisions in both the electricity sector (electricity production in Greece, E.ON electricity cases on the wholesale and balancing markets in Germany) and in the gas sector (long-term retail contracts in Belgium) which should improve competition to the benefit of consumers. Further, the Commission initiated a number of new cases, in particular as regards the use of networks to favour supply affiliates (*e.g.* gas networks of RWE in Germany and of ENI in Italy), as regards the foreclosure of markets through long-term contracts (in the French and Belgian electricity retail markets) and as regards possible cartels (E.ON-GDF gas case). In a number of cases (*e.g.* generation in Greece, E.ON electricity cases, RWE gas case) remedies have been adopted which will change the structure of the market: they will do so by either allocating new production facilities or reallocating exiting power plants to competitors or by putting network facilities in the hands of companies not active in the production and sales businesses.

Energy security

Security of supply is one of the core objectives of the EU's energy policy and is central to the Lisbon Strategy for Jobs and Growth. While the EU's "20-20-20 by 2020" objectives and energy market liberalisation policies will improve security of supply by reducing reliance on imported fossil fuels and raising incentives to invest in new generation and transmission capacity, the Commission considers that additional complementary policies are necessary. Consequently, in the 2nd Strategic Energy Review the Commission has proposed a five-point EU Energy Security and Solidarity Action Plan focusing on: infrastructure needs and the diversification of energy supplies; external energy relations; oil and gas stocks and crisis response mechanisms; energy efficiency; and making the best use of the EU's indigenous energy sources.

Of these priorities, raising investment in gas pipeline and other energy infrastructure to diversify supply is particularly important, as illustrated by the standoff between Russia and the Ukraine in winter 2008/2009 over gas supplies. For example, although gas supply is reasonably diversified for the EU as a whole, many member states rely on a single supplier for their gas (IEA, 2008c). Consequently, the Commission has identified six key infrastructure projects to be accepted as Community priorities that will help reduce countries' exposure to energy supply shocks from individual countries:

- A Baltic Interconnection Plan covering gas, electricity and storage to identify the necessary infrastructure for connecting the Baltic region with the rest of the EU.

- A Southern Gas Corridor to increase the supply of gas from the Middle East and Caucasus, including the Nabucco Pipeline project.

- A Liquefied Natural Gas (LNG) Action Plan to increase liquefaction facilities in producing countries and LNG terminals and ship-based regasification in importing countries.

- A Mediterranean Energy Ring to link Europe with the Southern Mediterranean through electricity and gas interconnections and help develop the region's solar and wind energy potential.

- North-South gas and electricity connections with Central and South-East Europe.

- A Blueprint for a North Sea offshore grid to interconnect national electricity grids in North-West Europe and facilitate the incorporation of new offshore wind projects into the grid.

Most of these priorities have already been identified under the Trans-European Networks-Energy (TEN-E) programme, which makes a small amount of public funding (EUR 21 million) available for mainly pre-feasibility studies of projects. The EU expects the energy industry itself to provide the bulk of the financing, though projects can often access funds from the EIB. The Commission has recognised that the TEN-E instrument was developed when the EU was considerably smaller and faced energy challenges of different dimension, and thus may no longer be sufficient. It has therefore begun the reflection process on whether the TEN-E instrument should be replaced by a new EU Energy Security and Infrastructure Instrument. The new instrument should make funds available for both pre-feasibility and feasibility studies, as in many cases major issues with projects can only be assessed during the feasibility phase. In addition, in its review of EU energy policy, the IEA (2008a) pointed out that as of 2007 only 16% of the TEN-E projects with a European interest had been finalised, and that incentives for investors to complete projects were inhibited by their other interests in generation and supply capacity. Any system for unbundling of TSOs should ensure the full effectiveness of their independence, in order to provide optimal investment in cross-border supply capacity. In addition, because firms do not have an incentive to internalise the energy security externality, there may be a greater role for public funding of infrastructure projects. Some of the other policy options for fostering cross-border transmission projects include:

- Nominating a European project co-ordinator for each major project or group project.
- Harmonising multi-jurisdictional regulatory frameworks (the adoption of the 3rd internal energy market package will contribute).
- Legislating time lines for qualified major transmission projects.
- Nominating designated transmission corridors for renewable energy development allowing faster siting and permitting.

The standoff between Russia and the Ukraine also underlines the importance of well-functioning markets, and the need for improved procedures for dealing with gas emergencies as well as harmonised security of supply standards. The Commission intends to table a proposal for the revision of the Gas Security of Supply Directive in 2009. Recent analysis by the IEA (2009) suggests that supply disruptions in Eastern European countries at the beginning of 2009 did not result in a large surge in spot natural gas prices in Western Europe and that as a result, price signals did not lead to changed consumption, production or inventory management patterns in Western Europe. In addition, very little gas supply was redirected to affected Eastern European countries because of the lack of East-flowing interconnection capacity. The IEA points to the oil market as one where market transparency better balances supply and demand and helps to mitigate crises, and suggests that European governments should consider co-ordinating their emergency policies. The IEA's recommended options that governments can draw on to improve their gas emergency policies include:

- Agreeing on clear definitions of reliability standards governing normal market operation.
- Defining the roles and responsibilities of market players in non-normal situations.
- Defining the role of transmission system operators during emergencies.
- Improving the understanding of the interdependencies between gas and power generation and the possible options for fuel switching.
- Improving the understanding of social, economic and other consequences of prolonged or sharp gas supply disruptions.

- Facilitating supply-side responses, such as short-term LNG purchases or diversions or swap arrangements with other suppliers, involving both pipeline and LNG supplies as well as alternate fuels.

- Developing relevant organisational capacities and links to existing energy emergency capacities, including stakeholder involvement.

- Improving the transparency of gas flows, stocks and other relevant data.

Another important priority is enhancing the powers of the EU over external energy policy, which is underdeveloped compared to areas such as trade and competition policy. The IEA's EU energy policy review argued that it was critical for Europe to speak "with a common voice" on external energy issues, and that the lack of co-ordinated action may have contributed to delays to projects like Nabucco, and weakened its position with major supplier countries such as Russia. The IEA believes that the EU's powers should be increased beyond its existing legal responsibilities to allow for greater co-ordination of member states. The Commission is responding to this by identifying specific mechanisms for increasing transparency between member states and the EU. The Commission is also considering revising the regulation that requires member states to notify the Commission about investment projects of interest to the Community in the petroleum, natural gas and electricity sectors.

Although diversification of EU energy supply is an important policy goal, it should not become a cover for policies that unnecessarily raise the cost of energy inputs. Europe is a net energy importer because many non-European countries have larger energy endowments and can produce energy at lower cost than European countries. If bio-fuels derived from sugar cane can be produced more efficiently outside the EU than within the EU, then tariffs and subsidies to promote domestic production are likely to distort resource allocation and unduly raise costs for end-users. Similarly, Europe could make greater use of nuclear fuels in electricity production to help meet its emission reduction goals without endangering security of supply, because uranium production is highly diversified across largely politically-stable countries.

Conclusion

The EU has an extensive agenda for creating a single internal energy market, diversifying energy supply, improving energy efficiency and reducing its carbon footprint by 2020. The EU should be praised for the comprehensiveness of its strategy and for leading the world in many of these areas. The actions it has undertaken so far will significantly increase the chances of an effective global agreement to mitigate climate change. The EU's 2020 goals are part of even more ambitious longer term objectives. The Commission plans to renew the Energy Policy for Europe with a 2050 "vision" and roadmap that could include: decarbonising the EU electricity supply by 2050; ending oil dependence in transport; and moving to a smart electricity network that can efficiently absorb new generation capacity from many small renewable energy producers.

Given the scale of its current and future ambitions, it is critical that the EU delivers its objectives in the most efficient manner. Policies to reduce European GHG emissions will lower potential growth. To keep the impact of mitigation policies on growth low, the EU must pursue least-cost abatement options and deliver a single, competitive internal energy market as soon as possible. For the most part, the EU is working towards this goal by: pricing the social cost of GHG emissions through the EU ETS, correcting market failures that cause energy to be used inefficiently and limit the development and use of renewable energy and other low-emission technologies; issuing directives that should speed progress toward the single energy market; and working closely with the member states that control many of the policy levers that determine whether the EU's objectives are met. The EU's framework for assessing the impact of Commission proposals also helps to ensure that the costs and benefits are examined carefully. Nevertheless, there are refinements that could be made to the instruments and policies that the EU has chosen to help meet its targets and goals.

Box 4.5. Recommendations concerning climate change and energy policies

To improve the equity and efficiency of the EU ETS during Phase III and beyond, the EU should:

- Analyse in more depth the pros and cons of broadening the ETS to include the road transport sector by shifting the point of obligation for the transport sector upstream to producers of transport fuel or fuel suppliers or the point of excise.

- Ensure that only sectors rigorously identified as being at genuine risk of carbon leakage continue to receive free allowances until 2020.

To ensure that the 20% renewable energy target is met in the most cost effective way, the EU should:

- Make sure that public procurement policies that actively favour renewables do not excessively increase the cost of providing government goods and services.

- Facilitate member states' use of statistical transfers and joint projects for renewables and maximise the cost effectiveness of renewable energy support measures.

- Move in the longer term to more co-ordinated or, if appropriate, a single harmonised European renewable energy support mechanism, and examine the options for including non-renewable, low-emission technologies.

- Assess the renewable transport fuels target in the light of further developments, in particular the future availability of second generation biofuels, reduce tariffs on imported biofuels and relax the requirement that all countries meet the target, rather than the EU as a whole.

- Increase funding for low-emission R&D.

- Consider phasing out all price support mechanisms for renewable technologies once renewable energy technologies compete fairly in the energy market to ensure that the ETS operates as efficiently as possible.

To make sure that the benefits of policies to reduce energy consumption exceed the costs, the EU should:

- Ensure that the mandatory EU-wide minimum energy performance standards for appliances are implemented effectively and focus on performance rather than specific technologies and remove the least energy-efficient products from the market. Targets should be flexible enough to ensure ongoing incentives for innovation.

- Remove reduced VAT rates that favour fossil-fuel intensive goods and services, rather than cutting rates on low-emission goods and services.

Box 4.5. **Recommendations concerning climate change and energy policies**
(cont.)

To speed progress toward a single, diversified, secure and competitive European energy market, the EU should:

- Ensure that the Commission has binding oversight over the certification procedures for TSOs.

- Undertake a review of the ITO option for effective unbundling within two years of the legislation as soon as is practicable.

- Ensure that ACER is adequately staffed to effectively carry out its responsibilities for co-ordinating cross-border access and investment issues and ensure that ACER has the powers to effectively contribute to a single energy market.

- Encourage member states to abolish tariff regulation. Member states' concerns about the impact of high or volatile energy prices on the welfare of disadvantaged groups can best be addressed through targeted transfers that do not distort investment and consumption decisions.

- Improve procedures for dealing with gas emergencies.

- Enhance the powers of the EU over external energy policy, which is underdeveloped compared to areas such as trade and competition policy.

Notes

1. The exceptions are developing countries such as Brazil, Indonesia and Papua New Guinea, whose forestry practices contribute to very high per capita emissions.

2. Note that the 20% target is a reduction compared to 1990 to be achieved by 2020. It is an independent commitment which has legal ground in a Directive amending the Emission Trading Scheme (ETS) and a Decision on the effort to reduce emissions in the sector not covered by the ETS. Specific reduction targets for the ETS as a whole and the individual targets for member states for the sectors not covered by the ETS are expressed as reductions compared to 2005 and not 1990. Choosing 2005 was necessary in order to be able to distinguish between the ETS and non ETS sectors. The first year specific data was available for the ETS was 2005.

3. While a large literature is available recommending the upstream approach for the transport sector, the EU believes that using an upstream approach involves risks because there is no practical experience of whether an upstream approach creates the same behavioural incentives at the point of emissions as the carbon price signal is transmitted to the emitters.

4. Other barriers include different allowable offsets under the two schemes, and the difficulty of verifying emissions in other jurisdictions.

5. The stationary energy sector includes all energy production and consumption, including electricity and direct uses of energy for heating and industrial processes, but excluding transport.

6. Annex 1 refers to the developed country signatories to the Kyoto Protocol that were required to reduce their greenhouse gas emissions by prescribed amounts by 2012.

7. However, it is worth noting that in contrast to the first two trading periods of the ETS where operators have been allocated allowances for free, the level of auctioning will increase significantly from 2013 onwards.

8. The EU ETS Directive acknowledges that as the world moves toward a global carbon price, that the competitive situation and thus the risk of carbon leakage may change in case there is an international climate change agreement. Therefore, by June 2010, the Commission has to report to the European Parliament and the Council and make any appropriate proposal in the light of the outcome of the international negotiations in Copenhagen in December 2009. If the negotiations are successful, the Commission may review the levels of free allocation.

9. On the other hand, excise rates on trucks are lower than for passenger vehicles in many EU countries.

10. As regards measures adopted (or in the process of being adopted) under the Ecodesign Directive (and some for Labelling), the total estimated annual energy savings by 2020 (compared with business-as-usual) account for about 343 TWh which correspond to 12.5% of the total EU electricity consumption. Converted to primary energy it is about 74 Mtoe which is 18.8% of the annual EU saving objective by 2020 (20% saving target compared to a business-as-usual scenario).

Bibliography

Anderson, D. (2006), "Costs and Finance of Abating Carbon Emissions in the Energy Sector", *Background Report for the Stern Review*, Imperial College London.

Bosetti, V., C. Carraro, E. Massetti and M. Tavoni (2008), "International Energy R&D Spillovers and the Economics of Greenhouse Gas Stabilisation", *Energy Economics*, Vol. 30(6), November.

Burniaux, J.M. *et al.* (2008), "The Economics of Climate Change Mitigation: Policies and Options for the Future", *OECD Economics Department Working Paper*, No. 658, OECD, Paris.

Duval, R. (2008), "A Taxonomy of Instruments to Reduce Greenhouse Gas Emissions and Their Interactions", *OECD Economics Department Working Papers*, No. 636, OECD, Paris.

EEA (2007), *Greenhouse Gas Emission Trends and Projections in Europe, 2007*.

EEA (2008), *Greenhouse Gas Emission Trends and Projections in Europe*, 2008.

Ellerman, A.D. and B.K. Buchner (2007), "The European Union Emissions Trading Scheme: Origins, Allocation, and Early Results", *Review of Environmental Economics and Policy*, Vol. 1, No. 1.

Enkvist, P.A., T. Nauclér and J. Rosander (2007), "A Cost Curve for Global Greenhouse Gas Reduction", *The McKinsey Quarterly*, No. 1.

European Group of Regulators for Electricity and Gas (2009), *Status Review of End-user Price Regulation*.

Garnaut, R. (2008), *The Garnaut Climate Change Review*, Cambridge.

IEA (2008a), *IEA Energy Policies Review: The European Union*.

IEA (2008b), *CO_2 Capture and Storage: A Key Carbon Abatement Option*.

IEA (2008c), *Energy Balances of OECD Countries and Energy Balances of non-OECD Countries*.

IEA (2008d), *Energy Prices and Taxes*.

IEA (2009), "Draft Proposal on Emergency Policy for Natural Gas for the October 2009 Ministerial Meeting", IEA/SEQ(2009).

IPCC (Intergovernmental Panel on Climate Change) (2007), *Climate Change 2007: Synthesis Report.*

IIASA (International Institute for Applied System Analysis) (2008), *GGI Scenario database*.

Jaffe, A., R. Newell and R. Stavins (1999), "Energy-Efficient Technologies and Climate Change Policies: Issues and Evidence", *Resources for the Future Climate Issue Brief, No.* 19, Resources for the Future, Washington DC.

Jamet, S. and J. Corfee-Morlot (2009), "Assessing the Impacts of Climate Change: A Literature Review", *OECD Economics Department Working Paper*, No. 691, OECD, Paris.

McKibbin, W. and P. Wilcoxen (2006), "A Credible Foundation for Long-Term International Co-operation on Climate Change", *Brookings Discussion Papers in International Economics*, No. 17.

National Oceanic and Atmospheric Administration Earth System Research Laboratory (2008), Press Release, 23 April 2008.

Neuhoff, K., K.K. Martinez and M. Sato (2006), "Allocation, Incentives and Distortions: The Impact of EU ETS Emissions Allowance Allocations to the Electricity Sector", *Climate Policy, No.* 6.

Nordhaus, W.D. (2004), "Life after Kyoto: Alternative Approaches to Global Warming", *NBER Working Paper*, No. 11889.

OECD (2007), *OECD Economic Surveys: European Union*, OECD, Paris.

OECD (2008), *OECD Environmental Outlook*, OECD, Paris.

Reinaud, J. (2008), "Issues Behind Competitiveness and Carbon Leakage: Focus on Heavy Industry", *IEA Information Paper*.

Schneider, L. (2007), "Is the CDM Fulfilling its Environmental and Sustainable Development Objectives? An Evaluation of the CDM and Options for Improvement", *Oeko Institute Report*.

Stern, N. (2007), *The Economics of Climate Change: The Stern Review*, CUP, Cambridge.

Tol, R. (2005), "The Marginal Damage Costs of Carbon Dioxide Emissions: An Assessment of the Uncertainties", *Energy Policy*, Vol. 33.

Wara, M. and D.G. Victor (2008), "A Realistic Policy on International Carbon Offsets", *Stanford Program on Energy and Sustainable Development Working Paper*, No. 74.

Weitzman, M. (1974), "Prices *vs.* Quantities", *Review of Economic Studies*, Vol. 41, No. 4.

World Bank (2008), "Rising Food Prices: Policy Options and World Bank Response", *World Bank Policy Note*.

Chapter 5

Further opening the European market to the rest of the world

The global financial crisis and associated recession are putting pressure on many countries to increase protection for domestic firms. The next few years will be very challenging for global trade policy. The EU has a significant interest in opposing rising protectionist sentiment and undertaking further trade liberalisation. Historically, trade liberalisation in the EU has followed a number of tracks: multilateral through the WTO; reciprocal through bilateral and regional preferential trade agreements (PTA); and non-reciprocal through initiatives such as the General System of Preferences (GSP), GSP+ and Everything But Arms (EBA) initiative that give special access to European markets to the developing and least developed countries. As a result, the European market is already significantly open to the rest of the world. An important challenge for the EU is ensuring that its initiatives in all of these areas are mutually reinforcing and that resources devoted to negotiating new PTAs do not detract from efforts in the multilateral sphere. The efficiency of the Common Agricultural Policy (CAP) has improved considerably during the course of this decade as payments to producers have become increasingly decoupled from production. Nevertheless, the overall size of support to the agricultural sector remains close to the OECD average and the biggest farms continue to receive the bulk of funds under the Single Payment Scheme. There is still considerable scope to improve the targeting of payments under the CAP. As is the case for the other OECD countries, further reducing export subsidies and tariffs on agricultural imports as already proposed by the EU in the context of the Doha Round would benefit consumers.

Selected issues in EU trade policy

The state of play in EU trade and trade policy

Until 2007, EU27 exports (either including or excluding intra-European trade) grew at an average annual rate of just under 4% this decade (Figure 5.1). Behind this average, there was a great deal of variation across countries and sectors. The most rapid export growth occurred in the recent accession countries in Central and Eastern Europe, as those countries became more firmly integrated with the rest of the EU economy. At the other end of the spectrum, export growth was very weak in some of the large EU countries, such as the United Kingdom, France and Italy. For the EU as a whole, growth in goods exports outpaced growth in services exports, and growth in machinery and transport equipment exports was particularly strong. Overall, the importance of trade to the EU27 has gradually increased over the past decade; excluding intra-European trade, exports and imports reached just over 23% of GDP in 2008. The EU has also run a small but persistent trade deficit, which at the end of 2008 was around 2% of GDP (Figure 5.2). The trade deficit was primarily attributable to the EU's large fuel and energy deficit; the EU runs a trade surplus in chemicals, machinery and equipment and services (Figure 5.3). Overall, the EU27 accounts for around 20% of world trade and 50% of global FDI, making it an extremely important player in global trade and investment (WTO, 2007).

Figure 5.1. **EU export volume growth**[1]

Average annual growth, 2000-08

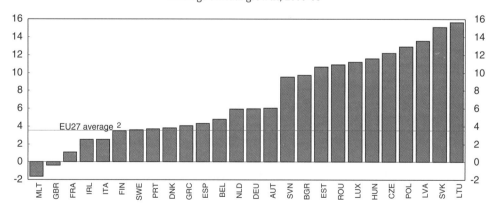

1. Including intra-European trade.
2. Using GDP weights.

Source: Eurostat.

StatLink http://dx.doi.org/10.1787/712825207506

The European Union currently makes use of a number of trade policy instruments, including tariffs, tariff quotas, export subsidies, customs controls, prohibitions relating to broader international agreements, and trade defence instruments such as anti-dumping measures (WTO, 2007). The EU's average applied most favoured nation (MFN) tariff has fallen

Figure 5.2. **The growing importance of external trade**

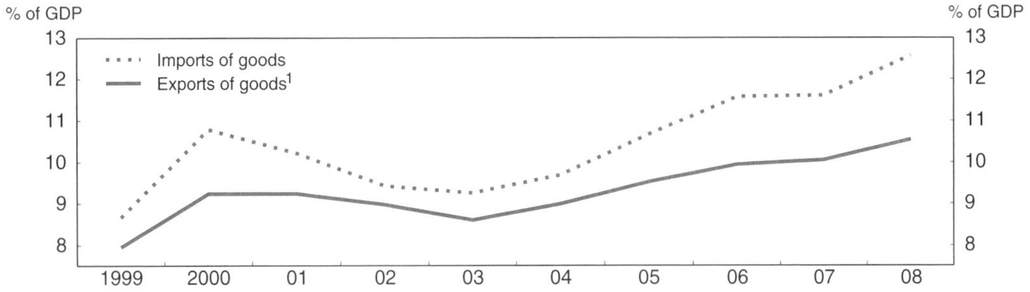

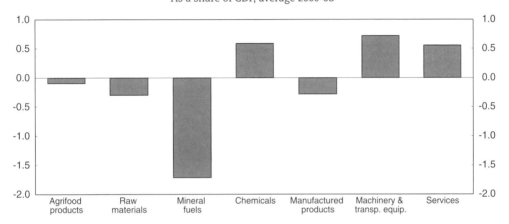

1. Excluding intra-European trade.
Source: Eurostat.

StatLink http://dx.doi.org/10.1787/712845144234

Figure 5.3. **Trade balance by commodity**
As a share of GDP, average 2000-08[1]

1. Average 2004-08 for services.
Source: Eurostat.

StatLink http://dx.doi.org/10.1787/712848450100

slightly over the past two decades, to around 5%. Average non-agricultural MFN tariffs are lower, at around 4%, than average agricultural tariffs, which were just under 15% in 2007. Applied tariff rates vary considerably across agricultural commodities, ranging from an average of just over 60% on dairy products to zero on cotton (Table 5.1). In 2007, close to 30% of tariff lines were duty free and 98 tariff lines, mostly in agricultural goods, were subject to tariff quotas. These figures all refer to tariffs applied on an MFN basis and do not take into account lower tariffs agreed in the numerous preferential trade agreements concluded by the EU. In practice, the average tariffs taking into account preferential trade are much lower. In 2007, 90% of all WTO notified export subsidies by value originated in the EU.[1] Total spending on export subsidies fell by more than 60% between 2006 and 2008. This was the combined effect of the reforms of the wine, sugar and dairy regimes and rising world prices. As a result of the fall in market prices, export subsidies for milk and milk products were reintroduced at the beginning of 2009 and import duties on cereals (except oats, buckwheat and millet) were reintroduced in October 2008. Over the decade to 2006, the EU introduced just under 200 anti-dumping measures, which were mainly applied to exports from China and India.

Table 5.1. **Tariffs and imports by product groups in the EU**[1]

Product groups	Final bound duties			MFN applied duties			Imports
	Average	Duty-free in %	Maximum	Average	Duty-free in %	Maximum	Share in %
Animal products	26.8	20.6	215	25.9	23.6	215	0.4
Dairy products	66.8	0.0	237	62.4	0.0	215	0.1
Fruit, vegetables, plants	10.7	22.8	231	11.6	18.5	231	1.6
Coffee, tea	6.9	27.1	88	6.9	27.1	88	0.7
Cereals and preparations	24.3	6.3	116	19.8	10.7	116	0.4
Oilseeds, fats and oils	5.6	48.2	113	6.0	43.1	113	1.2
Sugars and confectionery	29.5	0.0	133	29.8	0.0	133	0.2
Beverages and tobacco	23.2	23.0	210	20.0	19.8	191	0.6
Cotton	0.0	100.0	0	0.0	100.0	0	0.0
Other agricultural products	5.1	67.1	120	5.6	65.1	119	0.5
Fish and fish products	11.2	10.7	26	10.6	14.1	26	1.1
Minerals and metals	2.0	49.6	12	2.0	50.7	12	17.4
Petroleum	2.0	50.0	5	2.3	41.1	5	21.7
Chemicals	4.6	20.0	7	3.8	34.4	13	9.6
Wood, paper, etc.	0.9	84.1	10	0.9	81.3	10	3.1
Textiles	6.5	3.4	12	6.6	2.1	12	2.4
Clothing	11.5	0.0	12	11.5	0.0	12	4.8
Leather, footwear, etc.	4.2	27.8	17	4.1	26.1	17	2.5
Non-electrical machinery	1.7	26.5	10	1.7	27.3	10	13.1
Electrical machinery	2.4	31.5	14	2.6	28.3	14	6.3
Transport equipment	4.1	15.7	22	4.1	17.0	22	6.1
Manufactures, n.e.s.	2.5	25.9	14	2.5	24.2	14	6.3

1. Binding refers to concessions under WTO rules whereby members agree to "bind" their maximum tariff levels for a product by placing that tariff level on record with the WTO. These bound tariff rates become part of a state's schedule of concessions. However, in practice, many states apply lower duties than their bound tariff rates. These are called applied tariffs. Countries that do not apply their bound tariff rates can cut bound rates without providing new market access.

Source: WTO (2008), World Tariff Profiles 2008.

The years leading up to 2008 had seen a boom in trade as the global economy expanded at a rapid pace. However, following the dramatic decline in economic activity associated with the economic crisis, global trade has collapsed. The OECD's most recent projections are for global trade to decline by 18% in 2009, the largest fall in decades, and pick up only moderately in 2010 (Figure 5.4). This is putting pressure on many countries to increase protection for domestic firms and implies that the next few years will be some of the most challenging for global trade policy seen for some time (Baldwin and Evenett, 2009).

The EU has a significant interest in opposing rising protectionist sentiment through multilateral forums such as the WTO and the G20 and by undertaking further liberalisation at home. On the export side, freer trade helps open up new markets for domestic firms. On the import side, freer trade improves domestic access to new ideas and technologies, puts downward pressure on consumer prices and firms' input costs, and contributes to more rapid innovation and economic growth. Both sets of benefits are recognised in the Lisbon Agenda for Jobs and Growth. Moreover, any policies in response to the financial and economic crisis that unduly favour domestic firms over foreign firms will increase the incentive for other countries to do the same, leaving everyone worse off. As is the case with other OECD countries, further trade liberalisation by the EU would send a powerful free

Figure 5.4. **Export volume growth in OECD countries**

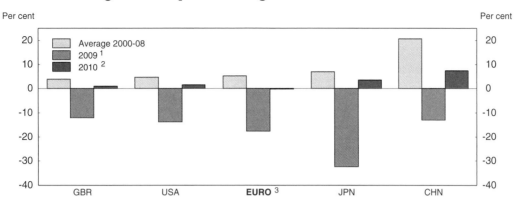

1. OECD estimates.
2. OECD projections.
3. Due to unavailability of EU projections, the euro area is being used instead.

Source: OECD, OECD Economic Outlook 85 database.

StatLink ᶟ *http://dx.doi.org/10.1787/712872158316*

trade message to the rest of the world and deliver benefits to consumers. Historically, trade liberalisation in the EU has followed a number of tracks: multilateral through the WTO; reciprocal through bilateral and regional preferential trade agreements (PTAs); and non-reciprocal through initiatives such as GSP, GSP+ and Everything But Arms (EBA) that give special access to European markets to the developing and least developed countries (LDCs) and are aimed at enhancing broader development goals in those countries. The EU's GSP scheme provides preferential access to the EU market for a larger number of beneficiaries and for a larger number of products than the comparable non-reciprocal preference schemes of other major developed countries. In addition, under an innovative incentive regime for sustainable development and good governance (known as the GSP+) the EU offers additional tariff preferences as an incentive to vulnerable developing countries to adhere to and implement international standards in the area of human and labour rights, environmental protection and good governance. It is important for the EU to continue to ensure that its initiatives in all of these areas are mutually reinforcing and that resources devoted to negotiating new PTAs do not detract from efforts in the multilateral sphere. In this spirit, the EU has, under the Global Europe framework, set an ambitious agenda for new generation bilateral trade agreements to complement multilateral liberalisation efforts.

Continuing efforts to secure further multilateral trade liberalisation

The Doha round of WTO negotiations commenced in 2001. Although estimates vary due to the complexity of the negotiations and different modelling assumptions, the global benefits of concluding the Doha round could be up to EUR 300 billion (House of Lords, 2008). While this represents a very small share of global GDP, any further liberalisation should be seen as progress in the current economic environment as cuts in bound tariff rates would contribute to strengthening the multilateral trading system. The main improvements on the table include: some cuts in applied tariffs and large cuts in bound tariffs (when applied tariffs are much lower than bound ones, this can translate into small cuts in applied tariffs), largely in agriculture; some liberalisation of barriers to trade in services is expected; and abolition of agricultural product export subsidies and of other measures with equivalent effects, as well as significant cuts in trade distorting support for farmers. Major potential gains from the Doha round can also be achieved in the area of trade facilitation. The EU is notably seeking:

- Improvements in market access for non-agricultural products on the basis of a non-linear formula that will cut the highest tariffs the most and offer flexibility for developing countries. Further to the July 2008 negotiation, this is now agreed (though conditional to agreement on the overall Doha package). The EU also favours additional industrial sectoral liberalisation, notably in the chemicals sector.

- Further liberalisation of the services sector.

- To further facilitate the protection of geographical indications.

- Incorporation of development priorities.

In return, the EU has offered to: cut its own agricultural tariffs by an average of more than 54%; cut the tariffs of the most protected agricultural products the most; reduce trade distorting subsidies by at least 75%; and eliminate export subsidies by the end of 2013, should other countries also eliminate all forms of export subsidisation.

Although negotiations stalled during 2008, there has been considerable progress in many areas, as set out in the latest negotiating texts of December 2008. In considering the reasons for this breakdown, it is important to remember that a number of earlier sticking points had been resolved. The so-called Singapore Issues – trade and investment, competition policy, transparency in government procurement, and trade facilitation – had (with the exception of trade facilitation) been taken off the table because there was no agreement on how they should be negotiated (House of Lords, 2008). At the Hong Kong meeting in 2005, countries agreed to phase out agricultural export subsidies and to discipline all export measures with equivalent effects as part of a Doha outcome. Developed countries had also agreed to improve access to generic drugs, while WTO members agreed on the objective of duty-free, quota-free access for all imports from all least developed countries, set an initial target for all developed countries to meet and encouraged developing countries in a position to do so to contribute as well. Importantly, the EU has already implemented duty and quota free access for all least developed countries under its Everything But Arms scheme. However, not all developed countries have followed the EU's lead. In the broader agriculture negotiations, the refusal of some more advanced developing countries to make further concessions in non-agricultural market access or to compromise on the Special Safeguard Mechanism (SSM) for agricultural products has also made a deal less likely.

The failure so far to secure further multilateral liberalisation through the Doha round, combined with the pressures generated by the global recession, has raised concerns that the long-term trend toward freer trade could be reversed. These fears have not been helped by some governments attempting to attach conditions to government spending and bailouts of firms that restrict their use to domestic activity. Nevertheless, such concerns should not be exaggerated. Among the OECD members of the WTO, applied tariffs are generally at or close to the bound rate (i.e. there is little scope to raise tariffs). According to François (2008), approximately 30% of world trade is locked in at zero tariffs through various European agreements, another 8% of trade is under zero tariffs locked in through NAFTA, and another 40% involves OECD importers where tariffs are at or very close to bound rates. On top of this, the commitments undertaken by China when it joined the WTO constrain its room for manoeuvre. Thus, due to binding regional and multilateral agreements, a large unwinding of trade through widespread hikes in applied tariff rates is unlikely unless the EU, NAFTA and WTO unwind as well. Although the risk of widespread rises in tariff rates therefore seems limited, attention will have to be given to an increased use of non-tariff instruments such as antidumping, countervailing duties, safeguard protection and excessive public subsidies (François, 2008). While tariff bindings do limit countries' possibility to increase tariffs, it must be remembered that many non-OECD countries do have plenty of room for manoeuvre. This implies that the value of a Doha deal has actually increased with the crisis.

For its part, the EU has affirmed its commitment to trade liberalisation, both through its actions in multilateral settings such as the WTO and the recent G20 meetings, and through the actions of the European Commission in establishing guidelines and putting pressure on member states that have attempted to tie new funds to particular industrial sectors such as automotives to maintain domestic production. The EU must continue to prioritise openness throughout the current global economic downturn and work with other countries to ensure that measures in response to the crisis do not discriminate against foreign interests or foreign workers (Dhar et al., 2009). Aid to financial institutions, automotive companies and policies to support the development of domestic renewable energy firms should be examined very carefully in this light and quickly unwound once a recovery is underway (Baldwin and Evenett, 2009). It is important that the EU continues to prioritise multilateral trade liberalisation as this is more likely to be welfare enhancing for the world as a whole and for its own consumers than greater fragmentation of global trade through further PTAs. As is the case with other OECD countries, further trade liberalisation by the EU would send a powerful free trade message to the rest of the world.

Ensuring that regional and bilateral trade agreements are consistent with freer global trade

When the Doha round began, the EU suggested it would devote most of its resources available for trade negotiations to multilateral rather than bilateral and regional trade liberalisation. However, in parallel with the Doha round, the EC has strengthened its efforts in securing further liberalisation through bilateral and regional preferential trade agreements (PTAs). By the end of 2007 there were some 200 PTAs in effect globally. The EU already has the most extensive network of preferential agreements of any WTO member and as a result applies the MFN to only nine countries - Australia, New Zealand, Canada, Hong Kong China, Republic of Korea, Japan, Singapore, Chinese Taipei and the United States (WTO, 2007). Other nations enjoy preferential tariff treatment that varies according to the terms of different agreements, or autonomous measures such as GSP. The EU's PTA policy has two main aims; the first involves securing PTAs and strengthening bilateral trading relationships with important trading partners such as the ASEAN and MERCOSUR countries, the Gulf States (GCC), Mediterranean countries, Central America, Andean Community, Korea, Canada, India and Ukraine, while the second replaces the Cotonou Agreement governing non-reciprocal trade agreements between the EU and the African, Caribbean and Pacific (ACP) countries, with Economic Partnership Agreements (EPAs) that will strengthen regional integration and provide a strong basis for partner countries' development.

The Commission has identified a number of criteria for determining which countries should be candidates for PTAs, including: their market potential; existing protection against EU export interests; potential partners' trade negotiations with EU competitors; and the impact of undermining preferential access to EU markets for existing PTA partners and developing countries. The EU wants new agreements to have provisions addressing services, investment, intellectual property rights, opening up of public procurement, competition policy, sanitary and phytosanitary barriers and environmental and social issues. In prioritising such provisions the EU is arguably choosing to pursue wider objectives through trade policy and insert provisions that could not be addressed in the context of the Doha round negotiations. The Commission undertakes a wide range of analytical exercises surrounding proposed PTAs. Preliminary Impact Assessments are carried out before the Commission proposes a negotiation mandate to the European Council. Sector specific and formal modeling exercises are undertaken to examine the impact of proposed PTAs on trade, welfare, production and employment. Sustainability Impact Assessments provide estimates of the potential social and environmental impacts of the trade agreement.

PTAs are controversial within the trade policy community because they are inherently discriminating; they reduce trade barriers for members but not non-members. This means that PTAs can potentially divert trade from efficient, low-cost non-members to inefficient, higher cost members facing lower tariffs. Thus an important question is whether the trade creation from PTAs more than offsets any trade diversion. Bhagwati (2008) sets out several elements of PTAs that can limit their net trade creation:

- Fierce competition between countries means that even small discriminatory tariffs against non-members can be consistent with trade diversion.

- The thinness of comparative advantage means that non-member countries facing differential tariffs from their competitors can lose that advantage quickly.

- Tariffs applied to non-member countries can be raised when they are bound at higher levels than applied tariffs.

- Complex rules of origin (ROO) within PTAs can lead to countries forgoing preferential tariff treatment and exporting under most-favoured nation terms instead, and sourcing inputs from more expensive member countries.

Despite the theoretical possibility for PTAs to divert trade, most empirical evidence suggests that trade creation from PTAs exceeds trade diversion and that therefore PTAs are welfare enhancing. Most of the existing evidence for PTAs to which the EU is a party (including those commissioned by the Commission), which comes from computable general equilibrium (CGE) models, is consistent with this broader evidence. One of the limitations of CGE modeling is that it can be difficult for non-specialist staff within trade and development ministries to understand the underlying assumptions that drive their results, especially within developing countries. Recognising this, economists at the University of Sussex have developed a more straightforward analytical framework for evaluating PTAs to complement CGE analysis (Rollo, 2006). Their checklist approach examines factors such as the details of the agreement, trade flows, macroeconomic variables and rules of thumb assessing the impact of shallow economic integration, to determine the potential welfare costs or gains that arise from agreements. For example, the rules of thumb they apply are that:

- The effects of a PTA will be greater the higher are initial tariff rates.

- The greater the similarity in the product mix and the higher the elasticities of supply the more likely it is that trade creation will exceed trade diversion.

- The greater the number of partners in the PTA the more likely it is that trade creation will exceed trade diversion.

- A PTA is more likely to be welfare enhancing when there are large differences in comparative advantage across the parties to the agreement.

- A PTA is more likely to be welfare enhancing when the proportion of trade between potential partners is high.

- A PTA is more likely to be welfare enhancing when trade is initially a small share of GDP.

Their application of the framework to recent EU PTAs, such as the EU-Egypt agreement, suggests that they have been welfare enhancing but that trade diversion issues have undermined many of the welfare gains from the agreements. Despite the limitations of this approach, a key implication is that the shallower the trade and economic integration that stems from a PTA, the lower are the welfare advantages that flow from the agreement. However, unlike CGE studies, these *ex ante* analyses do not capture all the complexities and interactions in an economy following a shock in terms of tariff reductions and should thus be interpreted accordingly.[2]

Because nations have multiple PTAs with other nations, which in turn have their own PTAs with different sets of nations, the EU's network of trade agreements appears chaotic. Bhagwati has dubbed it the "spaghetti bowl" (Baldwin, 2006). Debate about the welfare effects of PTAs and the implications of the regionalisation of global trade are likely to rage for some time. Yet, because regionalism is here to stay, a more productive way forward may be to consider how to multilateralise the world's existing and emerging regionalism (Baldwin, 2006). Superficially this seems like it will be very difficult to achieve. However, Baldwin (2006) argues that the relentless logic of globalisation's unbundling of the value chain within firms is likely to transform some of the beneficiaries of regionalism into losers, which in turn could help to build momentum toward harmonising the world's various PTAs and regional agreements. Baldwin develops an analytical framework that explains the spread of regional PTAs through a domino effect. The decision to join a PTA is determined by a domestic political equilibrium that balances the desire of exporters to join a PTA with the desire of import-competing firms to stay out of a PTA. Shocks that deepen a PTA's integration generate new political economy forces within non-member states that favour membership if the industrial output of exporters exceeds that of importers. He argues that regionalisation has left the world with three main trade blocs – Europe, North America and East Asia that are both fuzzy and leaky. For example, the EU trade bloc is fuzzy because the geographic boundary of the European trade bloc is not a straight line because some of the spokes of the EU customs area such as EFTA and Turkey themselves have bilateral agreements with countries outside the European area. The EU trade bloc is leaky because each bloc's tariff wall against the other blocs has holes in the form of cross-bloc Free Trade Agreements (FTAs). For example, Mexico is a member of NAFTA but it also shares a PTA with Europe.

According to Baldwin the way forward may be to use Europe's Pan-European Cumulation Scheme (PECS) as a model, although following the 2004 and 2007 enlargements of the EU its effects are somewhat more limited. Under PECS, all the FTAs between Western Europe and Eastern Europe were amended by substituting a common set of rules of origin and allowing for diagonal cumulation whereby firms in the then EU economies could source inputs from any nation in the PECS system without losing the origin status on sales to the EU. Through this process, Europe transformed itself from a fuzzy, leaky trade bloc to a relatively harmonious trade bloc (Figure 5.5). However, PECS also came with a cost; it harmed the export interests of non-members, and encouraged other countries to join to avoid the costs of staying out.

Figure 5.5. **The European spaghetti bowl**

Before harmonisation

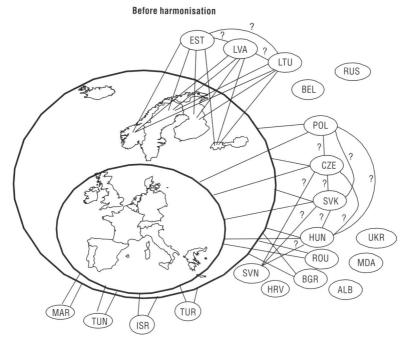

After harmonisation

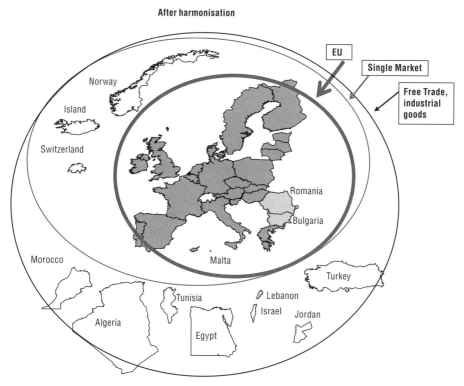

Source: Baldwin (2006), *Multilateralising Regionalism*.

The long-term challenge for Europe will be to try and replicate the harmonising benefits of PECS, while minimising the distorting elements as the EU extends its network of PTAs and the global unbundling of European firms becomes more common. EU trade negotiators should keep in mind that the design of PTAs may also be stumbling blocks to further multilateral liberalisation. Limao (2005) argues that large trading blocs (such as the United States and the EU) maintain higher multilateral tariffs on products imported from the PTA partner relative to those on similar products imported from the rest of the world. The higher MFN tariffs are then used as bargaining chips when negotiating new PTAs and therefore provide an incentive not to reduce MFN tariffs. PTAs can also be difficult to unravel and harmonise as tariff rates, sector coverage, rules of origin, and newer topics (such as environmental provisions and trade related intellectual property rights) all vary across PTAs. On the other hand, PTAs covering substantially all trade can also act as building blocks for multilateral negotiations by road-testing rules that multilateral negotiations could extend at a later stage, and go further and faster in promoting openness and integration. The EU also appears to be using PTAs as a mechanism for encouraging some degree of regulatory or policy convergence in areas such as competition policy, environment, energy, human and labour rights, that go beyond the multilateral commitments entered into by countries within the WTO framework (Horn *et al.*, 2009). However, many of these provisions are not enforceable through the withdrawal of trade benefits. This is in contrast to US PTAs, which include fewer "extra" WTO clauses, but those that are included tend to be enforceable under the general dispute settlement mechanisms of the PTAs. Given that the United States and the EU have some PTA partners in common (such as Mexico) but do not always share the same regulatory approaches, the inclusion of such "extra" WTO clauses in PTAs potentially raises difficult questions about the future harmonisation of PTAs with multilateral agreements.

Encouraging trade with developing countries and simplifying rules of origin

Developing countries are entitled to preferential access to European markets through several channels: all developing countries enjoy trade preferences under the Generalised System of Preferences (GSP), and the Everything But Arms initiative provides duty-free and quota-free access to the 49 least-developed countries (LDCs) as recognised by the United Nations. Moreover, the EU and the African Caribbean and Pacific countries are currently pursuing the negotiation of Economic Partnership Agreements (EPAs) to replace the system of one-way preference arrangements that had been in place under the Cotonou trade regime that expired in 2007. Under the EPAs, the EU has agreed to remove all remaining quota and tariff limitations on access to the EU market for ACP goods. This covers all products, including agricultural goods and will apply immediately following the initialing of the agreements, with a phase-in period for rice and sugar ending in 2009. Moreover, the rules of origin under the EPAs will be less stringent than those that apply under the existing GSP for developing countries. The main objective of the EPAs is to promote regional integration and development. EPAs aim to support the development of regional policies among ACP countries in trade in services and foreign direct investment, constraints on anti-competitive practices, greater transparency in public procurement practices and intellectual property rights. The global scope of the EPAs will depend on the level of preparedness and the decision of the ACP regions. The EU has successfully completed an EPA with 15 Caribbean ACP countries. It is also negotiating full EPAs with the Economic Community of West African States, the Economic and Monetary Community of Central Africa, Eastern and Southern

Africa, the East African Community, the Southern African Development Community (SADC) and the Pacific region. As a transitory measure before the completion of the negotiation of full EPAs, end 2007 "stepping stone" agreements have been initialed between the EC and key countries or regions, notably with a view to avoiding any trade disruption for the non LDCs and finalising negotiations of full EPAs.

EPA negotiations have proved both complex and in some ways controversial [see House of Lords (2008) for a discussion of the issues below]. Non-governmental organisations have expressed concerns that: the EU has not prioritised negotiations of the EPAs; negotiations are being treated as conventional free trade negotiations based on market opening rather than as tools for development; some countries have limited negotiating capacity because of both inexperience and a lack of resources, which may be hindering their ability to negotiate agreements in their interests; bargaining power may be asymmetric, as some countries feel like they have no choice but to join an EPA; and the EU is taking advantage of its superior bargaining position with some countries by reintroducing the Singapore Issues and other non-trade issues. However, the EU emphasizes that EPAs are important tools to support ACP countries' own development. In addition, the original Cotonou system of non-reciprocal preferences was no longer achieving its goals (the relative share of ACP countries on the EU market was falling and ACP countries were not successfully diversifying their exports) while the regime was also inconsistent with WTO obligations. In order to promote ACP countries' further development, these EPA agreements are highly asymmetric, requiring much lower levels of commitments from developing countries, and also deal with trade-related issues like trade facilitation or investment in a manner that takes into consideration the ACPs' capacities and development needs. The Everything But Arms initiative also complicates the process of negotiating EPAs because countries with duty-free and quota-free access through that programme (only those that are LDCs) may have less incentive to negotiate an EPA. Nevertheless, a number of these countries appear to see the wider advantages of EPAs, with nearly half of the countries that initialed interim EPAs in Africa being LDCs. There is also controversy about the requirement agreed in Cotonou that negotiations occur on a regional basis. The regional approach requires close co-operation between countries with, in some cases, limited experience of doing so. On the other hand, this is an ongoing process and consistent with the ambition to support regional integration through the EPA process. There are also issues arising from overlapping membership in regional associations in Africa. For example, all member states of SADC belong also to one or more other regional integration groupings with partly conflicting objectives. Bilateral negotiations could raise the issue of countries liberalising their trade with the EU before liberalising trade with each other, which could be distorting. To counter this risk, the EPA concept foresees an explicit clause that ensures that the EU in no case is granted any more concessions than regional ACP partners grant to each other. Regional groupings also allow countries to work together to increase trade and could facilitate the development of free trade areas within the regional groupings. Overall, the agreements involve trade-offs for developing countries; research by the International Centre for Trade and Sustainable Development (2008) suggests that the proposed EPA with the Caribbean countries will grant deeper and more stable access to the EU market than previous agreements, but will require more commitments from developing countries in the areas of intellectual property, services and investment. The EPA should nonetheless stimulate regional integration within the Caribbean countries and the development of larger, better functioning regional markets.[3]

An area of special concern is the complex rules of origin that apply under the EBA initiative and the prospective EPAs. Rules of origin determine whether the imported product was produced in the beneficiary country for tariff preferences purposes. They are designed to ensure that third party exporters cannot circumvent tariffs and examine whether there has been sufficient transformation in the exporting country. Rules of origin are unavoidable in a global trading regime where countries liberalise their trade with one another unevenly, but may imply that actual preferential access for many developing countries is less generous than it first appears. Earlier research suggests that although product coverage for developing countries is high under EU preferential agreements, take-up rates of preferential duties are low (Amiti and Romalis, 2007). More recent work suggests that preference utilisation rates for developing countries in 2008 were more than 75%, and for ACP countries were about 90% (Eurostat, 2009). Some middle-income developing countries actually pay higher average tariffs than developed countries under current preference schemes (Amiti and Romalis, 2007). These problems have been recognised by the Commission and the EPAs under negotiation will contain improvements compared to the Cotonou rules of origin, in areas such as fisheries, textiles and agriculture. The EU is also currently reforming its rules of origin under the GSP, with the aim of making them simpler and more development-friendly. There are concerns that rules of origin have been designed to force developing countries to source higher-cost intermediate inputs from developed countries and that the restrictiveness of rules of origin are greater than is necessary to offset trade deflection (Cadot and de Melo, 2007). The Commission for Africa (2005) has proposed that the EU should apply a 10% value added rule, which would allow producers to import low-cost inputs, undertake some work, and then qualify for duty free access. They argue that such a rule would benefit developing countries with minimal risk of damaging the integrity of existing preference arrangements. The EU should give this proposal consideration. However, currently the Commission considers that the development impact of such a low level of value added would be questionable, as beneficiary countries would not see a major upswing in manufacturing and processing activity. The EU considers that its rules of origin for developing countries compare favourably in relation with the preferential regimes granted by other major donor countries.

Reforming Trade Defence Instruments

There may be room for refinement to the EU's and other WTO members' trade defence instruments. These instruments – anti-dumping, anti-subsidy and safeguard measures – allow the EU to defend its producers against unfairly traded or subsidised imports and against dramatic shifts in trade flows insofar as these are harmful to the EU economy. Dumping occurs when a firm exports under normal value (prices and cost below those of home markets). Between 1996 and 2005, the EU imposed 194 definitive anti-dumping measures, with China and India being the most frequent targets. In 2006, the measures in place covered around 0.5% of the value of total imports. In comparison, the United States imposed 201 measures over this period. Globally, the imposition of anti-dumping duties increased by 22% in 2008, with developing countries accounting for the bulk of initiations and developed countries the bulk of impositions (Gamberoni and Newfarmer, 2009). The EU applies a Community interest test before applying anti-dumping measures which is not undertaken by most of the other WTO Members. Although Article VI of the General Agreement on Tariffs and Trade allows anti-dumping duties to be imposed as long as they are not exceeding the difference between the export price and their normal value (the dumping margin), the use of anti-dumping duties is contentious. Trade defence measures must not limit fair competition and normal business practices, but instead contribute to free trade in a way that encourages competition and international division of labour. Many economists also argue that anti-dumping measures cannot be justified from the perspective of overall welfare, as opposed to the more narrow interests of import-competing producers, and therefore unduly restrict trade. Others, however, hold that dealing with anti-competitive practices like dumping through anti-dumping measures restores balanced competitive conditions.

In 2006, the European Commission published a Green Paper that posed a series of questions to stakeholders about ways in which the use of trade defence instruments can continue to best serve European interests. Some of the issues the Commission put on the table included whether:

- There were alternatives to the use of trade defence instruments in the absence of internationally agreed competition rules.

- The interests of companies that have moved part of their production out of the EU and consumers should receive a heavier weight in the Community interest test and what sort of economic analysis could be used to assess these broader factors.

- The EU should make a formal distinction between least-developed and developing countries in the application of trade defense measures.

- The viability of the industry in the EU should be a factor in reaching decisions about the use of trade instruments and what the most appropriate measures of viability are.

- The EU should review the standing requirements that may have the effect of lowering the number of companies required to establish standing in a given case and exclude companies that may object to a complaint.

- The EU should refine the approach on "start-up costs" for dumping calculations in anti-dumping investigations in order to give a longer "grace period" to exporters in start-up situations.

- It should be possible for definitive measures in anti-dumping investigations to last less than the current five-year timeframe.

- There should be greater transparency in trade defense investigations.

The Commission should be praised for issuing the green paper and bringing some of these questions into the open. No specific policy initiatives have arisen from the subsequent consultation process so far. While the issues surrounding trade defense instruments are very complex, some progress on concrete proposals could perhaps be made given the importance of this issue. A successful outcome of the Doha Round rules negotiations would make the revival of this process more opportune.

Making more of existing market access

The EU employs considerable resources to improve market access for EU firms through PTAs and multilateral forums. However, it is equally important that EU firms make the most of their existing market access. A recent study conducted by the European Commission suggests that differences in external competitiveness among the euro area member countries are widening (Figure 5.6). In particular, Germany and some other mainly northern European countries improved their competitiveness in recent years while France, Italy, Portugal and Spain became less competitive. By putting more emphasis on

Figure 5.6. **Nominal unit labour costs in selected European countries**
Index 2000 = 100

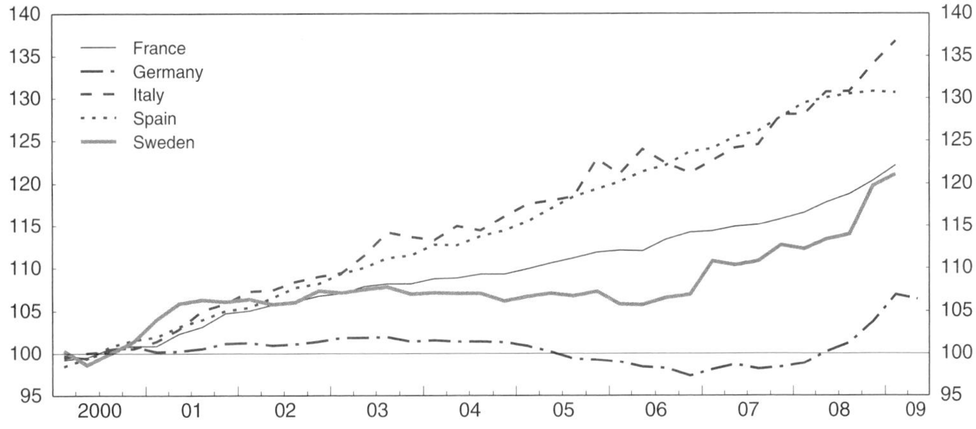

Source: OECD, OECD Economic Outlook database.

StatLink ⌸ http://dx.doi.org/10.1787/712885752442

productivity and ensuring that wage increases in the traded goods sector are in line with productivity gains, firms in the latter set of countries will be in a better position to maintain or increase their market share.

Recent joint research by Mayer and Ottaviano (2007) suggests that, at present, a handful of "superstar" firms account for the bulk of EU exports and that there is wide variation in the extensive margin (the number of firms exporting) across European countries. For example, there is a proportionately larger set of medium-sized firms involved in exporting in Germany than in other European countries. This research also suggests that firms score better than non-exporters in terms of the size of their value added and employment, as well as their capital and skill intensity, a finding consistent with the broader literature (Helpman, 2006). Some of the questions arising from this research are whether policies to improve firms' use of existing market access should focus more on increasing the number of firms that export or on encouraging existing firms to export more, and whether firm size is causally related to the propensity to export. More empirical research is needed on the questions to help inform policymakers about the right policy strategies for bolstering EU exports.

Because trade promotion is a competence of member states, encouragement for European firms to make more of existing market access is mainly undertaken by them and their business organisations. However, EU policies are supporting European companies to be present in global markets such as by maintaining open global markets through the commitment to the WTO, the multilateral trading system and the Doha Round and regulatory dialogue. Another effective tool is the Market Access Strategy which not only provides information for EU exporters on market access conditions in third countries, as a lack of knowledge about export markets and the combination of EU and non-EU regulations is a significant trade barrier, especially for services sectors, but also deepens the co-operation among the Commission, member states and business with the aim to support the EU exporters' competitiveness in third country markets. Perhaps the most important way for the EU to promote export growth is by pressing on with its agenda to complete the single market and liberalise internal trade in services. Limits in market size and market segmentation in general reduce economies of scale, thereby negatively affecting the performance of firms.

The Common Agricultural Policy

The EU's Common Agricultural Policy (CAP) is a policy for providing income support to farmers, guaranteeing a safety net for agricultural prices, ensuring that the agricultural sector respects environmental standards and provides land management and amenity public goods. The CAP aims to achieve: a competitive agricultural sector; production methods that support environmentally-friendly, quality products that the public wants; a fair standard of living and income stability for the agricultural community; diversity in the forms of agriculture, maintaining visual amenities and supporting rural communities; simplicity in agricultural policy; and the sharing of responsibilities among the Commission and the member states. In 2008, the CAP accounted for around 40% of the EU budget but less than 2% of total EU public expenditure. The OECD uses indicators for estimating total support granted to the agricultural sector, both in terms of market price support and budget transfers. In 2008, total support to the agricultural and rural sector was estimated around 1% of GDP, slightly above the OECD average (Figure 5.7). Producer receipts are estimated to be just under 40% higher in the EU than would have been the case in the absence of support. The OECD's key indicator for evaluating changes in agricultural support is the Producer Support Estimate (PSE). It is the total estimated value of policy transfers (in the form of price support and budget transfers) to producers as a share of gross producer receipts. Since 1986-88, the EU's PSE has shown a steady and substantial decline, from 40% down to 29% in the period 2005-07 (OECD, 2008). This was in large part due to successive policy reforms. However, other factors also have an impact on the PSE calculations, especially movements in global agricultural prices and exchange rates.

Figure 5.7. **Total agricultural support in OECD countries**

In per cent of GDP

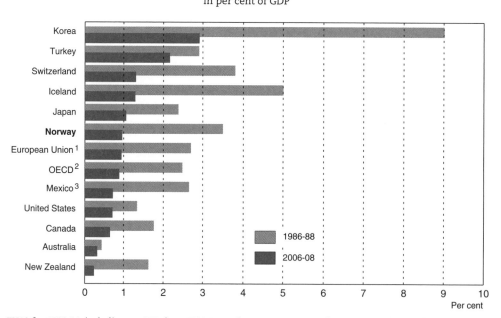

1. EU12 for 1986-94, including ex-GDR from 1990; EU15 for 1995-2003; EU25 for 2004-06 and EU27 from 2007.
2. Austria, Finland and Sweden are included in the OECD total for all years and in the EU from 1995. The OECD total does not include the non-OECD EU member states. Total support estimate as a share of GDP for the OECD total in 1986-88 excludes the Czech Republic, Hungary, Poland and the Slovak Republic as GDP data is not available for this period.
3. For Mexico, 1986-88 is replaced by 1991-93.

Source: OECD, PSE/CSE database 2009.

StatLink 🔗 http://dx.doi.org/10.1787/713003132150

Post 2003 reforms to the CAP

In 2003, the EU started to implement a series of reforms to more effectively implement the objectives of the CAP. The measures aimed to enhance competitiveness with significant adjustments in market measures in the sectors of cereals, dairy and rice. They promoted more market orientation by decoupling direct payments in the arable crops, beef and dairy sectors by introducing the Single Payment Scheme (SPS).[4] SPS is based on fixed levels of support. Member states had the option of basing payments on either the historic level of support received by individual farms (historic model with the farm the fixed reference for support), of averaging out the level of support received in a region (regional model with the area the fixed reference for support) or of using a combination of the two models. Rural development was strengthened with the shift of funds from the 1st pillar (direct payments and market measures) to the 2nd pillar (rural development) *via* modulation.[5] With the reforms implemented in 2005-07, it is still too early to make a comprehensive assessment. However, in general they went in the right direction in terms of decoupling payments from production, and thereby reducing the distortionary impact on production decisions.

Greater decoupling was a major improvement from the previous system of payments linked to production of specific commodities. In 2008, just over 30% of the PSE did not require production, up from near-zero in the mid-80s, and the share will increase further when the reforms agreed for the sugar, banana, fruit and vegetables and other sectors have been fully implemented. Single commodity transfers are very low for some commodities (largely grains and cereals) but still high for commodities such as sugar, beef and lamb. Some payments remain commodity specific so that countries can ensure that farms are not abandoned. Countries also retained some choice over whether aid would be made commodity specific; less than 1% was commodity specific in Germany, Greece, Ireland and the United Kingdom, while more than 20% was commodity specific in France, Spain, the Netherlands and Portugal (OECD, 2007). Overall, the share of the most distorting types of payments fell and is now below the OECD average.

Figure 5.8 shows how payments under the CAP have evolved over time. In the late-1980s, the PSE made up just under 40% of gross farm receipts, with over 90% of support tied to single commodity production. Two decades later, CAP support had fallen to just over 25% of gross farm receipts and less than 45% of support was tied to single commodity production due to successive reforms that reduced support and changed its composition towards less distorting mechanisms. Preliminary projections by the OECD suggest that producer support, as measured by the PSE, could increase marginally by 2013 as a share of gross farm receipts, though the share of single commodity transfers is likely to decline. However, there is considerable variation across the different agricultural commodities (Figure 5.9). The estimates should be interpreted very cautiously because they are based on a number of important assumptions. Estimates for gross farm receipts are based on forecasts for agricultural prices that in turn depend on the OECD's economic projections for the coming years. However, agricultural price developments are uncertain even in normal economic circumstances, let alone in the midst of a deep global recession. On the payments side, estimates take into account the additional decoupling of payments agreed in the CAP Health Check (see below), as well as other planned changes to the CAP, but otherwise make no assumptions about potential changes in policy over this period.[6] Critically, the slight increase in the PSE over the projection period is not driven by increases in payments (which are projected to decline slightly in nominal terms), but by projected falls in agricultural commodity prices related to improved global supply conditions and

Figure 5.8. **Producer support estimates by support category[1] in EU27**
In per cent of gross farm receipts[2]

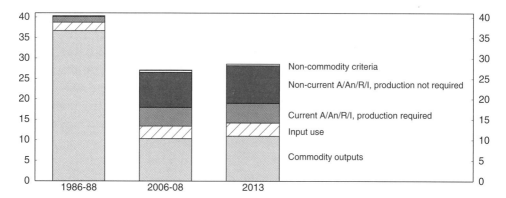

1. The categories "Non-current A/An/R/I, production required" and "Miscellaneous" do not show up because they are too small.
2. Provisional data for 2006-08 and estimates for 2013.
Source: OECD, PSE/CSE database 2009 and Secretariat calculations.

StatLink ⧉ http://dx.doi.org/10.1787/713031735874

Figure 5.9. **Producer single commodity transfers by commodity in EU27**
As a percentage of producer support estimates[1]

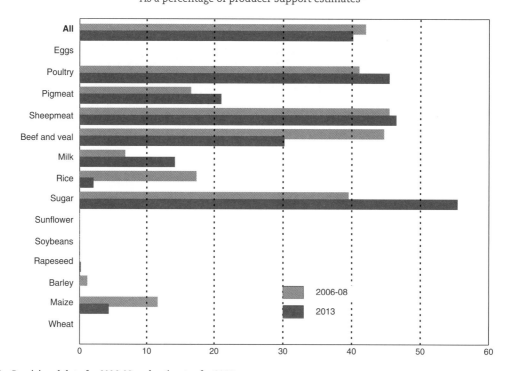

1. Provisional data for 2006-08 and estimates for 2013.
Source: OECD,PSE/CSE database 2009 and Secretariat calculations.

StatLink ⧉ http://dx.doi.org/10.1787/713044620506

weaker global demand growth. It should also be noted that the European Commission's own measures of support, which are based on narrower budgetary transfers, suggest that just over 90% of direct agricultural payments will be decoupled from production by 2013.

The 2007 *Economic Survey of the EU* (OECD, 2007) concluded that the 2003 reforms largely altered the composition of support, but not the level. Moreover, the most production and trade distorting measures still dominated and the reforms have not entirely eliminated incentives to produce. Significant market price support remained, largely because of border protection, especially in meat, milk and sugar. In addition, export subsidies were worth 2% of the value of agricultural exports in 2007 for the EU27. The *Survey* concluded that all commodity specific payments should be replaced by the Single Payment Scheme and that the positive aspects of the reform could be reinforced by a reduction in the overall level of support and by improvements in market access. The OECD's 2008 *Survey of Agricultural Policies in Member Countries* (OECD, 2008) argued that further reforms were necessary to give farmers the greatest possible incentive to respond to market signals and to target payments at low income farms to provide a genuine safety net.

The CAP Health Check

In 2008, the Council agreed on the CAP Health Check, which aimed to further reform the CAP so that farmers could better respond to price signals and face new challenges such as climate change, improve water management, protect biodiversity and produce green energy. Some of the key changes that have been decided are:

- Phasing out milk quotas by 2015 by increasing quotas by 1% every year from 2009/10 to 2013/14.
- Extending the decoupling of support so that only payments to suckler cow, goat and sheep premia will be linked to production by 2013.
- Give EU member states the possibility to move towards more uniform rates for direct payments (flatter rates) at a regional level.
- Shifting additional money from direct aid (Pillar 1) to rural development (Pillar 2) by reducing direct aid to farmers receiving more than EUR 5 000 by 10% by 2012 (was previously 5%) and introducing an additional cut of 4% on payments above EUR 300 000.
- Abolishing the set-aside that currently requires arable farmers to leave 10% of their land fallow.
- Simplifying cross-compliance rules that link the payments farmers receive to the respect of specific environmental, animal welfare and food-quality standards by withdrawing standards from the Cross Compliance list that are either no longer relevant or not linked to farmer responsibility.
- Reforming price intervention mechanisms by abolishing intervention for pig meat, setting intervention at zero for barley and sorghum and reducing the intervention price for wheat.

In its impact assessment of the Health Check proposals, the Commission identified a number of potential problems with the SPS framework and its implementation. The historic model, whereby SPS payments reflect previous production structures and agricultural support of individual farms is arguably less equitable than a regional model as it gives aid to farmers based on individual levels of past support. There is no adequate instrument for addressing the uneven distribution of payments. It was also pointed out that there was no provision for member states to adjust their SPS model based on recent experiences. The receipt of a large share of payments by a few beneficiaries means that large sums of payments went to very large farms. The receipt of payments by small enterprises meant that payment levels could be exceeded by administration costs. And partially coupled support and cross-compliance measures could be complicated. There was a wide variation in the average direct payment per hectare (Figure 5.10) and the average direct payment per beneficiary (Figure 5.11). The countries with the largest

Figure 5.10. **Average direct payment per hectare**
In EUR per hectare

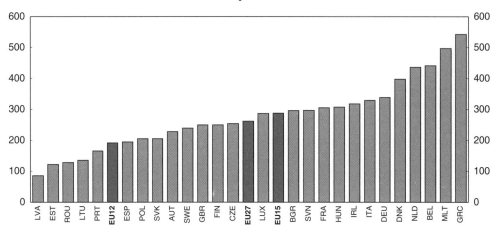

Source: European Commission, DG Agriculture.

StatLink ⟨⟩ http://dx.doi.org/10.1787/713068141246

Figure 5.11. **Average direct payment per beneficiary**
In thousand EUR per beneficiary

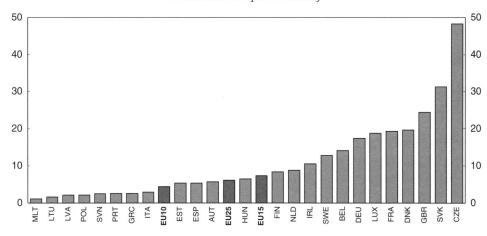

Source: European Commission, DG Agriculture.

StatLink ⟨⟩ http://dx.doi.org/10.1787/713074083307

payments per hectare were Denmark, the Netherlands, Belgium and Greece. The countries with the largest payments per beneficiary were France, Denmark, the United Kingdom, Slovakia and the Czech Republic. These differences reflect factors such as differences in crops, the average size of farms and historical levels of support. Assistance as a share of GDP varied considerably across countries.

The Commission examined four options for moving toward a flatter rate of SPS payment across agricultural producers: an EU-wide flat rate per eligible hectare; the Single Area Payment Scheme (SAPS) for new member states becomes the model for all;[7] a regional flat rate per hectare; and a regional flat rate per entitlement.[8] The Commission concluded that the reform options considered would all lead to more equal rates of payment per hectare or entitlement, but none would result in a fundamental change in the distribution of support amongst farms because most of the inequality in payments across farms is attributable to the unequal distribution of land amongst farmers. Because targeting regional flat rates would reduce the impact on land values and ensure that more support would remain among active farmers, the Commission argued that a regional flat rate per entitlement was the superior option.

The Commission considered different options for the currently partially-decoupled support schemes. The options considered included full decoupling and targeted selective decoupling. In its assessment the Commission argued that full decoupling would have its biggest impact on sectors and regions where the coupled premiums are an important share of the farmer's margin such as suckler cows and sheep. The big advantage of full decoupling would be in greater market orientation, more efficient income transfers and reduced administrative complexity and costs. However, the Commission concluded that selective decoupling (retained for livestock meat production) would be superior because of positive social and environmental impacts from lower rates of land abandonment.

The issue of whether the distributional fairness of the CAP could be improved by reducing payments to larger, more profitable farms was also examined. Around 80% of direct payments go to just 20% of producers (Figure 5.12). Before the Health Check, the only method of redistribution was through the linear 5% reduction of payments above EUR 5 000 from compulsory modulation. In the Health Check this was increased to 10%. The Commission considered a number of options for both upper and lower payment limits. With regard to upper limits, the Commission examined capping payments above a particular threshold, and progressively reducing payments above particular thresholds; payments above EUR 100 000 would be reduced by 10%, payments above EUR 200 000 by 25% and payments above EUR 300 000 by 45%. With regard to lower limits the Commission considered compulsory applications of current individual limits (EUR 100 or 0.3 hectares of agricultural land) and increased lower limits. A payment threshold of EUR 100 000 would result in budgetary savings of 8% and affect just over 25 000 farms. The progressive cut option would result in budgetary savings of just 2%, as large firms would still receive large payments. Raising the minimum payment to EUR 250 would exclude just over 30% of farms

Figure 5.12. **Distribution of average direct payment per beneficiary in EU25**

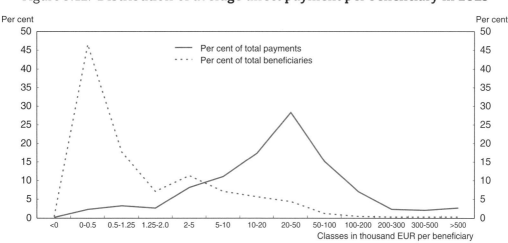

Source: European Commission, DG Agriculture.

StatLink 📊 http://dx.doi.org/10.1787/713107446278

from the cap that collectively receive 0.84% of payments. In its analysis the Commission rejected a cap on payments because it assessed the impact on large farms with high employment levels as being too great and instead endorsed the progressive individual limits option. In the Impact Assessment the Commission also analysed the effect of raising the minimum payment. It is pointed out that this would simplify the SPS but would affect member states in different ways and that better adjustment to specific situations could be achieved by giving member states the competence of setting the limits.

Modulation shifts payments under the CAP away from production subsidies toward the European Agricultural Fund for Rural Development (EAFRD). The Common Monitoring and Evaluation Framework (CMEF) provides a single framework for monitoring and evaluation of all Rural Development interventions for the programming period 2007-13. The CMEF establishes means for improving programme performance, ensuring the accountability of programmes and allowing an assessment on the achievement of established objectives. To ensure a targeted use of resources, rural development policy has adopted a strategic approach involving three consecutive steps. First, the Council Regulation and Community strategic guidelines set priorities for rural development which reflect EU policy priorities. Second, each member state submits a national strategy plan which is consistent with the Community strategic guidelines and the national and regional priorities. From a menu of approximately 40 support measures, member states select those best suited to address the specific strengths, weaknesses and opportunities of individual programming areas. Third, from 2010, member states will submit a summary report setting out progress in implementing the national strategy plan and objectives and its contribution to the achievement of Community strategic guidelines. To ensure spending takes place efficiently, national rural development priorities are translated into quantified targets using a range of common output, result and impact indicators complemented, where relevant, by programme-specific indicators. Additionally, baseline indicators have been provided by member states during the process of programme approval, thereby assessing the situation of each programme at the beginning of the programming period and providing the basis for the establishment of *ex ante* targets through the support of independent *ex ante* evaluators. This aims to provide effective monitoring and ongoing evaluation by ensuring that there are explicit, measurable objectives that can be assessed over time.

Assessment

It is welcome that the Commission is continuing to consider how the CAP can be better targeted and hence become more efficient and equitable. The Health Check builds on the 2003 reforms that enshrined a significant increase in the degree of decoupling of agricultural payments from production decisions. Nevertheless, there are still areas for improvement. The CAP allows countries to give commodity specific support within an envelope of 3.5% of the SPS (within the so-called article 68) and full decoupling has not been fully extended to the livestock meat production sector. The Commission's impact assessment argues that full decoupling would lead to a net adverse social impact through lower production or land abandonment and a net adverse environmental impact through reduced biodiversity, landscape losses and reduced forest fire protection. However, this analysis of the social impact of decoupling may assess social issues too narrowly. For the EU as a whole, the adverse social impact of reduced production in some areas may be offset by the more efficient allocation of resources that full-decoupling would bring. Social impacts on particular regions could be addressed through other targeted support measures. Concerns about biodiversity, landscape losses and forest fire protection could also be addressed through measures addressing these problems directly, although transaction costs have to be taken into account. The Commission examined a range of options for flattening payments across agricultural producers, and recommending a movement, on a voluntary basis for the member states, toward a regional flat rate per entitlement. The political agreement by EU agriculture ministers gives member states the possibility to move towards flatter rates for direct payments at a regional level, although currently it is not clear how many member states will take up this option.

The distribution of payments under the SPS is a complex issue. Agricultural production varies enormously across EU member states in terms of the types of agricultural goods produced, the efficiency and scale of farms, historic levels of income support, environmental impacts and the public goods provided by producers. Existing levels of support are also capitalised into land values, implying that any changes in policy and the distribution of payments will affect both the incomes and wealth of agricultural producers. Nevertheless, the Health Check reforms only partially address legitimate concerns that the CAP does not adequately target farmers most in need of income support.

In particular the income support objectives of the SPS are defined too loosely and the income and profitability of EU farm households are inadequately measured. The distribution of payments reflects largely the distribution of land and past patterns of production which result in payments that are not targeted specifically at those farm households most vulnerable to fluctuations in agricultural earnings, and farmers in different regions are not treated equally. It is not clear why large profitable farms with the means to manage the risk of their operations should receive income support above and beyond what is necessary to counteract specific market failures. For example, Baldwin (2005) argues that some countries could cut their CAP payments by 25% without affecting the amount given to 95% of farmers, and that such cuts would be unlikely to make large farms unprofitable enough to go out of business. In addition, much of the losses from such a reform would be borne by landowners rather than farmers; in 2003 around 40% of EU farmland was not farmed by the landowner (Baldwin and Wyplosz, 2003). The Commission's original proposals under the Health Check assessed and recommended that payments above specific thresholds be progressively reduced. Instead, however, the political agreement reached in the Council simply cuts all payments above EUR 5 000 by a further 5% and payments above EUR 300 000 by an additional 4%. This will reduce the regressivity of the CAP by much less than the original Commission proposals.

A related problem is that there has not been a serious attempt to separately quantify the payments that are necessary to offset public good externalities and those necessary to meet income support objectives. This is important because it is hard to address both with a single payment instrument (Moreddu, 2007). A risk with the existing system is that, because of the grandfathering of payments, many landowners receive payments that exceed what is necessary to provide public goods and provide them with adequate incomes. It also makes it more difficult to target payments to overcome specific, well-measured problems, such as environmental under-performance. Although the increased use of modulation will shift funds from direct support to support for rural development, reductions in direct payments could also be used to reduce the overall level of support to the EU agricultural sector. This would be particularly beneficial in the medium term as EU governments look to close the large budget deficits that are opening up during the current recession and address long-term fiscal gaps. Rigorous cost-benefit analysis and *ex post* analysis of rural development programmes is necessary to ensure that the funds do not overcompensate farmers and a greater proportion of the funds should be made available to non-farmers as well as farmers. Support for rural development should also not unduly inhibit necessary adjustments to structural economic change.

In the medium term, the Commission should give more consideration to moving to a better mechanism for providing income support to farmers. Options include making greater use of the tax-transfer system in member countries and thus integrating income support for farmers with income support for other workers, and subsidised private insurance schemes targeted at those farm households most exposed to earnings volatility (Zarhnt, 2008). Although the Commission has undertaken some analysis that suggests that an insurance-based instrument would be inferior to the existing system of income support, more detailed analysis of different options is necessary. A more radical option that merits detailed examination is a system of income contingent loans (Botterill and Chapman, 2009). Farmers would receive regular annual payments only for the rigorously measured public goods they provide. Temporary income support would be provided through low-interest loans, with eligibility triggered by shocks that temporarily reduce the income of farm households that are heavily reliant on the income from farm production. Farm households would repay the loans over time once their incomes had returned to more normal levels. Such a policy could have a number of advantages. The budgetary costs of agricultural support would be reduced because payments during periods when farm incomes were low would be offset by repayments during periods when farm incomes were high. The only permanent cost to the EU budget would be the interest subsidy. Support would be targeted at only those farm households that required support at a particular time, not all farm households. Because loans would have to be repaid, there would be less incentive for farm households to remain in the sector if their farms are not viable in the long run. However, before such a policy would be practical, much preparatory work and analysis would have to occur including: defining the relevant public goods and non-prohibitive and reliable methods to measure the public goods produced; estimation of transaction costs; measuring the incomes of all farm households, including off-farm income; organising the appropriate administrative arrangements for managing the scheme; determining the change in income or type of shock that would trigger eligibility for loans; and determining the income that would trigger repayment of the loans. Income contingent loans are also not a solution to permanent farm poverty as they are aimed at smoothing farm income over time, not lifting overall income levels. Persistent farm poverty is best addressed through member states' welfare policies.

Box 5.1. **Recommendations concerning trade and agricultural policy**

- Continue efforts to secure further multilateral trade liberalisation.
- Contribute to the success of Doha negotiations, including by a substantial reduction of agricultural duties and of trade distorting domestic support, as well as through the elimination of export subsidies.
- Continue to prioritise openness throughout the current global economic downturn and work with other countries to ensure that state measures in response to the crisis do not discriminate against foreign interests or foreign workers.

Box 5.1. **Recommendations concerning trade and agricultural policy** (cont.)

- Continue to work to ensure that regional and bilateral trade agreements are trade-creating and support broader trade and developmental objectives.

- Further simplify rules of origin for developing countries and ensure that they are fully consistent with both the EU's trade and development goals.

- The EU and other WTO members should continue their efforts to achieve multilaterally-agreed trade defense rules in order to make them more effective to react to changes in the structure of the global economy.

- Full decoupling could be extended to the livestock meat production sector, if adverse social and environmental impacts can be addressed more efficiently through more targeted support measures.

- Work toward further reforms of the Single Payment Scheme so that:

  ❖ Variations in payments per entitlement are further flattened.

  ❖ Payments to offset public good externalities are better targeted and in line with the rigorously measured size of those externalities.

  ❖ The income support component of the scheme acts as a genuine safety net for vulnerable farm households.

Notes

1. However, following the Uruguay Round agreement, notifications relating to export competition are limited to export subsidies.

2. The OECD (2007) has also examined selected regional trade agreements (Mercosur, Comesa, Asean). Although the EU was not a party to these agreements, they are of special interest to the EU, as it is engaged in negotiations with these regions (or their members). The study, focusing on agriculture, concluded that those regional trade agreements are net trade creating and did not find strong evidence of trade diversion.

3. Services and intellectual property rights were jointly foreseen by ACP and EU in Cotonou; they are concretely designed and integrated into the EPAs in negotiations and co-operation between EU and ACP partners. According to the EU, stakeholders in the Caribbean region as in many other ACP regions see this as an opportunity to attract more investment and create jobs rather than a trade-off.

4. A similar path was followed in: olive oil, cotton and tobacco (2003); sugar (2006); fruit and vegetables (2007); and wine (2007).

5. The rural development fund focuses on agri-environmental plans, payments in areas with natural handicaps and investment assistance. Only a small proportion of funds are for broader economic development of rural areas.

6. The Producer Support Estimate is the annual monetary value of gross transfers from consumers and taxpayers to agricultural producers, measured at the farm gate level, arising from policy measures that support agriculture, regardless of their nature, objectives, or impacts on farm production or income. It includes market price support, budgetary payments and budget revenue foregone (OECD, 2008). In estimating transfers through to 2013, most area and headage payments (except suckler cow premium and sheep and goat premium) are transferred to the Single Payment Scheme to reflect the additional decoupling under the Health Check. The single payment to new member states is doubled. Top-up payments are reduced to zero, as are transitional payments. Single payments are reduced to reflect the additional modulation under the Health Check. The modulated single payment is reduced by 10% and reallocated to Article 68 measures.

7. Under the Single Area Payment Scheme (SAPS) agricultural producers in new members states receive a uniform payment per hectare of agricultural land up to a national ceiling as per accession agreements.

8. The regional flat rate per entitlement is determined by dividing the total value of payment entitlements within a region by the area corresponding to those entitlements. It would differ from the regional flat rate per hectare of agricultural land mainly on its impact within regions because the amount of naked land would be unchanged and only those producers holding existing entitlements would be affected.

Bibliography

Amiti, M. and J. Romalis (2007), "Will the DOHA Round Lead to Preference Erosion?", *NBER Working Paper*, No. 12971.

Baldwin, R. (2005), "The Real Budget Battle: Une crise peut en cacher une autre", *http://hei.unige.ch/~baldwin*.

Baldwin, R. (2006), "Multilateralising Regionalism: Spaghetti Bowls as Building Blocs on the Path to Global Free Trade", *World Economy Annual Lecture*, Nottingham, 22 June.

Baldwin, R. and S. Evenett (eds) (2009), *The Collapse of Global Trade, Murky Protectionism, and the Crisis: Recommendations for the G20*, VoxEU.org.

Baldwin, R. and C. Wyplosz (2003), *The Economics of European Integration*, McGraw Hill.

Bhagwati, J. (2008), *Termites in the Trading System: How Preferential Agreements Undermine Free Trade*, Oxford University Press.

Botterill, L.C. and B. Chapman (2009), "Income Contingent Loans for Drought Relief: Delivering Better Outcomes for Farmers and Taxpayers", *Australian National University Centre for Economic Policy Research Discussion Paper*, No. 597.

Cadot, O. and J. de Melo (2007), "Why OECD Countries Should Reform Rules of Origin", *World Bank Research Observer*.

Commission for Africa (2005), *Our Common Interest* – Report of the Commission for Africa.

Dhar, B. *et al.* (2009), "Disavowing Protectionism: A Strengthened G20 Standstill and Surveillance", in Baldwin, R. and S. Evenett (eds) (2009), *The Collapse of Global Trade, Murky Protectionism, and the Crisis: Recommendations for the G20*, VoxEU.org.

Eurostat (2009),

François, J. (2008), "The Economic Crisis, DOHA Completion, and Protectionist Sentiment", *www.voxeu.org/index.php?q=node/2703*.

Gamberoni, E. and R. Newfarmer (2009), "Trade Protection: Insipient but Worrying Trends", in Baldwin, R. and S. Evenett (eds) (2009), *The Collapse of Global Trade, Murky Protectionism, and the Crisis: Recommendations for the G20*, VoxEU.org.

Helpman, E. (2006), "Trade, FDI and the Organisation of Firms", *Journal of Economic Literature*, Vol. 44, No. 3.

Horn, H.P., C. Mavroidis and A. Sapir (2009), "Beyond the WTO? An Anatomy of EU and US Preferential Trade Agreements", *Bruegel Blueprint Series*.

House of Lords (2008), "Developments in EU Trade Policy", European Union Committee 35th Report of Session 2007-08.

International Centre for Trade and Sustainable Development (2008), *Trade Negotiation Insights*.

Limao, N. (2005) "Preferential Trade Agreements as Stumbling Blocks for Multilateral Trade Liberalization: Evidence for the US.", *CEPR DP*, No. 4884.

Mayer, T. and G.I.P. Ottaviano (2007), "The Happy Few: New Facts on the Internationalisation of European Firms", *CEPR Policy Insight*, No. 15.

Moreddu, C. (2007), *Effective Targeting of Agricultural Policies: Best Practices for Policy Design and Implementation*, OECD, Paris.

OECD (2007), *OECD Economic Surveys: European Union*, OECD, Paris.

OECD (2008), *Agricultural Policies in OECD Countries: At a Glance*, OECD, Paris.

Rollo, J. (2006), "The Sussex Framework: Developing a Useful Analytical Tool for Policymakers Negotiating Free Trade Agreements", presentation to the ECIPE in Brussels.

WTO (2007), *Trade Policy Review of the European Communities*: Report of the Secretariat.

WTO (2008), *World Tariff Profiles 2008*.

Zahrnt, V. (2008), "Reforming the EU's Common Agricultural Policy: Health Check, Budget Review, Doha Round", *ECIPE Policy Brief*, No. 06/2008.

Glossary

ACER	Agency for the Co-operation of Regulators
ACP	African, Caribbean and Pacific
CAP	Common Agricultural Policy
CCS	Carbon Capture and Storage
CDM	Clean Development Mechanism
CEBS	Committee of European Banking Supervisors
CEIOPS	Committee of European Insurance and Occupational Pensions Supervisors
CEPR	Centre for Economic Policy Research
CER	Certified Emission Reductions
CESR	Committee of European Securities Regulators
CGE	Computable General Equilibrium
CIP	Competitiveness and Innovation Framework Programme
CIS	Community Innovation Survey
CLP	Community Lisbon Programme
CMEF	Common Monitoring and Evaluation Framework
CRD	Capital Requirements Directive
EAFRD	European Agricultural Fund for Rural Development
EBA	European Banking Authority
EBA	Everything But Arms
ECB	European Central Bank
EEAP	Energy Efficiency Action Plan
EERA	European Energy Research Alliance
EIA	European Insurance Authority
EIB	European Investment Bank
EFC	Economic and Financial Committee
EFTA	European Free Trade Association
ELFD	Energy Labelling Framework Directive
EPA	Economic Partnership Agreements
EPBD	Energy Performance of Buildings Directive
EPL	Employment Protection Legislation
EPO	European Patent Office
EQF	European Qualifications Framework
ERA	European Research Area
ESA	European Securities Authorities
ESCB	European System of Central Banks
ESFS	European System of Financial Supervisors
ESRB	European Systemic Risk Board
ESRC	European Systemic Risk Council

ETS	Emissions Trading Scheme
EUAs	European Emissions Allowances
EU ETS	European Emissions Trading Scheme
EUROHORCs	European Heads of Research Councils
FP	Research Framework Programme
FP7	7th Framework Programme for research funding
GDP	Gross Domestic Product
GHG	Greenhouse Gas
GSP	Generalised System of Preferences
IAB	Impact Assessment Board
IEA	International Energy Agency
IECCP	Integrated Energy and Climate Change Package
IP	Intellectual Property
IPCC	Intergovernmental Panel on climate change
IPRs	Intellectual Property Rights
ISO	Independent System Operators
ITO	Independent Transmission Operator
JI	Joint Implementation
LDCs	Least Developed Countries
LMI	Lead Market Initiative
MFN	Most Favoured Nation
NAFTA	North American Free Trade Agreement
NAP	National Allocation Plan
PECS	Pan-European Cumulation Scheme
PROs	Public Research Organisations
PSE	Producer Support Estimate
PTA	Preferential Trade Agreements
R&D	Research and Development
SADC	Southern African Development Community
SAPS	Single Area Payment Scheme
SE	Societas Europaea
SET	European Strategic Energy Technology Plan
SGP	Stability and Growth Pact
SMEs	Small and medium-sized enterprises
SPE	European Private Company
SPS	Single Payment Scheme
TSOs	Transmission systems operator
TEN-E	Trans-European Networks Energy
TFP	Total Factor Productivity
VAT	Value added tax
WEF	World Economic Forum
WTO	World Trade Organisation

OECD PUBLISHING, 2, rue André-Pascal, 75775 PARIS CEDEX 16
PRINTED IN FRANCE
(10 2009 13 1 P) ISBN 978-92-64-05445-5 – No. 56977   2009